FEMINIST POLITICAL THEORY

Feminist Political Theory

An Introduction

Valerie Bryson

Foreword by Elizabeth Meehan

PARAGON HOUSE
NEW YORK

First U.S. edition, 1992

First published in the United States by
Paragon House Publishers
90 Fifth Avenue
New York, N.Y. 10011

First published in Great Britain in 1992 by
THE MACMILLAN PRESS LTD
Houndmills, Basingstoke, Hampshire RG21 2XS and London
ISBN 0–333–51635–4 hardcover
ISBN 0–333–51636–2 paperback

Printed in Hong Kong

Library of Congress Cataloging-in-Publication Data
Bryson, Valerie, 1948–
    Feminist political theory : an Introduction / Valerie Bryson.
        p.   cm.
    Includes bibliographical references and index.
    ISBN 1–55778–562–7 (cloth)—ISBN 1–55778–563–5 (paper)
    1. Feminist theory.   2. Political science.   3. Feminism—United
States.   4. Feminism—Great Britain.   I. Title.
HQ1190.B79   1992
305.42'01—dc20   92–2669
                                                  CIP

To my parents, Heather and Alan Poole

Contents

PART II   MODERN FEMINIST THOUGHT

Foreword

I am delighted to be able to introduce readers to this book, having been 'in on it' from the beginning when the publisher asked me to review the original proposal. Initially, I thought that if Valerie Bryson could bring off what she intended she would make a unique contribution to the literature on feminist theory and politics. Throughout the progress of the manuscript, it was clear that this was exactly what was going to happen. There are many things that are important about this book; here, I shall mention three.

First, her scope is remarkable. The historical and conceptual sweep of the book is comprehensive, beginning with the seventeenth century and continuing to explain the linkages and points of departure among mainstream schools of political philosophy and feminist ideas. All of this illuminates her discussion of disagreements in modern feminist theory. It is very difficult to do this without being simplistic or repetitive. This book is neither.

Second, while the business of understanding and explaining entails categorizing and labelling, Valerie shows how the usual way of classifying feminist approaches tends to 'obscure the sophistication of . . . [their] . . . ideas and activities'. As she explains, 'modern feminism involves a dynamic and exciting body of thought that is highly controversial and that is constantly challenging its own assumptions'. In her outstanding exposition of both concepts and the history of ideas, Valerie has written a book that deserves to be a standard text for undergraduates and which will be a constant source of stimulation to experienced researchers.

Third, the book addresses issues that preoccupy readers outside the academic world. As Valerie says, feminist thinking is an enterprise that seeks to understand society in order to challenge and change it. The goal is 'knowledge that can be used to guide and inform feminist political practice'. She shows, like Dale Spender in *Women of Ideas*,[1] that many guides from the past have been lost – a loss that is important as early writings are of interest, not only in their own right, but because they are often strikingly modern in the issues they deal with and their forms of analysis. There has had to be too much 'starting from scratch'. In recent decades, the revival of feminism has often provoked two counter-claims. One, heard even in the 1950s, is that feminism is redundant because most goals have been met. The other is that, for one reason or another, feminism is no longer interesting, politically or intellectually. Yet, as I was thinking about what to say in this preface, one of my sisters told me that she could not borrow *Women of Ideas* from Inverness Public Library for the customary four weeks because there was such a queue of readers waiting for it. In the two weeks allotted to her, older relatives in Edinburgh, where she was reading it, were keenly interested in the snippets they were able to share. Without simplifying her complex and difficult themes, Valerie uses a language of beautiful simplicity that will capture the attention of women outside the universities and colleges. I know what to give some of my relations for Christmas!

I think the capacity to span audiences is vitally important to society in all sorts of fields. Too often, the idea that 'ordinary people' cannot understand, or be objective about, matters of principle (to do with business, constitutions, electoral systems, the public interest, and so on) is used as a pretext for restricting participation to elite groups. If Valerie's subject-matter 'is a dynamic and exciting body of thought' that challenges social practice, then her exposition of it is the most universally exciting and challenging that I have read.

Department of Politics   Elizabeth Meehan
Queen's University of Belfast

Note

1. Spender, D. (1983) *Women of Ideas and What Men have Done to Them* (London: Routledge).

Acknowledgements

There are many people without whose help this book would not exist. My thanks are due above all to Sonia Florent who has been involved from the beginning, and whose sisterly advice and criticism have been invaluable. Elizabeth Meehan has provided help and encouragement throughout, and her enthusiasm has helped me through many a difficult patch. Ursula Vogel too has been extremely supportive, and has provided a consistent source of stimulating and challenging ideas.

Thanks also to Catherine Smith and Marilyn Dunn for their work on the word-processor above and beyond the call of duty, and to Roger Rendell for proof-reading and scholarly advice.

Thanks to the friends who have helped in so many different ways.

And, of course, thanks to David, Patrick and Lucy Bryson.

VALERIE BRYSON

Introduction

For most of its history, Western political theory has ignored women. We seldom appear in its analyses of who has or should have power; when it has deigned to notice us it has usually defended our exclusion from public affairs and our confinement to the home; only rarely have we been seen as political animals worthy of serious consideration. Even today, this exclusion of half the human race is in general either perpetuated or dismissed as a trivial oversight; the inequalities that may exist between men and women are deemed practically unimportant and theoretically uninteresting. Feminist political theory, however, sees women and their situation as central to political analysis; it asks why it is that in virtually all known societies men appear to have power over women, and how this can be changed. It is therefore *engaged* theory, which seeks to understand society in order to challenge and change it; its goal is not abstract knowledge, but knowledge that can be used to guide and inform feminist political practice.

The term 'feminist' first came into use in English during the 1880s, indicating support for women's equal legal and political rights with men. Its meaning has since evolved and is still hotly debated: in this book I will use it in the most broad and general terms to refer to any theory or theorist that sees the relationship between the sexes as one of inequality, subordination or oppression, that sees this as a problem of political power rather than a fact of nature, and that sees this problem as important for political theory and practice. This means I will anachronistically apply it to some who wrote before the term existed, and to some who themselves rejected it (most often because they understood it to refer only to the concerns of middle-class women). I will also provisionally allow it to include some men who contributed to feminist debate; here, however, it should be noted that many

1

modern feminists argue that men can never be feminists, either because they are 'the enemy' or because, lacking first-hand experiences, they can only be at best 'feminist supporters'.

The following chapters trace the development of feminist political theory from the seventeenth century to the present day. This is not, however, a record of systematic progress, for many ideas and writers disappeared from history, and it is only recently that the rich heritage of feminist thought has been rediscovered. This means that new generations of feminists have often had to start almost from scratch; it also means that although some early writings inevitably appear naive and simplistic, they can at times seem strikingly modern, and they can offer insights that still seem relevant today. They are also frequently written with a passion and wit that sparkle across the centuries and that reflect their basis in women's lived experience: here Mary Wollstonecraft's difficulty in organising her personal life, Elizabeth Cady Stanton's impatience with domesticity or Simone de Beauvoir's rejection of 'respectability' are not simply interesting biographical facts, but may affect both their theories and our perception of them.

The development of feminist thought has not only been uneven, but it has also always involved deep theoretical disagreements. These partly reflect the varied needs and perceptions of women in different societies and situations, but also stem from feminism's mixed origins in both the liberal and the socialist traditions of 'male-stream' political thought as well as in women's own experiences. Rather than talking of feminism as a unified body of thought, many modern commentators therefore identify a number of distinct feminist positions. Here the approaches most commonly identified are those of liberal, Marxist and radical feminists; the term socialist feminism is also, rather confusingly, used to describe both all theories that see socialist and feminist goals as related (whether or not they are based on a specifically Marxist analysis) and some modern attempts to synthesise the ideas of Marxist and radical feminisms.

According to such classifications, liberal feminism essentially claims that because women are rational beings like men, they are entitled to the same legal and political rights; liberal feminists have therefore argued and campaigned over the last three hundred years for women's right to education, employment, political participation and full legal equality. Liberal feminism concentrates on rights in the public sphere and does not analyse power relationships that may exist within the home or private life; it assumes that the justice of its cause will ensure its success and that men will have no reason to oppose it. Although it is premised upon the perception that women as a group are now disadvantaged, it argues that it is up to individual women to make the most of their opportunities once political and legal equality have been won.

Marxist feminists however argue that in class society such rights can benefit only a few middle-class women; most women, like most men, will remain oppressed until the capitalist economic system is replaced by communism. From this perspective, the key to women's liberation is their entry into the paid labour market and their participation in the class struggle; it is only in communist society that the economic dependency that is the basis of women's oppression will disappear, and communal childcare and housekeeping free them from domestic drudgery and allow them to participate fully in productive life. Such changes cannot be achieved simply by demanding justice, for they are the product of a particular stage of economic development; sexual equality cannot therefore be achieved at will, but only in specific historical circumstances.

According to radical feminists, both these theories ignore the nature and ubiquity of male power. Radical feminism was first fully articulated in the late 1960s, and it argues that men's patriarchal power over women is the primary power relationship in human society. It further argues that this power is not confined to the public worlds of economic and political activity, but that it characterises all relationships between the sexes, including the most intimate. This insistence that 'the personal is political' involves a re-definition of power and politics and hence a challenge to the assumptions of political theory, which is itself seen as an instrument of male domination that justifies or conceals the reality of male power and its bases in 'private' life. Some radical feminists argue further that differences in behaviour and attributes between men and women are biologically determined rather than socially acquired, and that women embody superior qualities; for some, this means that all men are to be considered 'the enemy', and lesbian separatism becomes the only viable feminist option. Others reject this, but agree that men as a group oppress women in all areas of life, and that an understanding of this must be central to any feminist politics.

Some modern socialist feminists claim to combine the best of both Marxist and radical feminism. They agree with radical feminism's insistence on the ubiquity of male power and its insistence that all areas of life be seen as political. They seek however to give patriarchal power a history and to understand its relationship with other forms of domination; in particular, they try to explore the ways in which class and sex oppression interact in capitalist society. In terms of feminist politics they advocate struggle at all levels; this will sometimes involve autonomous women's organisations, but will also involve working with men. Unlike liberal and orthodox Marxist feminists, these socialist feminists argue that men have at least a short-term interest in maintaining present gender inequalities; unlike some radical feminists, however, they do not see the interests of men and women as permanently opposed.

Such classification suggests that there are four distinct feminist approaches which attribute women's situation to bad laws, a bad economic situation, bad men or to a combination of these. This is however to caricature complex theories which cannot be neatly slotted into such distinct categories and which are constantly evolving; the use of such labels can therefore at times obscure the sophistication of feminist ideas and activities. The classification of theories must therefore be approached with caution. In this book I shall use it as a convenient starting-point into the maze of feminist theories that acknowledges their interrelationships, but that allows different assumptions to be disentangled and contradictions exposed. This will involve an exploration of the ways in which the different approaches have interacted and fed off each other, and I will argue that although many disagreements remain there has been in recent years a certain convergence of feminist ideas, involving at the very least a rejection of the easy certainties and simplicities of some past approaches.

A key area of disagreement, however, remains in the 'difference/ equality' debate. Many feminists have always been unwilling to grant any political significance to the biological differences between men and women, on the grounds that these will always be used to women's disadvantage. Nevertheless, some feminists have long argued that women are innately superior, and there is now a strong strand within modern radical feminism that insists that biological differences colour the whole of our lives. In particular, it is argued that men are innately competitive, aggressive and sexually predatorial, while women's biological capacity to give birth means that they embody the 'womanly virtues' of peace, nurturing and co-operation. Some argue further that women actually think differently from men, and that intuition and empathy can give rise to a higher understanding than male calculation and reason; for some, it is the diffuse nature of women's sexuality that gives them access to 'non-linear' forms of understanding, outside the confines of male logic. Such arguments may provide a useful corrective to traditional views of human nature and rationality whereby male-identified modes of activity and thinking are uncritically taken as the norm, and 'objectivity' is in fact a guise for male bias. It can also allow us to 'envalue' activities and attributes traditionally associated with women. However, such biological determinism seems to represent something of a dead-end for political theory; although influential, it is therefore also strongly resisted by many modern feminists.

Another contentious area is the alleged racism of modern Western feminist theory. Much as feminists have attacked traditional political theory for excluding or marginalising women, feminism itself has been accused of universalising the assumptions and needs of white women in Europe and America and largely ignoring the very different perspectives of black and third world women – indeed its very use of such terms suggests that white first world women are seen as the norm to which other groups may be added, as well as concealing the vast differences amongst the women so labelled. Some women are now demanding that the experiences of women who have hitherto been marginalised become a central starting point rather than an optional extra for feminist theory and practice, and that existing approaches be discarded along with male theory. Others argue that the limitations of present theories can be overcome, and there is in general a greater sensitivity to such issues than amongst Western feminists in the past. Nevertheless the huge question of whether there can even in principle be a global movement of women remains unresolved, and will be a key area of debate in the next decades.

Recent feminist criticisms of traditional theory have coincided with a crisis in 'male-stream' political thought and philosophy. Not only have political changes in Eastern Europe left many Marxists in a state of confusion, but the whole of Western political thought has been attacked by 'post-modernist' theories which deny in principle the possibility of certainty and objectivity. From this new perspective, there can be no ultimate truth or final knowledge, concepts such as 'justice' or 'right' lose their meaning, and the certainties of liberalism and Marxism are alike rejected as the partial products of particular historical moments. Post-modernism has been welcomed by some feminists, who see in it a way of demystifying and reconstructing theory with an understanding of the power relations and partial perspectives that this must necessarily involve; it can also break down the category 'women' to alert us to the diversity of experiences that this includes. However it is necessary to disentangle genuine theoretical insights from academic fashion, and other feminists are most cautious, arguing that post-modernism can never provide the basis for a feminist politics; some argue that it is indeed an inherently conservative theory that delegitimises any attempt to challenge the status quo.

Such debates will be explored in later chapters, and mean that, far from constituting a body of received truths, modern feminism involves a dynamic and exciting body of thought that is highly controversial and that is constantly challenging its own assumptions. Earlier writings too are not simply 'dead theories', for they involve issues that are still being argued over today; as such they are both fascinating in their own right and highly relevant to current feminist politics. I therefore argue that we can learn from all of the ideas discussed in the following pages for those that do not provide insights may help us to avoid earlier mistakes. In particular, although many writers have claimed to have found clear solutions, in practice such ideas have always become modified. Awareness of this means that new ideas can now be welcomed and used, while claims that they provide *the* answer are rejected; we are perhaps moving towards a position in which we can both identify the structures and processes that are contrary to the interests of women, and understand that none of these on its own provides the key to change, for each is inevitably interconnected with all the rest. This means that different forms of feminist activity may often be understood as complementary rather than alternative approaches, for if there are no easy answers, there is no one form of feminist politics appropriate for all women, in all circumstances and in all societies. Real differences of course remain, and feminists are not even in agreement as to their goals, let alone the means of achieving them. Good theory can, however, allow us to distinguish between genuine disagreements and failures of communication or differences of emphasis, and to identify possible forms of appropriate political action and the ways in which these may interconnect.

What I have discovered in writing this book is above all the complexity of feminist political theory as it has developed both now and in the past, the extent to which 'new' debates and ideas have been anticipated by earlier writers, and ways in which feminism consistently spills over the boundaries of conventional political debate, challenging its assumptions and forcing new issues onto the agenda. This means that feminist political theory cannot be conveniently 'ghetto-ised', for the issues it raises are of vital importance to any understanding of political power; in seeking to explain and challenge the situation of women, it increases our understanding of all areas of political life, and any political theory that ignores it is inevitably partial and impoverished.

Part I

The precursors

1

Early feminist thought

Contrary to popular opinion, feminist theory did not begin with Mary Wollstonecraft at the end of the eighteenth century, but goes back at least to medieval times (and no doubt found private expression much earlier). As far as we know, the earliest public debate was conducted entirely by men, but from the fifteenth century women's voices were beginning to be heard, and the first woman to write about the rights and duties of her sex seems to have been the Frenchwoman Christine de Pisan (1364–1430). From the point of view of feminist political theory, what is interesting about the earliest writings is not so much the details of what individual writers of the time had to say, for these did not yet constitute an analysis of power relations or any kind of political programme, but rather the fact that debates over women's role in society that include a recognisably feminist perspective go back further than had been commonly assumed. It is also interesting to note that from the first such debates had an international character so that, for example, de Pisan's influence can be traced to the debates in England at the end of the seventeenth century (Ferguson, 1985, p. xi; see also de la Barre,1990; Willard, 1975; Shahar, 1983).

Mary Astell and the seventeenth-century debate

Ferguson has seen in this period 'the first sizable wave of British secular feminist protest' (Ferguson, 1985, p. 15), when for the first time significant numbers of women challenged received ideas about their sex in pamphlets and in books. Some of these were published anonymously, but by no means all, and of these writers the best known are the dramatist Aphra Benn (1640–89), and Mary Astell (1666–1731), who has recently been described as 'The First English Feminist' (Hill, 1986, her book title) and 'arguably the first systematic feminist theoretician in the west' (Catherine Stimpson, Introduction to Perry, 1986, p. xi). (See also Smith, 1982; Kinnard, 1983; Browne, 1987.) Discussion at this time differed from the earlier debates, partly because of the unprecedented scale of women's own involvement, but also because it occurred at a time of rapid economic, social and political change. As such, it both expressed the needs and tensions of a modernising society, and employed new philosophical concepts and political terminology; the questions it raised and the language it used are with us today.

Any attempt to 'read off' feminist theory from the social situation of women should be approached with extreme caution; but it does seem that the increased scale and intensity of the debate stemmed at least in part from the challenge to women's traditional role that occurred in these early years of capitalist development. Changes in agriculture were creating a new and growing class of wage labourers, and as the division of labour became more complex and units of production larger, the old system of family-based domestic industry gradually declined, creating for the first time a distinction between the public world of employment and the private world of home and family. At the same time women were progressively excluded from trades and professions in which they had previously been active, such as brewing, printing and medicine, while aristocratic women who had formerly played an important role in running their husbands' estates were increasingly restricted to the domestic sphere. After the Reformation, the traditional refuge of the convent was no longer available, and for growing numbers of women marriage became an economic necessity and their dependence on their husbands increased; demographic factors were, however, increasing the numbers of 'surplus women', and for an unmarried woman such as Mary Astell there seemed to be no respectable means of earning a living. In this context it is not surprising that the role of women should have been debated, moreover it was only once the public and the private could be clearly distinguished that it made sense to ask about the appropriate sphere of women's activity; this distinction was alien to medieval society, but remains central to many discussions of feminism today.

Politically, the seventeenth century was of course one of extreme turmoil and questioning of traditional authority, and it was inevitable that the events of the Civil War and the Interregnum would politicise many women as well as men. As well as the traditional 'behind the scenes' involvement, there is evidence of women demonstrating, rioting and petitioning parliament. Even more dramatically, a number of the radical religious sects that sprang up challenged received notions as to appropriate sexual roles and behaviour: for example, the Ranters preached extreme sexual permissiveness, while the Quakers argued that men and women were not only equal in God's eyes, but were equally eligible for the ministry.

Questions of authority in state and family were, moreover, intimately linked in the political theory of the time. Conservative defenders of absolute monarchical power argued that the authority of the king over his people was sanctioned by God and nature in exactly the same way as that of a father over his family; this meant that 'patriarchy' (the rule of the father) in the home was used as justification for a parallel power in the state. Opponents of such state power, who argued that authority was *not* divinely ordained but must rest on reason and consent, were therefore forced to re-examine arbitrary power within the family as well; logically, it seemed, patriarchy in state and home must stand or fall together. Perhaps unsurprisingly, this logic was not pushed to its conclusion, and although Hobbes and Locke, the foremost political theorists of the century, did examine relationships within the family at some length, they fell back on arguments of social convenience and men's superior strength to justify the continued subordination of women. This meant that while they saw men as independent and rational individuals capable of perceiving and pursuing their own self-interest, they saw women as wives and mothers, weak creatures unable to escape the curse of Eve, whose interests were bound up with those of their family, and who therefore had no independent political rights.

This at first sight appears to be the kind of inconsistency that a more rigorous application of the underlying principles could rectify; some recent theorists have however suggested that, despite their universalistic pretensions, the basic premises of these early liberal writers are inherently biased against women. Thus it is argued that they are based on an essentially male view of human nature that ignores human interdependence and attributes such as nurturing that have traditionally been associated with women (Jaggar, 1983). It is further claimed that the whole theory is predicated upon a distinction between the public and private which involves the exclusion of women from the former and a devaluation of the latter (Pateman, 1986a), and that it perpetuates a view of rationality that excludes women, because it defines reason in terms of *overcoming femininity* (identified with nature, particularity, biology, passion and emotion). (See Coole, 1988; Lloyd, 1984; Braidotti, 1986; Nye, 1990a.) These are complex arguments which will recur throughout the book; at this stage it is important to note simply that the extension of traditional theory to include women may not be as unproblematical as it at first sight seems, and that the concepts and assumptions made by male theorists may not be entirely adequate when it comes to expressing female needs and experiences.

It was not, however, Hobbes and Locke who were to provide the direct inspiration for this first generation of late-seventeenth-century feminists, but the underlying revolution in philosophy which had been started earlier in the century by Descartes. According to Cartesian philosophy, all people are possessed of reason, and therefore true knowledge, which is based on experience and self-discovery rather than study of the classics, is in principle available to all, and traditional authority is rejected in favour of rational analysis and independent thought. Despite his insistence that 'even women' are capable of rational thought, Descartes too has been accused of hijacking reason for his sex (largely because he strengthened and formalised the mind-body distinction) (see Lloyd, 1984). However at the time his ideas seemed purely liberating and provided inspiration for many feminist writers, for they meant that *all* authority could be questioned, and that women's lack of classical education need not exclude them from philosophy: as Mary Astell said, what is important is good ideas, and not 'what fanciful people have said about them' (*A Serious Proposal to the Ladies*, in Ferguson, 1985, p. 188).

(See also Perry, 1986; Hill, 1986; Kinnard, 1983; Smith, 1982; Rogers, 1982.)

Stemming from this new approach to philosophy, we find in Astell's writings a classic early statement of the core liberal feminist belief that men and women are equally capable of reason, and that therefore they should be equally educated in its use: 'Since God has given to Women as well as Men intelligent Souls, why should they be forbidden to use them?' (*A Serious Proposal to the Ladies*, in Ferguson, 1985, p. 188.) Here she anticipated the arguments of Mary Wollstonecraft and other later writers, by arguing that although women in the society of her day appeared frivolous and incapable of reason, this was the product of faulty upbringing rather than any natural disability; as such it was evidence of the need for improved female education rather than its impossibility. However, although Astell based her arguments on the liberal idea of rationality, she did not accept the liberal idea of political rights. Like most of the seventeenth-century feminists, she was a staunch Tory and defender of the monarchy; as such, she was more concerned to deny political rights to men than to attempt to extend them to women. Indeed the logic of her conservatism led her to a seemingly very unfeminist conclusion: accepting the parallel between authority in the state and in the home, she argued that a wife must obey her husband as a subject must obey the king; when a women enters marriage, she argued, she has chosen a 'monarch for life', and must therefore submit to his authority.

Astell's writings are at times heavily ironic, so that not everything she says should be taken at face value; nevertheless her conservatism does seem genuine enough. It has, however, more radical implications than at first sight appear, and in many ways she is carried beyond liberal feminist demands to a broader analysis of the relations between men and women. Firstly, she insisted that a woman's duty to obey her husband did not involve any recognition of his superiority; indeed there is throughout her writings a marked tone of barely disguised contempt for the male sex (for example, she said that men are not fit to educate children, for 'precepts contradicted by example seldom prove effective'; quoted in Kinnard, 1983, p. 37). Secondly, she argued that submission to male authority could *not* extend to single women, whether 'poor fatherless maids' like herself or 'widows who have lost their masters' (*Reflections Upon Marriage*, in Ferguson, 1985, p. 195). This meant, thirdly, that an educated woman should choose to reject the domestic slavery involved in marriage, and she therefore advised women to avoid matrimony (while cheerfully admitting that if they all followed her advice, then 'there's an End to the Human Race'; quoted in Perry, 1986, p. 9). From this it followed, fourthly, that women's activities need not be limited by the need to attract a husband, and they could therefore concentrate on improving their minds rather than their beauty: 'Were not a morning more profitably spent at a Book than at a Looking Glass?' (quoted in Perry, 1986, p. 92). Finally, as a practical means of freeing women from marriage and dependence on men, she advocated the establishment of female communities, rather like secular nunneries, where women could live and learn together without men, knowing themselves 'capable of More Things than the pitiful Conquest of some Wretched Heart' (quoted in Perry, 1986, p. 102). This idea excited considerable interest; it failed to attract sufficient financial support, not so much because of its feminism, but because of its dangerous associations with Roman Catholicism.

This means that far from her being simply an early feminist educationalist with unfortunate leanings to conservatism and an inability to come to terms with female sexuality, we can find in Astell some of the central ideas of modern radical feminism: the idea that man (whether as sexual predator or tyrannous husband) is the natural enemy of woman; the idea that women must be liberated from the need to please men (which Perry sees as an early form of 'consciousness-raising'; Perry, 1986, p. 103); the belief that this can be achieved only if women are enabled to live separately from men; and the perception that men have controlled and defined knowledge: 'Histories are writ by them, they recount each others great Exploits and have always done so' (quoted in Perry, 1986, p. 3). Underlying all this there is a clear rejection of the whole scale of values in which man is seen as the measure of women's success: it was not for nothing that her major work on education was entitled *A Serious Proposal to the Ladies . . . by a Lover of her Sex*.

While Mary Astell may have been the most radical and systematic feminist of her time she was, as has already been said, certainly not an isolated voice. This means that by the early eighteenth century we have a quite widely established perception of women as a group in society whose situation is in need of improvement, and it is this consciousness of women's group identity which Smith thinks distinguishes writers of this period from their predecessors (Smith, 1982). What we do *not* yet find, however, is any direct challenge to women's social and economic positions or to the sexual division of labour, nor do we find any coherent political programme or demand that the rights of male citizens be extended to women. For the most part socially and politically conservative, these early feminists addressed themselves almost exclusively to women of the upper and middle classes and there was no attempt to link the situation of women to other disadvantaged groups in society. For them it was through education and the exercise of reason that women could be made independent of men, and it is not until the third quarter of the eighteenth century that feminism was to become associated with wider demands for change.

The Enlightenment and early liberal feminism

In many ways, the middle years of the eighteenth century seem to represent a retreat from feminism, as arguments for women's rationality became less fashionable than belief in their innate weakness and dependence on men, the ideas of Astell and her contemporaries fell into disrepute, and the very names of these early feminists were forgotten. Nevertheless, although there was no systematic analysis of women's situation, individual complaints about their lot continued, and the question of women's education never completely disappeared from the agenda (Smith, 1982; Ferguson, 1985; Rogers, 1982; Spender, 1983a). Many women continued to write and publish throughout the period, and the most famous of these were the 'bluestocking' group of 'salon intellectuals'. Although they expressly opposed feminist ideas and accepted a place secondary to men in the literary world, their very existence as a group of intellectual women, publicly discussing and publishing from the 1750s onwards, could be seen as a statement about women's ability and role in society: no longer a silenced majority, women could not be entirely excluded from public debate. It is in this context that the ideas of the second 'wave' of feminists must be understood; there is no *direct* line between them and the writers of Mary Astell's day, but their ideas did not explode upon an entirely unsuspecting world, and this half-forgotten heritage contributed towards the rapid growth of feminist ideas in the last quarter of the eighteenth century.

This was a period in which the stress on rationality and the questioning of traditional authority which we saw beginning in seventeenth-century philosophy was to reach its fullest expression. It was also a period dominated by the experiences of the American and French revolutions, and in which philosophical debates on the nature of freedom and human rationality were to take tangible form in the American Declaration of Independence (1776) and the French Declaration of Man and Citizen (1789). What united the philosophers of this so-called 'Age of Reason' or 'The Enlightenment' was their optimism and their belief in progress through the onward march of human reason and knowledge; reason replaced God or antiquity as the standard of right or wrong, and no institution or authority was to be exempt from its judgement. Although many of the leading philosophers were in fact socially and politically conservative, the radical implications of these principles are obvious, and they provided the basis for the liberal belief that as rational beings individual men have rights that must not be violated by arbitrary power, that therefore any authority must rest upon the consent of the governed, and that the individual should be as far as possible self-determining and free from government control.

Although always expressed in terms of the rights of *man*, it might at first sight seem that this could be understood as a generic term that includes women; for the most part, however, the philosophers of the Enlightenment and the leaders of the revolutions did not simply fail to make this extension, but they denied that it could be made (see Kennedy and Mendus, 1987, Introduction). There was indeed a strikingly widespread consensus that the principles of rational individualism were *not* applicable to women, for it was held that by their very nature women were incapable of the full development of reason; thus we can find in the writings of Voltaire, Diderot, Montesquieu and above all Rousseau, the idea that women are essentially creatures of emotion and passion, who have an important role to play as wives and mothers, but who are biologically unsuited for the public sphere (see Rendall, 1985; Schapiro, 1978; Kennedy and Mendus, 1987).

This consensus did not, however, go unchallenged, and by the end of the century there were a number of attempts to show its inconsistency, and to demonstrate that the liberal ideas of the Enlightenment could be applied to women as well as men; of these the best known is Mary Wollstonecraft's *Vindication of the Rights of Women* (1792), but the fame of this work should not be allowed to obscure the extent of other feminist writing at the time. For example, the French writer Condorcet insisted that women *were* capable of reason and should be educated accordingly, that they had therefore the same political rights as men, and that to deny this was an unacceptable tyranny. In practice he did not anticipate the widespread involvement of women in politics, but this he said was no reason to deny them political rights in principle – indeed he argued that women could no more be logically excluded from politics on the grounds of menstruation or pregnancy than could a man because he was suffering from gout. (*On the Admission of Women to the Right of Citizenship*, 1790, and *Sketch for a Historical Future of the Progress of the Human Mind*, 1793, in Baker (ed., 1976); see also Schapiro, 1978, and Vogel, 1986.) Here we have a direct attempt to confront the inconsistencies of other writers and to claim that liberal principles have a universal application that includes women, so that 'Feminism was . . . an integral part of the complete pattern of liberalism that Condorcet so enthusiastically advocated' (Schapiro, 1978). The German, von Hippel, similarly rejected the idea that women's exclusion from civil and political rights could be justified in terms of a biologically given nature; it was men, he claimed, who had made women what they were, and he demanded that men and women be given equal rights and education for citizenship rather than their traditional sex roles. He went further than other writers of the time in blaming men for women's situation, and in denying that the traditional division of labour between the sexes was sanctioned by reason or nature; it was however, he argued, enlightened *men* who had to act to liberate women, for they themselves had been rendered incapable of independent political action (*On the Civil Improvement of Women*, 1793; see Vogel, 1986).

However, women at this time were themselves far from silent, and their voices were to be heard on both sides of the Atlantic demanding equal treatment with men. Thus in America Abigail Adams (1744–1818) wrote in 1776 to her husband (who later became the second president of the United States), employing the language that he had used against English rule to point out that her sex too needed protection from tyranny and 'will not hold ourselves bound by any laws in which we have no voice or representation'. John Adams' reply that 'As to your extraordinary code of laws, I cannot but laugh . . .' can have done little to change her opinion that 'all men would be tyrants if they could' (extracts in Schneir, 1972, and Rossi, 1973). Other correspondence of the period suggests that such ideas were commonly discussed by women of Adams's class (Rendall, 1985, Ch. 2; Spender, 1983a), while a more systematic analysis was given by Judith Murray (1751–1820) (see Spender, 1983a, and Rossi, 1973).

Meanwhile in England the historian Catherine Macaulay (1731–91) was arguing on similar lines. In her *Letters on Education* (1790) she insisted that the differences between the sexes were a product of education and environment and not of nature; she attacked the way in which women's minds and bodies had been distorted to please men, and she demanded that boys and girls be given the same education – and here she went beyond uncritical acceptance of male values to demand that the education of boys too be changed to provide them with traditional female skills. Macaulay's work has been overshadowed by that of her close contemporary Mary Wollstonecraft (1759–97), but at one time her fame extended across two continents: she was in correspondence with George Washington (Spender, 1983a, p. 127), and Abigail Adams asked a correspondent to find out all he could about her for 'One of my own sex so eminent . . . naturally raises my curiosity' (Spender, 1983a, p. 129). Whatever the reason for her rapid disappearance from public memory (an indigestible prose style, the offence caused to polite society by her marriage to a much younger man, and the inability of male historians to cope with the existence of more than one feminist writer at a time have all been suggested – see Spender, 1983a), it is certain that at the time her ideas were widely read and anticipated many of Wollstonecraft's – a fact which the latter readily acknowledged.

It was of course in France that women of this period were to play the most dramatic role: the women of Paris demanding bread, the *tricoteuses* knitting under the guillotine and Charlotte Corday's assassination of Marat have passed into legend, while a number of individual women such as the moderate republican Madame Roland were involved in the struggle for political power. Feminism as such was always marginal to the revolution; demands for improved female education were however included in the first petitions to the National Assembly (the French Parliament), and wider issues of women's rights and representation were soon fiercely debated in pamphlets and the radical press, and in the women's political clubs that sprang up between 1789 and 1793. With Condorcet, women were arguing that principles of the Enlightenment applied to them too, and that political rights belonged to them as much as to men: Olympe de Gouges' *Declaration of the Rights of Women* (1790, in Riemar and Fout, 1980) is the clearest example of this approach. (See also Rendall, 1985; Spender, 1983a; Evans,1977; Tomalin, 1974; Kelly, 1987.) As the revolution developed, however, such demands were silenced; in an anti-feminist reaction the women's clubs were closed and the most prominent writers and spokeswomen imprisoned or put to death; in the light of her own fate, de Gouges' claim that 'since a woman has the right to mount the Scaffold, she must also have the right to address the House' has a terrible irony (Riemar and Fout, 1980, p. 63).

However, although the articulation of feminist demands in the French revolution was short-lived, it did have an impact on the public imagination that was to affect popular reaction to feminism in other nations: 'The feeling was that the French were bad, revolution was bad, the French revolution had led to feminism, therefore feminism must be bad' (Rover, 1970, p. 13). It is therefore important to remember that liberal feminism could be seen as a revolutionary ideology in the most literal sense, if we are to understand the reception given to Mary Wollstonecraft's ideas in England; for despite her own revulsion from the extremism and violence of the revolution, 'Viewed through the smoke of the Bastille, Wollstonecraft loomed like a blood-stained Amazon, the high-priestess of loose-tongued liberty' (Taylor, 1983, p. 11). This meant that although her work was less original than both her admirers and detractors have claimed, its effect was maximised by its timing – she wrote it two years after the outbreak of revolution; and it was written with a force and passion which reflected the tumultuous times through which she was living.

Mary Wollstonecraft's *Vindication of the Rights of Woman*

Despite this reputation, Evans has described the *Vindication of the Rights of Woman* as 'really an educational tract' (Evans, 1977, p. 16), and certainly at one level it is simply a continuation of the old debate about women's nature and their capacity for reason. Here Wollstonecraft was particularly concerned to refute the ideas of the philosopher Rousseau who, in his work *Emile*, which described the ideal education of a young man, had included a chapter on the very different education of 'Sophy', Emile's future wife. For Rousseau, men's and women's natures and abilities were *not* the same, and these biologically given differences defined their whole role in society, with men becoming citizens and women wives and mothers. This meant that the education of boys and girls must both recognise natural differences in ability and inclination ('Little girls always dislike learning to read and write, but they are always ready to learn to sew', *Emile*, p. 331), and encourage the virtues appropriate to adult life: this involved a training in rational citizenship for boys and lessons in how to please a man and bring up his children for a girl. Rousseau's democratic radicalism had marked him out from the other philosophers of the Enlightenment, and it is partly because she shared his passion for liberty and justice in other spheres that Wollstonecraft was so enraged by his views on women; it is the radical nature of Rousseau's views on politics which give a revolutionary edge to her insistence that girls and boys should be educated alike.

Her quarrel with Rousseau was fourfold. First, like earlier feminists, she refused to accept that women were less capable of reason than men, or that vanity, weakness and frivolity were the natural attributes of her sex ('I have, probably, had an opportunity of observing more girls in their infancy than J J Rousseau', *Vindication*, p. 129); in phrases often strikingly reminiscent of Astell (of whom she had probably never heard) she roundly condemned the mindless vanity of upper class women of her day, but like Astell saw this 'femininity' as a social construct that distorted rather then reflected women's true ability. Secondly, Wollstonecraft argued that if men and women are equally possessed of reason they must be equally educated in its use: woman is *not* 'specially made for man's delight' (*Emile*, p. 322), but an independent being who is both capable of and entitled to a rational education. This much had, as we have seen, already been asserted by earlier feminists, but Wollstonecraft extended the argument in her third main point of disagreement with Rousseau: as men's and women's common humanity is based on their shared and God-given possession of reason, then *virtue* must be the same for both sexes – that is, it must be based on reason and it must be freely chosen. This meant that for Wollstonecraft the virtues of the good wife and mother could not be seen as 'natural', nor could they be based upon a male-imposed ignorance cunningly disguised as innocence, and she argued forcefully that a woman taught only passive obedience to her husband could never be fit to bring up children. Women must be given knowledge and education so that they can make rational choices, for it is only then that it makes sense to talk of their goodness.

The implications of this idea that women's actions must be freely chosen is radical indeed, and adds a new dimension to the debate for it challenges the whole idea of ascribed social roles and the rights and duties that accompany them. It is this fourth and final area that distinguishes Wollstonecraft and her contemporaries from the earlier feminists, for the idea of equal *worth* now leads irrevocably to that of equal *rights*. In Astell's time, belief in women's rationality had been combined with political conservatism, but now it was firmly linked to political liberalism, and the principles were established that were to lead to later campaigns for women's suffrage and legal rights and, eventually, to the demand for equal participation with men in the worlds of politics and paid employment.

The systematic articulation of these demands was however still very much in the future, and Wollstonecraft was much more concerned to establish the principle than to elaborate a detailed programme for change. She was writing at a time when although industrialisation was opening up new employment, this was, particularly for women, at very low wages and in appalling conditions, while in the middle ranks of society women's economic dependence on men had grown with the increased separation of home and work. As in Astell's day, employment prospects for middle-class women were almost non-existent (Wollstonecraft's own experiences showed her how degrading and unsatisfactory were the only available options of teacher, companion and governess), and increasingly a man's wife was seen as the purely ornamental symbol of his success and not in any sense his partner; this dependency was formalised in Blackstone's famous decree that within marriage 'the very legal existence of the wife is suspended . . . or at least is incorporated and consolidated into that of the husband' (quoted in Kramnick, 1978, p. 34). It was in this context that Wollstonecraft insisted that women had an independent right to education, employment, property and the protection of the civil law; this she argued was needed to ensure that women were not forced into marriage through economic necessity, and that wives were not entirely dependent on the goodwill of their husbands. Women therefore needed legal rights in order to make independent rational choices and achieve virtue; a woman who is forced to perform the traditional female roles will do so very badly, but if men

> would . . . but snap our chains, and be content with rational fellowship instead of slavish obedience, they would find us more observant daughters, more affectionate sisters, more faithful wives, more reasonable mothers – in a word, better citizens (*Vindication*, p. 263).

As the above quotation suggests, Wollstonecraft did not expect that education and freedom of choice would lead most women to reject their traditional role, but argued that they would enable them to perform it better. She did not accept the public/private split that runs through liberal thought and which insists on the superiority of the former over the latter; rather she sought to *envalue* women's domestic responsibilities (Thornton, 1986, p. 88), and to show that domestic duties, properly performed, were a form of rational citizenship; that is, they were to be seen as public responsibilities rather than a source of private satisfaction or tribulation (Vogel, 1986).

The problem with this, of course, is that in a world in which domestic duties are unpaid, the economic dependence of a woman upon her husband remains; Wollstonecraft had perceived the dangers of this, but does not follow its implications through. Similarly, her insistence that motherhood is a form of citizenship does not solve the problem of the male monopoly of formal political and legal power, which leaves women dependent on the goodwill of men to 'snap their chains'. Here she did briefly suggest that women should have representatives in government (*Vindication*, p. 260), but this was in no way central to her argument, and although she argued that women must be free to choose a career in business or public life, she never suggested that individual successful women might use their power to benefit their sex as a whole.

Another major problem arises from Wollstonecraft's and other liberal feminists' uncritical adoption of a concept of reason which is bound up with the need to subdue passion and emotion – qualities traditionally associated with the female. For Rousseau in particular, the rule of reason was to be achieved by the exclusion of the objects of passion – women – from public life; and some feminists have recently suggested that this exclusion is not simply an unfortunate product of Rousseau's personal prejudices, which could be ignored by modern theorists, but is basic to his whole theory. Here it is argued that women's confinement to the home represents a necessary precondition for his view of rational citizenship, for this presupposes not only the exclusion of passion from public life, but its containment and expression within the family. From this perspective, if women enter political life they not only disrupt it, but they destroy its domestic foundations (Coole, 1988; Canovan, 1987). It is also suggested that the stress on rational universalistic principles denies the possibility of other forms of knowledge traditionally associated with women, such as intuition, imagination, emotion and personal experience, and that it 'mistakes the masculine bias for a universal mode of enunciation' (Braidotti, 1986, p. 48).

Wollstonecraft's view that reason was the basis of rational citizenship, and that it involved the overcoming or control of love and passion also caused her problems at a more personal level. Although she recognised the existence of female sexuality, this was only to insist that it, like love, must be subordinated to reason, so that marriage and motherhood must be based on rational choice and duty: 'In the choice of a husband women should not be led astray by the qualities of a lover' (*Vindication*, p. 224), and more private and unruly emotions were allowed no place. This means that in print she often seemed a 'prim moralist' (Brody, 1983) with a very cynical view of marriage; in real life, however, she was to find such precepts unworkable, and many a modern feminist whose heart refuses to obey the dictates of logic and political correctness will empathise with her experience of her unhappy love affairs and sympathise with the conflict between love and reason articulated in her private correspondence (Walters, 1979). Ironically, it was the publication of this correspondence by her husband Godwin shortly after her death in childbirth that did most to discredit her ideas for the next generations of women: the association of feminism with 'immorality' effectively banished it from consideration in 'respectable' society.

All this suggests that the tasks facing liberal feminists are more complex than they might at first sight seem; these problems will be returned to in later chapters, but already in these early feminist writings we find suggestions that the consistent application of supposedly universal principles may call into question these principles themselves, and that ideas of individualism, the public and the private, and the supremacy of reason, may acquire new dimensions when viewed from a woman's perspective.

A further criticism that has frequently been made of liberal feminists is that they fail to recognise any non-sexual forms of oppression or to relate the situation of women to conditions in society as a whole; in particular they are accused of being class-blind, and interested only in the plight of middle-class women. Thus it has been said of Wollstonecraft that 'her feminism was basically a demand for equality with bourgeois man' (Walters, 1979, p. 320), and certainly the *Vindication* does address itself to women of the middle class, and she consistently seems to assume that the existence of servants is necessary if domestic work is to be more than mindless drudgery. However, her best-known work was preceded by her *Vindication of the Rights of Man* (1790) which defended equal rights against the claims of hierarchy and privilege, and attacked inheritance and property as causes of poverty and misery for working people; her last novel (*The Wrongs of Woman: or Maria*, published posthumously in 1798) was concerned to explore the predicament not only of the middle-class heroine, but also of a servant girl drawn to prostitution; so that a wider awareness of social issues is to be found if we look beyond the pages of the *Vindication of the Rights of Woman*. To describe her as a socialist would be an exaggeration, for her ideas on economics remain latent rather than systematically articulated, but there is in her writings a consistent insistence that a good social order is incompatible with a high degree of inequality: 'From the respect paid to property flow, as from a poisoned fountain, most of the evils and vices which render this world such a dreary place to the contemplative mind' (*Vindication*, p 252) and 'the more equality there is among men, the more virtue and happiness will reign in society' (*Vindication*, p. 96). Thus she went well beyond the defence of equal property rights normally associated with liberalism, and provides an interesting link with the ideas of the 'utopian socialists' to which we now turn – indeed one of the foremost of these, Robert Owen, was to say that he 'had never met with a person who thought so exactly as he did' (quoted in Rauschenbusch-Clough, 1898, p. 188).

The utopian socialists and feminism

The term 'utopian socialist' was used by Marx and Engels to refer to those who believed that competitive capitalist society should be replaced by a more equitably organised, co-operative and rational one, and that this could be achieved by demonstrating the reasonableness and desirability of reform: persuasion and example, not class conflict and revolution, were to be the agents of social change. The best known of these early socialists were the Frenchmen St Simon (1760–1825) and Fourier (1772–1837), and the British Robert Owen (1772–1837). They do not form a unified group and some of their ideas were eccentric in the extreme; they were, however, an important influence on later writers and, unlike most later socialists, they saw relationships between the sexes and within the family as central issues – changes here were not seen as simply the by-products of social change or class struggle, but were themselves a necessary precondition for the transformation of society. These feminist aspects of their thought were developed by their followers, and attracted widespread interest and excitement in both England and America. There was lively debate in the press and on the public platform, with lecture tours by prominent feminists requiring extensive policing (see Eckhardt, 1984; Taylor, 1983); in the numerous but short-lived socialist communities that the movement inspired, the role of women was a central concern (Muncy, 1973); while William Thompson's 1825 *Appeal on Behalf of Women* (the ideas of which he attributed to his friend Anna Wheeler) remains an outstanding contribution to feminist theory.

In this context the ideas of Wollstonecraft and other liberal feminists were but a starting point, and although socialist feminism was never a coherent movement, a number of key themes emerge. In the first place, the goal was not equal rights within the existing system, but within a radically transformed one in which private property was to be abolished or severely modified, and in which women would have economic as well as legal independence. Secondly, the traditional division of labour between the sexes was widely attacked: not only were women to be given a full place in productive life, but men were to share communal responsibility for domestic work. Thirdly, the family as an institution was widely condemned: it was seen as a source of male power, a bastion of selfish individualism incompatible with socialist co-operation, and as a coercive restraint on free choice. Following from this, some stressed, fourthly, the importance of the free expression of sexuality, and argued that 'free love' was the necessary basis of a free society. All this meant that the liberal claim for equal rights was now placed firmly within a social-economic context of which Wollstonecraft had shown only passing awareness, and power relationships were identified within the family as well as in public life. Recent writers have also seen in the new ideas on sexuality a symbolic challenge to the dualism of Western political thought, for reason and virtue no longer seemed to require the denial of passion, but rather its fullest possible expression (Coole, 1988).

Attempts to put this analysis into practice, however, met with little success. With their faith in reason and human perfectibility the leaders were very much children of the Enlightenment; they therefore expected that education and example would prove the moral and practical superiority of their system, and that capitalist funding would be found to further the cause of social transformation. Perhaps not surprisingly, such support was seldom forthcoming. Thus although Owen claimed to have shown that benevolence was not incompatible with capitalist self-interest in his famous model factory at New Lanark in Scotland, where improved conditions, health and housing had produced not only a healthy workforce but healthy profits too, other capitalists remained unconvinced that this represented a sound return on investment, and were frightened off the scheme by Owen's increasingly radical ideas on religion and the family. Owen himself came to see the establishment of socialist communities as a speedier means of regenerating society; as with those inspired by Fourier, the idea was not to 'drop out' of existing society, but to change it by force of example; in practice, however, the communities were to prove more of a warning than an inspiration.

America in the nineteenth century had seemed to offer an ideal opportunity for such experiments, and Emerson wrote in 1840 that 'Not a reading man but has a draft of a new community in his waistcoat pocket' (quoted in Muncy, 1973, p. 5). Of the five hundred or so secular and religious communities that were established, about 50 were inspired by Fourier and 16 by Owen (of which the most famous was New Harmony, founded in 1825 by Owen himself); there were also at least 7 Owenite communities in England between 1821 and 1845 (Lockwood, 1971; Harrison, 1969; Hardy, 1979; Garnett, 1972). However, none of these socialist communities lasted for more than a few years; this was partly because optimism and idealism could not compensate for lack of practical skills and financial resources, and partly because they tended to attract all kinds of opportunists and misfits and were torn by personality clashes and policy disputes; attitudes to women and to the family also seem to have played a crucial role.

For Owen private property, religion and marriage formed a kind of unholy and inseparable trinity; each was evil in itself, each upheld the others, and none could therefore be eradicated in isolation. Thus to stop the married woman being treated as the property of her husband, it was necessary to abolish not only marriage but also private property. To abolish private property, it was necessary to remove the major source of individualism and selfish gratification – the family. To do this, it was necessary to attack the cement that bound them together and upheld them both – religion. However, although the three institutions were logically entwined in theory, Owen found himself unable to abolish the family in practice: most of those entering the communities wished to live as couples, communal child-rearing and the separation of children from their parents was far too unpopular to carry out, and fear of scandal led him to downplay his attack on marriage (although in fact Owen never advocated promiscuity, but stable relationships based on free consent rather than legal constraint). The need for such caution was shown by the extent of public hostility to the Owenite community that had been established at Nashoba in 1825 by Frances Wright, with the rehabilitation of former negro slaves as a major aim (Eckhardt, 1984); Wright's unorthodox views on marriage ('she put an affirmation of sexual experience that no one else in nineteenth century America would approach', Eckhardt, 1984, p. 156) provoked widespread condemnation and effectively removed any chances of attracting 'respectable' financial support. Fourier's ideas on the liberating effects of sensuality were downplayed for similar reasons: he had advocated extreme sexual permissiveness both as a means of breaking down the ethics of individualism and possessiveness, and because he thought repression was harmful and incompatible with harmonious society; clearly his ideas could all too easily become an excuse for sexual exploitation, but in practice the Fourierite communities largely ignored this aspect of his thought and adopted a relatively conservative attitude to the family (Muncy, 1973, p. 70). This means that although the failure of the communities is often cited as proof of the inadequacy of the utopian socialists' theories, their theories on the family were never in fact put to the test.

As with the family and sexuality, so too with the division of labour, socialist theory was never matched by community practice. Here Fourier's views were again the most radical, for he demanded a total end to all specialisation and the entire division of labour: he argued that work could be fulfilling and creative only if it were freely chosen, and that an ideal community must be organised to allow all individuals to move freely from one occupation to another. He did seem to think that some jobs will naturally be more attractive to women and implied that they should care for very small children, but he also insisted that in any occupation at least some of the workers should be of the sex that does not normally perform it (Robertson, 1982). This meant that no man or woman would be bound to one task for life and that domestic tasks like all other work would be the willingly performed expression of creativity rather than mindless drudgery. In practice, however, Fourier's elaborate ideas were never systematically applied, and, despite the claims of the men to the contrary, it seems that responsibility for domestic life remained firmly with the women in all the communities. In this context it is perhaps not surprising that they should consistently be less enthusiastic in their support than the men; this was often taken as a sign of women's political backwardness, but as Barbara Taylor has argued it

> had less to do with any innate partiality for individual wash-tubs than a fear, often justified, of becoming embroiled in a hard life over which they would have too little control, and in which they would bear the brunt of utopian impracticality (Taylor, 1983, p. 250).

However, as indicated at the beginning of this section, the impact of utopian socialism and its importance for feminist theory was not limited to the experience of the communities, but became linked in the 1830s and 1840s to a revival of interest in feminist issues which although short-lived was international in character. Thus, for example, Frances Wright had contacts in England, France and America, while there were many direct links between Owenites in England and French feminists inspired by the ideas of St Simon and Fourier. Moreover, while previous generations of feminists had broken ground by going into print, women such as Frances Wright, Anna Wheeler and Frances Morrison were now stating their case in public and drawing huge crowds to their lectures and meetings (Taylor, 1983).

Enthusiasm for the feminist cause was however by no means universal amongst socialists, particularly in England where Owenism had by the 1830s built up a considerable basis of working-class support strongly linked to the co-operative and trade union movements. Owenism never became a mass movement on the scale of the Chartist campaign for the vote which reached its peak at about the same period, but its feminism posed problems for working-class supporters at a time when the idea of the male breadwinner and domestic wife was becoming increasingly popular amongst the working class. Women had been widely involved in political activity such as food riots and strikes earlier in the century, but with increased sexual competition for jobs they became excluded from trade union activity, and although they played an active role in both Chartist and Owenite organisations, particularly in the earlier years, this was often in support of male activity and did not necessarily involve any kind of feminist consciousness. By the 1850s political involvement by working-class women had sharply declined and active hostility to feminism had increased (Florent 1988).

Nevertheless for a brief period socialism and feminism had been united not only with each other but with the idea that it is only by transforming *personal* life that wider political and socio-economic changes can occur, and that such personal change itself can only succeed in the context of wider social transformation – so that the personal, the political and the socio-economic are inextricably linked and intertwined. Although latent in all utopian socialist theories, especially Owenism, these interconnections were made most explicit in the work of William Thompson (1775–1844), a leading Owenite and economist who gave feminism a centrality lacking in other writers, and whose most direct analysis of women's situation is to be found in his splendidly titled *Appeal of One Half of the Human Race, Women, Against the Pretensions of the Other Half, Men, to Retain Them in Political and Thence Civil and Domestic Slavery*, a work which he wrote in close co-operation with Anna Wheeler, a leading socialist feminist lecturer.

William Thompson's Appeal on Behalf of Women

This was formally a reply to James Mill's *Article on Government* (published 1824) in which Mill had claimed that as women have no interests separate from those of their husband or father, they have no need for independent political representation. As such, it ridiculed Mill's logic and vigorously restated the liberal case for equal rights; here Thompson went well beyond Wollstonecraft's tentative ideas on representation to insist that women are entitled to full political rights including representation and participation in affairs of state. Their intellectual capacity is, he argued, at least as great as men's, and biological differences can never be an argument against political rights. At present 'the law has erected the physical organisation into a crime' (*Appeal*, p. 171), but in fact, he asserts, the consequences of female biology are much less incapacitating than the diseases of excess to which male legislators are prone, while

Is it possible to conceive that legislative power lodged exclusively in the hands of women could have produced atrocities and wretchedness equal to those with which exclusive male legislation has desolated the globe? (*Appeal*, p. 131.)

However, Thompson was not simply a liberal feminist, and although he claimed these equal rights he argued that they could become meaningful only when common ownership and co-operation replaced private property and competition as a basis of social organisation. Until such time, he claimed, women could still be disadvantaged, for formal equality takes no account of actual difference of condition (such as responsibility for child-rearing), so that men will in practice be more successful than women and 'Superiority in the production or accumulation of individual wealth will ever be whispering into man's ear preposterous notions of his relative importance over woman' (*Appeal*, p. 198). Economic independence for Thompson therefore involved far more than Wollstonecraft's insistence that women have the right to follow a career, for it included the independence of a wife from her husband. This he argued, could only be achieved in a co-operative society in which the full worth of women's contribution would be appreciated, and in which there would be no motives for men to practice injustices or for women to submit to them – for only without the distorting influences of possession and property could men and women relate to each other as free and equal human beings.

However, although women's oppression was therefore seen as a product of capitalism reinforced by unequal laws, he also saw it as based on men's selfishness:

Whatever system of labour . . . whatever system of government . . . under every vicissitude of MAN's condition he has always retained woman his slave (*Appeal*, p. 196).

This led him to an analysis of the ways in which men have kept women as their slaves which has clear affinities to the radical feminist analysis of patriarchy and oppression in personal relationships. Thus, he argued that a husband (a man 'who has admitted a woman to the high honour of becoming his involuntary breeding machine and household slave') does not simply use legal or physical coercion to dominate his wife but insists on controlling her mind, demanding her love as well as her obedience and 'exacting from her trained obsequiousness the semblance of a *voluntary* obedience'. He saw the family too as a means of male domination, where women are 'isolated and stultified with their children, with their fire and food-processing processes' and reduced by their despotic husbands 'to a state of stupidity and apathy, rendering them incapable of a greater degree of happiness than that of the brutes' (*Appeal*, pp. 63, 66, 180 and 70).

All this is strong stuff, and provides an analysis of power in personal and family relations which is far removed from Wollstonecraft's ideal of the 'domestic citizen'. However it did not lead Thompson to condemn his sex in perpetuity or to advocate the kind of separation envisaged by some modern radical feminists (and by Mary Astell, see above). Rather he believed that the true interests of the sexes could be reconciled, for if women were free then men would find the pleasures of equal companionship far outweighed those of despotism; on a larger scale, the ending of relations of dependency and possession in personal life would make possible a new and higher order of society and

> As women's bondage has chained down man to the ignorance and vices of despotism, so will their liberation reward him with knowledge, with freedom and with happiness (*Appeal*, p. 213).

This conclusion blends liberal, socialist and radical analysis as it shows the interconnections of political, economic and personal power, and as such it has much in common with modern socialist feminist analysis. It also frequently bears a startling resemblance to the ideas put forward by John Stuart Mill (the son of James Mill) in his famous *On the Subjection of Women* some 24 years later; and it is based on a philosophy, utilitarianism, which is usually associated with liberal theory but which Thompson uses throughout his analysis. The implications of this will be discussed in the next chapter, but at this stage it is important to note that Thompson's use of utilitarian theory suggests that liberal concepts may be more flexible than some feminists have claimed, and not necessarily incompatible with other approaches.

The utopian socialists failed to achieve their aims, and they have generally been seen as merely an eccentric footnote to the history books. However their ideas represent an important if brief alliance of liberal, socialist and feminist ideals which challenged the distinction between the private and the public and saw the interconnections between legal, political, economic and personal subordination. For the next 150 years, liberal campaigns for political and legal rights were largely separate from socialist preoccupations with the class struggle, while the idea of personal oppression frequently disappeared from the agenda; it is only in the work of some modern feminists that these separate strands are being drawn together again.

2

Liberalism and beyond: mainstream feminism in the nineteenth century

During the nineteenth century, earlier feminist demands were increasingly translated into mainstream political action, inspiring movements for educational, legal and political reform and culminating in the mass campaign for the vote. Feminist politics did not however simply reflect the application of liberal principles to women, for it also owed much to the influence of evangelical Christianity and associated movements for moral reform; these not only led many women directly into political activity but they also provided a justification for feminist demands based on the very unliberal idea of sex *difference*. Here it was claimed that an essential feature of this difference is women's moral superiority, and that women's sex-specific qualities should be allowed to influence public life; this meant that apparently liberal demands for legal or political equality often rested on quite unliberal theoretical assumptions.

Nineteenth-century feminism was also in many ways more radical than many accounts suggest. The writers to be considered in this section were essentially 'reformist' in that they did not seek to deny the rule of law but rather to extend legal protection and rights to women, neither did they provide a systematic attack on the socio-economic system, or on marriage and the family. Nevertheless, their sense that women were a separate group in society with shared interests and experiences led them at times to an analysis in which women were seen as a class with interests distinct from and opposed to those of men. This was frequently accompanied by a celebration of female solidarity and friendship that anticipates twentieth-century ideas of 'sisterhood', and also by the belief that changes in the public sphere could only be successful if they were predicated upon changes in private life, including sexual relationships. This is not to suggest that there existed at this period a fully-fledged theory of patriarchy; nevertheless any examination of the debates of the time shows that the ideas of radical feminists were being anticipated to a much greater extent than is generally realised, and that to label the approach of the nineteenth-century writers and reformers simply as 'liberal feminist' is to impose an inappropriate classification based on conventional politics, and hence to obscure its nature and diversity (Maynard, 1989; Levine, 1987).

This very diversity also makes it extraordinarily difficult to gain a clear overview of the development of feminist thought during the period. What we find is an almost exponential growth of ideas and activities; particular analyses or campaigns could lead off in all kinds of directions, or they could disappear only to emerge years later in a different guise; groups and campaigns sometimes seem to grow, divide, coalesce and fragment almost at random. Any attempt to understand such a complex movement is likely to involve an arbitrary selection of issues and ideas. The problem may, however, be side-stepped by studying the ideas of outstanding individuals and their interaction with the movement as a whole: here I have chosen to concentrate on Elizabeth Cady Stanton in America and John Stuart Mill and his wife Harriet Taylor in England. This selection involves the exclusion of notable feminist writers such as Margaret Fuller (1810–50) and Harriet Martineau (1802–76), and marginalises activists such as Sarah and Angelina Grimké (1792–1873 and 1805–1879), Susan Anthony (1820–1906) and Lucy Stone (1818–93) in America, and Barbara Leigh Smith Bodichon (1827–91) and Josephine Butler (1828–1906) in England (see Rendall, 1985; Rossi, 1973; Flexner, 1959; Sabrovsky, 1979; Herstein, 1985; Levine, 1987; Wheeler, 1983; Weiner, 1983; Urbanski, 1983; Dubois, 1981). However Stanton, Taylor and Mill do between them cover virtually all the ideas of 'mainstream' feminism during the period. Stanton was not only a highly original writer, but was active in the American woman's movement for over half a century; frequently highly controversial, she cannot be seen as representative of American feminism, but she was in touch with all of its aspects. Mill's *Subjection of Women* is frequently seen as the classic statement of liberal feminism, but I will argue that it was both less original and more radical than its reputation suggests; he and Taylor were not isolated voices in Victorian Britain, but were bound up with a more general development of feminist ideas.

Elizabeth Cady Stanton and feminism in America

Like many other American feminists, Elizabeth Cady Stanton (1815–1902) first developed her ideas in the context of the movement for moral reform that had emerged from the religious revivalism of the early years of the century. Although it is perhaps difficult for many twentieth-century feminists to empathise with the temperance campaigners, their activities rapidly developed a feminist dimension. As in England, a woman on marriage surrendered all independent legal rights, including protection from an abusive husband, the right to leave him and the right to keep her own property or earnings. Temperance campaigners soon demanded that women who were on the receiving end of male drunkenness should have legal protection and the opportunity to escape from a violent marriage. This led to demands for the reform of divorce and child custody laws, for women to have the access to education and employment that would give them economic independence, and, by the 1840s, to the first organised political campaign for a married woman's right to her own property.

The movement for the abolition of slavery was also related to the growth of feminist ideas in a number of ways. Most obviously, at a time when a married woman was effectively her husband's possession, there was a clear analogy between the situation of women and slaves. The movement was both a moral crusade and a liberal republican campaign, for the institution of slavery could be seen not only as an affront to God, but also as a violation of the spirit of the American constitution; in both cases the arguments against negro slavery could be used on behalf of women, while the frequently cited argument that slavery involved the sexual exploitation of women (both of the female slave by her owner, and of his wronged wife) introduced a gender-specific aspect to the debate. Perhaps more important, however, was the actual experience of those women who felt themselves morally bound to campaign for the abolition of slavery, but who found themselves precluded from an active role because of their sex. Even the collection of signatures for petitions was often frowned upon; while vehement opposition to their attempts to speak in public on the issue led Sarah and Angelina Grimké to a passionate assertion of the rights of women which went beyond the earlier ideas of Mary Wollstonecraft in demanding that women themselves act to secure their political, legal and economic equality with men (Sabrovsky, 1979; Rossi, 1973). (Here there is a clear parallel with the experiences of women in modern left-wing movements and the growth of modern radical feminism, see Chapter 10 below.) Stanton herself was incensed to find that she and other women delegates were excluded from an anti-slavery convention held in London in 1840, and that the suggestion of female participation in the proceedings led to an 'excitement and vehemence of protest and denunciation (that) could not have been greater, if the news had come that the French were about to invade England' (quoted in Buhle, 1978, p. 79). It was this experience, coupled with Stanton's personal frustrations with the demands of domesticity, that provided the direct inspiration for the first ever women's rights convention – the Seneca Falls Convention of 1848, which Stanton later claimed represented 'the inauguration of a rebellion such as the world had never seen' (quoted in Rossi, 1973, p. 144).

The Seneca Falls Convention

At one level the Declaration of Sentiments and the Resolutions resulting from the convention (which were signed by 68 women and 32 men) can be seen as a straightforward demand that the principles of liberal republicanism be applied to women as well as to men. Indeed the Declaration was deliberately modelled on the 1776 Declaration of Independence, down to its assertion that 'We hold these truths to be self-evident: that all men *and women* are created equal . . .' (Rossi, 1973, p. 416; my italics); and it used the language of mainstream American politics to demand the rights of women as citizens to the vote, to property, to education, to employment and to public participation in politics and the church. In this respect it marked an important milestone for liberal feminism; women's rationality and equality with men were now taken as given, and the tentative ideas of earlier writers were brought together in concrete demands for legal change and for collective action to achieve it; the basis was now laid for the emergence of feminism as a political movement as well as a theory.

Critics of liberal feminism have, however, argued that this position contained a number of contradictions. Firstly, although it recognised the collective interests of women and their oppression by men, it ignored the vested interests of men in continuing their subordination. Thus although we find a recognition of male rule which would not seem out of place in a modern radical feminist account of patriarchy ('The history of mankind is a history of repeated injuries and usurpations on the part of man towards women, having in direct object the establishment of absolute tyranny over her' [in Rossi, 1973, p. 416]), this was coupled with an assumption that, by appealing to principles of reason and justice, women and men could work together to change the law and abolish male tyranny. This, critics argue, ignores the fact that a ruling class does not normally surrender power simply because that power is found to be contrary to reason. However, although this position was true of some feminists, Stanton herself became increasingly suspicious of male support, particularly after the feminist cause was set aside by most male abolitionists after the Civil War on the grounds that 'this is the negro's hour'. This betrayal, as she saw it, led her to the belief that women's emancipation must be won primarily by women themselves, and that all men, whatever their race or class, formed an 'aristocracy of sex' with vested interests opposed to women. This belief was one of the issues that separated Stanton from more 'moderate' campaigners, and contributed to a split in the organised women's movement which was not reunited until the 1890s; and it means that in her writings we can find a clear analysis of women as an oppressed class which could only be freed by its own collective struggle.

Another criticism that has been made of liberal feminists in general and of Stanton in particular, is that to demand rights for women as individuals on the same basis as men is to ignore the fact that their shared domestic situation prevents full exercise of these rights. Stanton had seven children and frequently complained of the problems of combining motherhood and political activity. However, she never really questioned female responsibility for home and children, and Eisenstein says that in wanting women to become citizens without questioning their role in the family, 'Stanton's understanding of how motherhood and woman's domestic responsibility exclude her from public (male) life appears to be forgotten' (Eisenstein, 1981, p. 162). In other words, despite her perception of women as a sex class, her appeal to principles of liberal individualism ignored the collective and sex-specific restrictions on women's lives, and she failed to see that this private oppression could negate the achievements of public equality.

A further problem arises from the implication that the male world of politics and paid employment is a source of fulfilment and 'republican virtue' in a way that women's domestic sphere is not, so that women can only realise their human potential when they enter the public sphere. As we saw earlier, this idea had been rejected by Mary Wollstonecraft, who argued that responsible motherhood could be an important source of citizenship, but is perhaps inherent in the liberal elevation of mental over bodily activity – from which perspective all manual and physical work is inferior to a life of reason, and the activities of the middle-class male are seen as the most truly 'human'. Stanton herself was ambiguous on the matter, and had found motherhood to be a source both of great satisfaction and of intense frustration. At times she suggested that woman's capacity to bear children made her superior to man, and, like Mary Wollstonecraft, she argued that good mothering was a public responsibility that must be based on education and the exercise of reason. Here her accounts of her battles with male 'experts' on how to feed and care for her children make for amusing reading: she rejected the contemporary practice of swaddling (which was based on the belief that unbound infant limbs would break under their own weight), and the medical opinion that a baby's stomach could only hold one tablespoonful of milk (an opinion which she held responsible for many infant deaths through malnutrition); when her own childrearing methods proved successful she was congratulated on her 'female instinct', but she preferred to think that her practices were based on reason (Rossi, 1973, pp. 396–401). However, she also claimed that motherhood 'calls out only the negative virtues that belong to apathetic classes, such as patience, endurance and self-sacrifice' (*History of Woman Suffrage*, vol. I, p. 22), and in general her writings imply that public life is both more fulfilling and more important than the domestic sphere. Some modern feminists argue that such a view is the inevitable outcome of liberal premises, which involve an uncritical adoption of male values and a devaluation of traditional female activity.

However, much of this criticism is to miss the point that for many of the Senecca Falls delegates, and for many activists throughout the century, public rights were demanded not for their own sake, but as a practical means of improving women's daily lives. It was not that, as Eisenstein has claimed (Eisenstein, 1981), these feminists believed that private oppression could be simply legislated away, but it seemed clear that the lot of a woman trapped in a violent marriage would be better if she had the legal right to leave her husband and to achieve economic independence; rights of education and employment were clearly also of practical importance to single women who would otherwise have no role in society or reasonable source of income. The vote itself did not become a central campaigning issue until after the American Civil War when black men were enfranchised (see p. 48), and it was only towards the end of the century, when most other rights seemed to have been won, that the organised woman's movement could be largely equated with the suffrage campaign. This reduction of the movement to a single issue was vigorously opposed by Stanton, who consistently argued that women's oppression involved not only the denial of her rights as a citizen but her sexual exploitation. She further insisted that this was related to her economic situation and to the whole system of social and religious indoctrination: 'The battle is not wholly fought until we stand equal in the church, the world of work, and have an equal code of morals for both sexes' (quoted in Eisenstein, 1981, p. 112).

The analysis of sexual oppression

This claim that women's problems lie not only in the denial of political and legal rights, but also in an oppressive sexual morality goes well beyond traditional liberal concerns, and it was already present at Seneca Falls, where delegates demanded a rejection of the dual standard of morality 'by which delinquencies which exclude women from society, are not only tolerated, but deemed of little account in man' (Rossi, 1973, p. 147). For virtually all the 'mainstream' feminists of the nineteenth century this did not mean that women should be freed from repressive sexual morality but that men should submit to it too; unlike the early socialists, the goal for most feminists was chastity for both sexes. This was in line with the ideas of both the evangelical movement, with its stress on self-discipline and traditional virtues, and the liberal suspicion of the body which, with its stress on reason, elevated mental over physical activity and tended to equate sexual enjoyment with animal self-indulgence. Stanton herself did not deny that sex could be pleasurable to both men and women, and in the late 1860s she worked briefly with Victoria Woodhull, a notorious exponent of free love. However, she shared the belief that sexual desire was a source of weakness and exploitation that must be strictly controlled, both because it constituted an inferior form of human behaviour, and because of the practical consequences for women's health. Here she shared the dominant view that women were more able than men to control their sexual appetites, and that the unrestrained exercise of male sexuality caused great misery and degradation to the female sex. Thus in marriage a woman had no right to deny her husband's sexual advances and was at risk from both unwanted pregnancy and venereal disease; it was therefore male lust that drove many women to seek abortion (which Stanton opposed on health grounds while refusing to blame the women who had recourse to it); prostitution was a clear consequence of both male sexuality and the unjust economic system that drove some women to such desperate measures; all women, moreover, were united by a fear of rape. Indeed, like some modern radical feminists, Stanton went so far as to see rape as synonymous with the condition of her sex: 'Society, as organised today under the man power, is one grand rape of womanhood, on the highways, in our jails, prisons, asylums, in our homes, alike in the world of fashion and of work' (Dubois, 1981, p. 123).

All this means that issues of power and domination were identified not only in public political life, but also in the most intimate relationships; and Stanton campaigned publicly to change conditions of family life and marriage. Here she went well beyond existing claims for married women's property rights to attack the institution of marriage itself, seeing it as a form of unpaid prostitution and domestic labour, rather than a religious sacrament based on love and mutual obligation. Her own ideas on this were reinforced by her experience in talking to small women-only groups in the late 1860s; these seem to have been very similar to modern consciousness-raising groups (see Chapter 10 below), where personal problems could be explored with other women, and frequently found to reflect a shared situation. A central issue was women's loss of sexual autonomy on marriage, for a wife had no right to deny her husband sexual access to her body; and Stanton increasingly saw this as a root cause of women's oppression: 'Women's degradation is in man's idea of his sexual rights. How this marriage question grows on one. It lies at the very foundation of all progress' (in Rossi, 1973, pp. 392–3). In one sense this position can be seen simply as a logical extension of the premises of liberal individualism, whereby the idea that an individual has rights in his or her person gains specific meaning when applied to women. The issue could therefore be expressed using the language of the liberal tradition; thus Lucy Stone, who was generally seen as a more 'moderate' and 'respectable' feminist than Stanton, wrote: 'It is very little to me to have the right to vote, to own property etc if I may not keep my body, and its uses, in my absolute right' (quoted by Wheeler, 1983). However, it also involved a redefinition of power and politics that anticipated the modern radical feminist claim that 'the personal is political'; private life was seen as an arena in which power is both exercised and can be challenged, and this meant that women's freedom was to be won, not simply by allowing them to enter into public life, but by transforming their situation at home.

Eisenstein has complained that here Stanton failed to match her analysis with an adequate solution: having shown the collective and all-pervasive nature of women's oppression by men, she relied on formal legal and political changes to end it – a solution which falsely 'assumes that all the relations of marriage are embedded in law' (Eisenstein, 1981, p. 159). This is, however, to over-simplify the nature of Stanton's demands. Certainly she wanted full legal and political rights for women, and she attached great importance to changes in the law. However, she did not see these legal changes as occurring in isolation, or as sufficient in themselves to bring about the changes she desired: this would require a major shift both in women's and men's consciousness, and in socio-economic conditions. In a sense, the process of demanding change was radical in itself, as it undermined the dominant consciousness by challenging the legitimacy of male power, and placing hitherto unmentioned issues on the public agenda. An assault on the formal collective powers of men therefore brought into question the morality of each individual oppressor. This power was also attacked by challenging conventional as well as legal rights, and it is in this context that we can understand some feminists' insistence on retaining at least part of their own name on marriage, and their experiment with the 'Bloomer costume' in the early 1850s. To refuse to be known as 'Mrs Henry Stanton' and to dress for comfort and convenience rather than male approval was, Stanton believed, to assert her own autonomy and to reject the slave status implied in the loss of name – although the Bloomer costume (a full, calf-length skirt over baggy trousers) attracted so much hostility and ridicule that it distracted from all other issues, and Stanton soon stopped wearing it in public. Relations between husband and wife could also, Stanton believed, be changed through education, and here as so often she went beyond 'moderate' feminist demands for women's access to education, to insist that the sexes be educated *together*. She saw co-education as important, not simply because women have a right to knowledge and qualifications, but because it would help change the attitudes of the sexes towards one another: by working and learning together boys and girls would see each other as equals, so that their adult relationships, including marriage, could be based on respect, equality and companionship.

Religion and the Woman's Bible

Towards the end of her life, this concern with changing the attitudes that underlie sexual subordination led Stanton to attack what she saw as a major agent of indoctrination: religion. *All* forms of organised religion were, she argued, hostile to women: the Hindu widow on the funeral pyre, the Turkish woman in the harem, the American mother refusing chloroform in childbirth because she must suffer for Eve's original sin – all were victims of male-dominated religion. Although some individual ministers were supportive, she found the churches in America to be an enormously powerful force against her feminist ideas, and as her

early evangelicalism turned into agnosticism (although not athe-
ism), she adopted an increasingly anti-clerical position. This culmi-
nated in the 1890s when she attempted to make the attack on
religion a focal point for the organised women's movement; and
in 1895 she published, in collaboration with other women, *The
Woman's Bible*, a feminist critical commentary which denied that
female subordination was divinely ordained, and claimed that men
had manipulated religion to legitimise their power (extracts in
Dubois, 1981). However, this 'monument to feminist religious
polemical scholarship' (Banner, 1980, p. 164) did not achieve what
she had hoped; religious leaders refused to take her arguments
seriously, and the new generation of feminist leaders was increasingly reluctant to become involved in any issue other than the
suffrage campaign.

Class, race and feminism

Although throughout the century more 'respectable' feminists
were anxious to distance themselves from Stanton's seemingly
intemperate attacks on the church and her willingness to debate
sexual affairs in public, she was far from alone in seeing women's
emancipation as a matter of more than legal and political change;
frequently it was the manner and timing of what she said, rather
than its content, that antagonised erstwhile co-workers. On economic matters, however, she sometimes went further from the
'mainstream' position, particularly in the period from 1868 to 1870
when with Susan Anthony she edited a feminist journal, *The
Revolution*. This took a decidedly pro-labour, anti-capitalist stand,
and made a serious, although unsuccessful, attempt to organise
women workers. It is therefore untrue to say of Stanton that she
was concerned only with the problems of middle-class women;
like Mary Wollstonecraft she consistently criticised economic
inequalities, and she showed a keen interest in the ideas of the
Utopian socialists. However, she never developed a sustained
economic analysis of capitalism; and although she worked in the
early 1870s with Victoria Woodhull, who published the first
American edition of the *Communist Manifesto*, and who was president of the small American branch of the First International (see
Banner, 1980, pp. 125–30), she appears to have had no knowledge

of Marxist economic theory. Moreover, far from focusing on the problems of the working class as a whole, like many other nineteenth-century feminists her concern for the situation of working-class women was combined with extreme hostility to working-class men. In part, this stemmed from resentment of the fact that the most ignorant man had political rights denied to middle-class women like herself. For Mary Wollstonecraft, writing at a time when most men were denied the vote, the franchise had been a marginal matter (*Vindication*, p. 259), but to the nineteenth century American woman 'to have drunkards, idiots, horse-racing rum-selling rowdies, ignorant foreigners and silly boys fully recognised . . . is too grossly insulting' (Stanton's *Address to the Seneca Falls Convention*, in Dubois, 1981, p. 32). As the century progressed, the feminist movement increasingly preyed upon the class prejudices of middle-class women, and Stanton's original demand for universal suffrage became a call for the 'educated vote' (that is, a literacy qualification for both sexes). She also maintained that rape was a crime only of working-class men, and towards the end of her life she advocated birth control as a means of limiting the numbers of the working class.

Intertwined with this class hostility was a considerable amount of racism. This is at first sight surprising in view of American feminism's origins in the Abolitionist movement, when Stanton and others had frequently equated the conditions of black men and women: 'the black man and the women are born to shame. The badge of degradation is the skin and the sex – the "scarlet letter" so sadly worn upon the breast' (in Dubois, 1981, p. 83). Some modern feminists argue however that such comparison of the situation of women and black men is itself racist, as it forgets that not all women are white and means that black women disappear from the agenda. Moreover, in the aftermath of the Civil War, Stanton refused to support the enfranchisement of the black man if the vote were not also given to women; she argued that white women were *more* entitled to the vote than were former slaves and, furious at the betrayal of the women's cause by those for whom she had worked, she did not scruple to attempt to 'build feminism on the basis of white women's racism' (Dubois, 1981, p. 92).

Until recently, the political activism of black women has been largely written out of history by white commentators. It is however now being rediscovered by black feminists who are both redefining the concept of political activity from a black perspective and rescuing the ideas of such eminent foremothers as Maria Stewart and Sojourner Truth (see Collins, 1990, ch. 1). Truth (1797?–1883) was a former slave who travelled the country talking on black and women's issues; her most famous speech was at a women's rights convention at Akron in 1851 where she poured scorn on the male claim that women were too weak and frail to deserve the vote, with a reminder of the strength and trials of those like herself – 'And ain't I a woman?' (in Schnier, 1972, pp. 94–5). In general, however, much black women's activism remained marginal to the suffrage campaign, and by the end of the century their involvement was actively discouraged by its white leaders, lest their presence antagonise white women from the south (see Davis, 1981; Spender, 1983a, pp. 357–74).

The difference/equality debate

Such discrimination on grounds of race is quite clearly at odds with the sentiments of individual rights proclaimed at Seneca Falls half a century before. However, by this time American feminists were abandoning equal rights arguments for those based on women's moral superiority – a view of natural difference that could also encompass ideas of racial inequality. According to the cult of 'true womanhood' which was enjoying increased popularity by the end of the century, it was not women's shared rationality but their uniquely female qualities that entitled them to the vote; arguments that had formerly been used to deny women a role in public life were now used to demand such a role, and to insist that the 'womanly values' of purity, temperance and peace find expression in affairs of state. Although Stanton quite often referred to women's superior qualities, and she was not adverse to using this position in support of her cause, her feminism differed from the later suffragists in that her claims rested much more clearly on liberal ideas of equal rationality leading to equal rights; and despite her analysis of sex, class and the multi-faceted nature of women's oppression, these rights were in the last analysis the rights of each woman *as an individual* (on this, see a famous late essay *The Solitude of Self*, in Dubois, 1981).

Stanton's active political life spanned over half a century; her output of lectures, essays and letters was enormous, and included an attempt to document the entire course of the feminist struggle in the massive *History of Woman Suffrage* (she co-edited the first two volumes with Susan Anthony and Matilda Gage; the remaining four volumes take the story up to the 1920 Amendment to the American Constitution which gave women the right to vote). By the time of her death in 1902, important gains appeared to have been made, and even women who opposed the suffrage campaign could play a public role in a way that would have been unthinkable in Stanton's youth. As her lifelong friend Susan Anthony said, by 1902 all the legal changes demanded at Seneca Falls had been granted, except for the vote (*History of Woman Suffrage*, vol. 4, p. xiii), and from 1890 the moderate and radical wings of the organised feminist movement had been united, and increasingly concentrated on this one remaining demand. Stanton, however, consistently refused to narrow her interests to this one issue. As we have seen, although she has frequently been labelled a liberal feminist, she did not see women's problems as simply those of political and legal inequality, and throughout her life her own campaigns and interests were quite extraordinarily wide-ranging. The vote and the Bible, property rights and methods of child-rearing, trade unions and rational dress, education and rape, employment and marriage – all these were grist to her mill, for she saw male power as all-pervasive, and the public and private spheres as essentially interrelated. Although she never advocated separatism, she was also radical in her insistence that these changes must be fought for by women themselves, conscious of their shared interests and of the contrary interests of men; and she refused to moderate her demands and accusations to what might be considered 'ladylike' or 'respectable' – on the contrary: 'When I think of all the wrongs that have been heaped upon womankind, I am ashamed that I am not forever in a condition of chronic wrath, stark mad, skin and bone, my eyes a fountain of tears, my lips overflowing with curses . . . (quoted in Griffith, 1984, p. 164).

Nevertheless, as we have seen, some critics argue that Stanton's approach was inevitably restricted by its liberal premises, and that this was a general characteristic of American feminism, which grew during her lifetime into a significant, if frequently divided, mass movement. This same kind of combination of radicalism and conservatism was also to be found in British feminist politics and theory, to which we now turn.

John Stuart Mill and feminism in Britain

Organised feminism came later to Britain than to America, and discussion of feminist thinking in the mid-nineteenth century has tended to concentrate on the writing of John Stuart Mill (son of the James Mill who provoked Thompson's *Appeal on Behalf of Women*, see Chapter 1 above), who has been described as 'the only major liberal political philosopher to have set out explicitly to apply the principles of liberalism to women' (Okin, 1980, p. 197). Mill claimed that his philosophical readings had always convinced him of the need to give women equal rights; however, it was his close friendship with Harriet Taylor, whom he married in 1851 after the death of her husband, that gave an urgency to that intellectual conviction, and inspired his most famous feminist work, *The Subjection of Women* (written in 1861 and first published 1869). Although this book provoked considerable hostility and ridicule in England, and was the only one of his books to lose his publishers money, it had an enormous worldwide impact; it appeared in over a dozen countries in its first few years of publication, and 'It is difficult to exaggerate the enormous impression which it made on the minds of educated women all over the world' (Evans, 1977, p. 188). In America it was received with tremendous enthusiasm: Sarah Grimké (see above p. 39) at the age of 79, 'trudged up and down the countryside in Massachusetts' to sell one hundred and fifty copies of the book (Rossi, 1973, p. 296), and Stanton wrote 'I lay down the book with a peace and a joy I never felt before, for it is the first response from any man to show he is capable of seeing and feeling all the nice shades and degrees of woman's wrongs and the central point of her weakness and degradation' (Rossi, 1970, p. 62).

Recent feminist comment has, however, been generally much less flattering, and Mill's work is often seen more as an example of the inevitable *failings* of the liberal approach to feminism than of its triumphs. Its fame has led to an exaggeration of its originality by both contemporaries and later commentators: had Stanton read

William Thompson's earlier *Appeal on Behalf of Women* (see Chapter 1 above) she would have found an equally perceptive and sympathetic account of women's situation, while modern discussion of both his insights and shortcomings gains a new perspective when his ideas are placed in the context of their time.

The spread of feminist ideas

Although overshadowed by Mill and the later activities of the suffragettes, women themselves were, by the 1860s, far from silent or inactive. Harriet Taylor's *Enfranchisement of Women* (1851) is the most famous feminist work by a woman, but it was certainly not the only one, and many of her arguments were anticipated in Marion Reid's *A Plea for Woman* (1845). Only a few years later, women in Britain were not simply writing about the rights of their sex, but publicly campaigning for changes in the law. This had remained largely unchanged since Mary Wollstonecraft's time, so that a married woman was effectively her husband's possession, and she had no more legal status than a child: as Mill wrote 'There remain no legal slaves, except the mistress of every house' (*Subjection*, p. 147). For some 'factory girls', new employment possibilities offered a certain amount of economic independence, but this was lost on marriage (when a husband became legally entitled to his wife's earnings), and there was no opening up of careers for middle-class women, whose only source of economic security was to find a husband. Meanwhile the increased separation of the worlds of home and paid employment, and the strengthening of the idea of the male breadwinner, helped consolidate the 'separate spheres' ideology. According to this dominant view, woman's role was *naturally* and *essentially* domestic and family centred, while man's lay in the public world of work and politics – a view summed up in the often-quoted lines from Tennyson's *The Princess*:

> Man for the field and woman for the hearth;
> Man for the sword and for the needle she;
> Man with the head, and woman with the heart;
> Man to command and woman to obey;
> All else confusion.

In practice, this 'ideal' frequently did not correspond to reality. Many working-class households depended on the wife's earnings, and the line between home and work was far from clear, as there remained a considerable amount of domestic industry and many households tasks, such as washing, were still undertaken collectively. It also ignored the large numbers of women who must remain unmarried as there were, quite simply, not enough husbands to go round: the 1851 census found there to be about one third more women than men living in England. However, in a sense reality was less important than *beliefs* about appropriate gender roles; from the perspective of this dominant ideology, unmarried or working women were at best invisible, at worst unnatural failures.

All this means that in some ways the pressures on women were even greater than in Wollstonecraft's time; by the mid-nineteenth century, however, they were becoming increasingly challenged, and women themselves were campaigning to achieve changes in their situation. In particular, changes were demanded in relation to child custody, divorce and property laws, and for women's access to education and employment; by the 1860s the vote too was a prominent feminist demand. As Levine has pointed out (Levine, 1987), the early feminist movement in Britain was scarcely recognisable as such, as it involved a diffuse network of groups, rather than a centralised organisation with an effective leadership. From 1856 much activity centred around the 'Langham Place Group' and *The Englishwoman's Journal*, founded in 1858 by Barbara Leigh Smith Bodichon and Bessie Rayner Parkes, but there was also a nationwide growth of debating societies and social clubs in which feminist issues were discussed.

For some women, public rights were demanded as a way of imposing middle-class ideas of 'domestic virtue' and a harsh sexual morality on the poor; this was particularly true of those who claimed a role in the administration of the 1834 Poor Law, so that 'For many middle-class women, the claims that could be made on behalf of their gender were also the claims of class dominance' (Rendall, 1987, p. 27). More generally, membership of early feminist groups was largely middle or upper-middle class, and great stress was placed on the 'respectability' of their activities; unlike the utopian socialists, these ladies had no wish to offend polite society by appearing to attack the family, or by questioning conventional morality. Bodichon herself was illegitimate, although she was extremely well provided for by her father, and this meant that she frequently had to keep a low profile; similarly the support of Mary Ann Evans (George Eliot) for feminist campaigns was not publicised because she was known to be 'living in sin'. Nevertheless, the concerns of many mid-century feminists often went beyond those of their own class to stress the shared needs of all women, and their campaigns were not simply for formal legal rights. For example, the first organised group, the *Woman's Property Committee* (founded 1855), saw the importance for working-class women of the right to keep their own wages, and later campaigns around prostitution saw this as a product of poverty, legal powerlessness and male sexuality rather than the fault of the women themselves. This means that liberal ideas of individual rights coexisted with a growth of the idea that women as a sex have interests opposed to that of men. This was also at times accompanied by a self-conscious seeking out of female company and an assertion of female superiority than anticipates some strands of modern radical feminist thought. Moreover demands for political and legal rights did not necessarily involve an uncritical acceptance of male values and priorities, as some recent commentators have suggested. For some women, legal and political rights were a way of entering the male world, but for many they were seen as a means of improving conditions of domestic life that did not involve any challenge to the doctrine of 'separate spheres'; in general, they were demanded as a response to specific problems faced by women in their everyday lives, rather than ends in themselves, to which women were entitled according to principles of abstract justice. The ideas and activities of the period cannot therefore be described simply as 'liberal feminist', for this label conceals the diversity of aims, issues and assumptions that were involved. As in America, this was in part due to feminism's mixed heritage, whereby religious ideas about 'womanly virtues' mingled uneasily with liberal notions of equality and individual rights, to produce a widespread, but not necessarily coherent, demand for change.

There was, therefore, an ambiguity at the heart of Victorian feminism, an ambiguity from which John Stuart Mill was not exempt. Here I would argue that the inconsistencies and contradictions that critics have identified in his work were not unique to him, but reflected more widespread confusion. As in America, entitlement to rights was sometimes based on liberal ideas of shared rationality, and sometimes on the idea that women are in fact 'different', and that as a sex they possess qualities that deserve representation in public life. This means that rights might be demanded in order for women to 'be like men', *or* in order for them to realise their sex-specific virtues (either in the home or by raising the standards of political and intellectual life). It was therefore unclear whether women were to duplicate, complement or supplant the qualities of men, and whether their alleged political rights were to be seen as an individual entitlement, a means to general social improvement or a necessary weapon for a 'sex class' with interests opposed to those of men. As we saw, these problems were present in American feminist writings and activities, and they still beset modern feminist thought; it is in this context that we can understand some of the inconsistencies that are to be found in the writings of Mill.

J. S. Mill's Subjection of Women

At one level, Mill's *The Subjection of Women* is simply an extension to women of the Enlightenment belief that an institution can be defended only if it is in accordance with reason. Here he argued that women's subordination is a barbarous relic of an earlier historical period; far from being the inevitable outcome of natural attributes, it originated in force, and was now sanctified by custom so as to appear 'natural'. He agreed that women *appeared* to be in many ways inferior to men, but argued that this was a consequence of social pressure and faulty education, 'the result of forced repression in some directions, unnatural stimulation in others' (*Subjection*, p. 38). Women, therefore, must be given the same opportunities as men; only then will we know their true abilities, and only then will society reap the full benefit from the talents of all its members. This means that legal discrimination against women is wrong, and that 'it ought to be replaced by a principle of perfect equality, admitting no power or privilege on the one side, nor disability on the other' (*Subjection*, p. 1); in particular, women's legal servitude in marriage must be abolished, they must be allowed free access to education and employment, and they should be allowed both to vote and to hold political office.

This gives us a statement of the liberal feminist position that was clear and forceful, but by the 1860s hardly original; it was, however, qualified in certain important respects. Mill's initial position on the question of women's nature and ability is one of agnosticism, but it soon becomes apparent that the liberal idea that women are probably 'as good as men' coexisted with the suspicion that they are, in important respects, essentially 'different'. In the first place, he suggested that although women are like men possessors of reason, their mode of thinking tends to be more intuitive and 'down to earth', so that 'Women's thoughts are . . . as useful in giving reality to those of thinking men, as men's thoughts in giving width and largeness to those of women' (*Subjection*, p. 109). Some modern feminists have reacted angrily to this suggestion; thus Annas says that in identifying women's thought processes as essentially intuitive, Mill has fallen for 'the oldest cliché in the book' (Annas, p. 184), and that this gives rise to an intellectual hierarchy, in which the man of genius benefits from the lesser talents of his female research assistant. However, other recent commentators have denied that the identification of such sexual difference need involve ideas of superiority and inferiority, and Annas herself has been accused of an uncritical acceptance of conventional male values (Thornton, 1986; Mendus, 1989). Certainly Mill's other writings make it clear that he did not think that rational calculation is the only or the best way of reaching the truth, nor did he simply equate different ways of thinking with differences between the sexes. Thus he frequently stated that poets and artists have insights denied to a 'mere thinker', and in 1832 he wrote to the historian Carlyle that 'My vocation lies in a humbler sphere; I am rather fitted to be a logical expounder than an artist . . . it is the artist alone in whose hands Truth becomes impressive and a living principle of action' (in Schneewind, 1965, p. 84). In general he saw logical and intuitive thought as complementary rather than antagonistic; this means that the ideal partnership between man and woman is one of 'reciprocal superiority', so that 'each can enjoy the luxury of looking up to the other, and can have alternatively the pleasure of leading and being led in the path of development' (*Subjection*, p. 177). All this suggests that women should be admitted to intellectual life, not because they are in all relevant respects the same as men, but because they are quite probably different. This is not a liberal argument as usually understood, but, as stated above, it corresponds to a strong strand of Victorian feminism; it is also echoed in some modern radical feminist ideas about the superiority of female modes of thinking.

It is also clear that although Mill gave men and women equal political rights, and insisted that there must be no bar to women's education and employment, in practice he saw the sexes as playing very different roles in society – roles which largely conformed to the ideology of 'separate spheres'. Women, he argued, should be free to follow the career of their choice, and they should not be forced into marriage through economic necessity; if, however, they do choose marriage, then this is their career, and they should accept the responsibilities that it entails. This means that a married woman should be responsible for running the home, and 'the common arrangement, by which the man earns the income and the wife superintends the domestic expenditure, seems to me in general the most suitable division of labour between the two persons', so that 'it is not . . . a desirable custom, that the wife should contribute by her labour to the income of the family' (*Subjection*, pp. 87–8). Modern critics have not been slow to attack this conclusion, accusing Mill of betraying the very principles on which his feminism was based: 'The constraints which Mill believed should be imposed on married women constitute a major exception to his argument for equality of individual freedom between the sexes – an exception so enormous that it threatens to swallow up the whole argument' (Goldstein, 1980, p. 328). His conclusion seems to rest upon the belief that only women can or should perform domestic tasks, so that if a wife goes out to work, 'the care which she is herself disabled from taking of the children and the household, nobody else takes' (*Subjection*, p. 88); there is no suggestion that a man could ever share these tasks with his wife. Why self-determining individuals should have their roles prescribed for them in this way is completely unexamined; we can only assume that for Mill the point was so self-evident that it did not require discussion. This is surprising in the light of his otherwise consistent insistence that reason, not custom, should regulate human affairs; he was, moreover, well acquainted with and sympathetic towards the ideas of the utopian socialists who, as we saw earlier, did challenge the conventional domestic division of labour.

Mill's conclusions meant that women's opportunities were restricted by marriage in a way that men's were not, that they therefore could not be represented equally in the worlds of employment and politics and that a married woman would be economically dependent upon her husband – here Mill seems to think that a wife's *potential* ability to earn her own living would be sufficient to earn her husband's respect and ensure her position as an equal partner in the marriage. Such a view has been vigorously opposed by modern feminists, and also differs from the arguments of Mill's wife, Harriet Taylor, as expressed in the earlier *Enfranchisement of Women* (1851). There has been some doubt about the authorship of this essay, which was originally published under Mill's name; Mill himself, however, said that he was 'little more than an editor and amanuensis' (Introduction to *The Enfranchisement*, p. 1), and its arguments differ significantly from Mill's in *The Subjection*, confirming the view that it should be regarded as Taylor's work. In it Taylor argued that a married woman *should* contribute to the household income, 'even if the aggregate sum were but little increased by it', as she would then 'be raised from the position of a servant to that of a partner' (*Enfranchisement*, p. 20). This argument is clearly more in line with modern liberal feminist thinking than Mill's belief that female liberty is somehow compatible with economic dependency and full domestic responsibility. Nevertheless, Mill's ideas cannot be dismissed as the unthinking or self-interested response of a well-intentioned but essentially chauvinistic male, for they were shared with some feminist women of his day, including some members of the 'Langham Place Group' (see Rendall, 1987, chapter 4). Marion Reid had in 1845 argued on lines very similar to Mill that women were entitled to civil and political rights, but that married women should stay at home and that 'the best and noblest of women will always find their greatest delight in the cultivation of domestic virtues' (*A Plea for Woman*, p. 16). The problem was, however, compounded for Mill, because he combined his insistence that women take full domestic responsibility with a failure to discuss in any detail the value of domestic work. Reid had argued that the domestic sphere is 'not a mean ignoble one' (*Plea*, p. 21), but is as intellectually demanding as most male occupations. Like Wollstonecraft she insisted on the dignity and worth of women's traditional work and the need for female education if it is to be well performed. Mill on the other hand showed no sign of having such a high regard for domestic work. In an early essay he went so far as to deny that it could be regarded as a serious occupation; and here he argued that in an ideal marriage 'there would be no need that the wife should take part in the mere providing of what is required to *support* life; it will be for the happiness of both that her occupation should rather be to adorn and beautify it' (Rossi, 1970, p. 75). A benign interpretation might dismiss this statement as a product of the young Mill's initial infatuation with Harriet Taylor, whom he had just met; certainly by the time of *The Subjection* he saw domestic work as a serious, if tedious, business. Nevertheless it remains a mystery why Mill thought that a rational woman would freely choose to dedicate herself either to 'adorning and beautifying life' or to the wearying demands of household management; this choice makes sense only if a woman's true fulfilment lies, after all, in service to her husband – an idea which contradicts the main arguments of his book.

Critiques of Mill's liberalism

Thus far, Mill has been criticised for failing to follow his liberal principles to their logical conclusion. Other critics, however, argue that his analysis is flawed not because of an inconsistent application of liberal principles, but because of the limitations of these principles themselves. For some, this starts with his use of utilitarian theory. As originally propounded by Jeremy Bentham, a close friend of John Stuart Mill's father, James Mill, this stated that laws and moralities should be judged, not according to some abstract idea of right and wrong, but according to whether or not they increase the sum total of human happiness (*Introduction to the Principles of Morals and Legislation*, in Warnock (ed.), 1966). In calculating this (and Bentham provided complex guidelines as to how this should be done), it is assumed that all individuals seek to maximise their own pleasure, and that each person's happiness carries equal weight. This has obvious egalitarian implications, which has led Boralevi to claim that utilitarianism has a strong theoretical link with feminism, despite the unfeminist conclusions reached by James Mill and, at times, by Bentham (Boralevi, 1987; see also Ball, 1980). For some feminists, on the other hand, the assumption that people are to be understood as calculating, competitive, hedonistic and autonomous individuals is highly suspect, a paradigm based on male thinking and modes of behaviour, and one that ignores female nurturing and human interdependence (see Jaggar, 1983, chapter 3). From this perspective, classic utilitarianism involves a denial of female qualities, and cannot be the basis of an adequate feminist theory.

Mill, however, did not support this paradigm. He consistently denied that there is such a fixed, eternally-given human essence, arguing that human character is a variable product of society rather than a constant fact of nature (see *Logic*, Book 6). He also stressed the interconnectedness of human pleasures, arguing that in a properly organised society each individual would find happiness in the pleasure of others, so that 'a direct impulse to promote the general good may be in every individual one of the habitual motives of action' (*What Utilitarianism Is* in Williams (ed). 1985, p. 129). As Coole has pointed out (Coole, 1988, p. 160), similar qualifications had already been made by Thompson, and both writers used this modified utilitarian theory to demand political and legal rights for women. Here, therefore, Mill was not taking any original philosophical step, and there are striking similarities between his arguments and those of Thompson, whom he described as 'a very estimable man, with whom I was well acquainted' (*Autobiography*, p. 75). Both argued that women must be included in the utilitarian calculation of happiness, and that they require full legal and political rights to defend their interests and the opportunity to express themselves in whatever sphere of life they choose. They argued that men too would benefit if women became their equals, for the pleasures of intellectual companionship are far greater than those of despotism; thus men will gain when they no longer 'surrender the delights of equality . . . for the vulgar pleasures of command' (Thompson, *Appeal*, p. 70). Finally, and this was perhaps most explicit in Mill's work, the whole of society will benefit if relations between the sexes are based on justice and equality. Mill's arguments here are complex and cover a number of areas. Of these, the most important are, firstly, that the pool of talent available to society will be doubled, with obvious benefits for social prosperity and progress. Secondly, political life would improve as the family would become 'the real school of the virtues of freedom' (*Subjection*, p. 80), where citizens would learn the democratic virtues of self-reliance and mutual help and respect. Thirdly, the character of both men and women would improve, as 'All the selfish propensities, the self-worship, the unjust self-preference, which exist among mankind, have their source and root in, and derive their principle nourishment from, the present constitution of the relation between man and woman' (*Subjection*, p. 148). Mill further argues in other writings that if women had an alternative to marriage then this would go far to curb the evils of over-population (*Principles of Political Economy*, p. 459) – and population control was, for Mill and many other liberal economists, a prerequisite of economic prosperity.

Coole has argued that in thus stressing the benefits to men and to society, Mill has partly moved away from the stronger case that can be based on equal rights arguments. She claims that his utilitarian position opens the door to compromise, for if it could be shown that sex equality was *not* a means to the greatest happiness, then logically it would have to be abandoned, for 'Rights are now means to social well-being rather than absolute ends intrinsic in every individual' (Coole, 1988, p. 150). Here it could be that Mill's position was primarily intended to persuade the unconverted, rather than an integral part of his approach. However, as discussed above, he simply did not think that means and ends do ultimately conflict in this way; if they appear to, then this is a reflection of poor social arrangements and lack of education. A true child of the Enlightenment, be believed that the just society could be achieved through the advance of reason; there is no place in his thought for the possibility that the interests of one group or class in society could clash irrevocably with another; a harmonious society was, he believed, in the interests of all.

Another aspect of Mill's theory that has troubled modern feminists arises from a further qualification that he made to Bentham's utilitarian theory, by which he insisted that all pleasures are *not* equal, but that some are clearly superior to others; and here he argued that the 'higher' pleasures are those of the mind rather than the body. Critics say that this attitude devalues women's reproductive activity and denies the legitimacy of sexual enjoyment, and that it involves a concept of reason based on a rejection of all that has traditionally been associated with the female, so that 'the truly equal woman is she who eliminates all trace of femaleness' (Coole, 1988, p. 153). Certainly, as we saw earlier, Mill did not seriously evaluate women's domestic work, and he never suggested that their nurturing role might be a cause for celebration; on the contrary, he shared the negative view of Taylor that 'There is no inherent reason or necessity that all women shall voluntarily choose to devote their lives to one animal function and its consequences' (*Enfranchisement*, p. 18). Sex too could not be liberating or genuinely fulfilling, but must be strictly controlled; he wrote that there could be no great improvement in human life so long as 'the animal instinct of sex occupies the absurdly disproportionate place it does therein' (quoted in Mendus, 1989, pp. 178–9). His own friendship with Harriet Taylor caused considerable public scandal, but was almost certainly not sexual; his friend Thomas Carlyle wrote: 'His *Platonica* and he are constant as ever: innocent I do believe as sucking doves, and yet suffering the clack of tongues, worst penalty of guilt' (Hayek (ed.), 1951, p. 86); Mill himself wrote 'We disdained . . . the abject notion that the strongest and tenderest friendship cannot exist between a man and a woman without a sensual relation' (*Autobiography*, p. 137).

Mendus has argued that this attitude gave Mill an impoverished view of human nature, and she finds his ideal of marriage – that is, marriage of minds and not of flesh – and the accompanying image of women 'deeply depressing and distorted' (Mendus, 1989, p. 172). However, as so often, Mill's views here are not merely idiosyncratic; in seeing sex in purely negative ways he was reflecting a view dominant in Victorian Britain; we saw earlier that this was also a view held by most American feminists. Levine has pointed out that Victorian attitudes to sexuality were largely based on *fear* (Levine, 1987). This stemmed from an increased public perception of male violence towards women, a widespread concern about the incidence of prostitution (particularly child prostitution), and the related dread of contracting venereal disease. As in America, the solution was seen to lie in the control of male sexuality; from the 1850s there were campaigns against the way in which the 'dual standard' of morality was enshrined in the marriage code, and by the 1860s the issues were sufficiently well-aired for a change in the law on prostitution to be met with vigorous opposition. The aim of the notorious Contagious Diseases Acts (of which there were several, the first in 1864) was to reduce the high rate of sexually transmitted disease in the armed forces. The Act decreed that any woman living in a garrison town whom the police believed to be a prostitute could be forced to undergo regular medical examination to discover if she were infected; described at the time as 'medical rape', this examination involved an often brutal and semi-public internal examination. Opponents of the Acts, of whom the most famous leader was Josephine Butler, were appalled at the way in which they condoned male vice, while perpetuating a double standard that decreed that a 'fallen woman' had no rights; some were also prepared to sympathise with the prostitutes, blaming their situation on men's wickedness and on a system that denied them alternative employment. This means that the campaign had far-reaching implications. Firstly, it implied a common interest shared by all women (for the prostitute and the 'innocent' wife infected by her husband were both victims of male lust), and saw this in terms of men's power over women. Secondly, it involved a hostility to male sexuality which recurs at intervals in the history of feminism, and finds forceful expression in some sections of the movement today. Thirdly, it related women's sexual exploitation to issues of employment and education; and, finally it suggested to many that an individual's control over her own person could not be guaranteed without legal and political rights. All this was expressed within the framework of a highly negative view of sex very similar to that of Mill (who supported Butler's campaign), and it later broadened into a more general movement for moral reform which had strong links with the suffrage movement. This suggests that Mill's views on sex cannot be dismissed simply as the outdated prejudices of a prudish Victorian intellectual, for they may be compatible with quite radical feminist campaigns; they also have strong affinities with some strands in modern radical feminist thought.

Mill himself was particularly concerned with male violence within marriage, and with a wife's loss of sexual autonomy:

> however brutal a tyrant she may be unfortunately chained to – though she may know that he hates her, though it may be his daily pleasure

to torture her, and though she may feel it impossible not to loathe him
– he can claim from her and enforce the lowest degradation of a human
being, that of being made the instrument of an animal function contrary
to her inclinations (*Subjection*, p. 57).

This meant that, like many of the American feminists, he did not
see women's subordination as lying only in their exclusion from
public life; it was rooted in relationship within the family, as it is
there that men are free to act as petty despots, and many 'indulge
the utmost habits of excesses of bodily violence towards the
unhappy wife' (*Subjection*, p. 63). Again like the American feminists, he saw legislative change as an important way of ending this
private oppression. For women to be free from domestic tyranny
they needed access to education and employment, so that economic need would not force them into marriage; they also needed
the full protection of the law, and this included political rights.

Although Mill was far from the first writer to express such an
opinion, he was the first politician to make a serious attempt to
put it into practice. For a short period he was himself a member
of parliament, and he introduced an Amendment to the 1867
Reform Bill (which gave the vote to most of the urban working
class) which sought to enfranchise women on the same basis as
men. This was supported by a petition signed by nearly 1500
women; although defeated by 123 votes, a not insubstantial 73
were cast in Mill's support, and similar reforms were introduced
by other members in many subsequent sessions. Mill's arguments
in favour of his Amendment make it clear that he was not simply
demanding public political rights as a matter of abstract justice;
rather he saw the franchise as a way of improving women's conditions in the private sphere. He denied that a woman's interests
can be incorporated in her husband's, and he insisted that the
myth of male protection be exposed – he therefore demanded
that 'a return be laid before this House of women who are annu-
ally beaten to death, kicked to death, or trampled to death by
their own protectors' (Kamm, 1977, p. 160).

This belief that domestic tyranny can be tackled by granting
women legal and political rights, is very similar to Stanton's
approach and has been attacked on similar grounds. However,
although neither Stanton nor Mill tackled the questions of econ-

omic dependency within marriage, nor the sexual division of
labour, both insisted that legal and political reforms were *not* in
themselves sufficient to ensure the ending of female subordination; for this, they both argued that a change in men and
women's consciousness and their perception of each other is
required. Here Mill argued persuasively that male dominance is
maintained not only by the obvious methods of coercion and
denial of rights, but also by a more subtle and insidious control
of women's *minds*. Thus the whole of a woman's experience and
education instils ideas of dependence and voluntary submission;
they are trained not only to obey, but to love their masters, for
'Men do not want solely the obedience of women, they want their
sentiments . . . They have therefore put everything in practice
to enslave their minds' (*Subjection*, pp. 26–7). Although often
overlooked by critics, the sections in which Mill develops these
ideas are perhaps the most perceptive in *The Subjection*, and may
well have been those that so delighted Stanton; these ideas were,
however, not original, for very similar points had been made
earlier by Thompson.

Education therefore becomes an essential part of the process of
emancipation, not simply because it provides women with career
opportunities, but because it can help change their self-perception;
attracting a man will cease to be the prime goal of a woman's life.
Throughout Mill's philosophy, education in its widest sense is a
key means to social improvement, and, as we saw earlier, women's
position within the family is integrally linked to progress in other
areas: as public rights improve women's situation and status at
home, so the family becomes a place where the lessons of despotism and submission are replaced by those of partnership and
equality; the democratic family thus becomes a training-ground
for the democratic citizen.

A further criticism that is often made of liberal feminists is that
they are concerned only with the needs and interests of middle-
class women. Clearly Mill empathised strongly with the intellectual frustrations facing a woman such as Harriet Taylor, but he
did support Butler's campaign against the Contagious Diseases
Acts and, as we have seen, he was very much concerned with
working-class victims of male violence. He was, moreover, no
apologist for the socio-economic status quo, which he saw as one

in which the wealthiest were the most idle, while those who worked hardest were little better-off than slaves. He showed considerable sympathy with the ideas of the utopian socialists, and in comparing their proposals with existing society he concluded that 'The restraints of communism would be freedom in comparison with the present condition of the majority of the human race' (*Principles of Political Economy*, p. 129). His preferred solution, however, was for a reformed private property system in which rights of inheritance were strictly controlled and workers' co-operatives and profit-sharing schemes would be encouraged: 'it is not to be expected that the division of the human race into two hereditary classes, employers and employed, can be permanently maintained' (*Principles*, p. 460). It remains true that, unlike Thompson, Mill never developed an analysis of the ways in which the capitalist system systematically disadvantaged women, nor is there any room in his theory for the possibility of substantive conflict of interest between classes or between men and women; nevertheless his goal was equality between the sexes not within the existing unequal society, but within one in which both political and economic life had become significantly more democratic.

There is a sense in which Mill's feminism is significant not because of what he said but because of who he was. Virtually all of the points that he made in *The Subjection* had been made earlier by Thompson; many had also been made by Marion Reid, Harriet Taylor and the American feminists. Because of his fame, however, he has attracted more than his share of critical commentary, and he has been widely criticised both for failing to follow his principles of liberal individualism to their logical conclusion, and for failing to understand the limitations of these principles. Like the American feminists he failed to explore the critical questions of economic dependency and the division of labour, nor did he really examine the interrelationships of class and sex oppression, or see that the institutions of society might not be neutral, but might be systematically biased in favour of one class or sex. His repressive attitude to sex also finds little sympathy from contemporary feminists. Nevertheless, like so many nineteenth-century feminists his concerns were not as narrowly formal and legalistic as the 'liberal feminist' label suggests; at times his ideas have a surprising affinity with some strands of modern radical feminism. In terms of both his insights and his limitations he would seem to be a typical Victorian feminist; despite the attention which his work has received he did not produce any new theoretical insights.

Britain and America were not the only nations in which feminism developed in the nineteenth century. Although the timing and nature of feminist ideas and movements varied, Evans has claimed that there was a common pattern of development, whereby initial claims for property, education and employment rights became fused with campaigns for moral reform, and led eventually to the demand for the vote; liberal equal rights arguments, often associated with the rise of an independent middle class, were also important.

Thus similar arguments were being developed throughout the industrialising world, and there was a clear international dimension to the growth of feminist ideas. Mill's *Subjection* was published in a dozen countries and was associated with the founding of feminist movements in Finland, France and Germany (Evans, 1977, p. 19). Similarly Ibsen's play *The Dolls House* (1879), which proclaimed that a woman has rights as an individual as well as a wife and mother, had an international impact (extract in Schneir, 1972). The nineteenth century cannot, however, be seen simply as a time when the justice of mainstream feminist demands was gradually accepted. As we shall see in the following chapters, the success of feminist movements varied widely, and although many men and women came to believe that women should have full legal rights, when it came to political rights many others agreed with Queen Victoria who wrote in 1872 that: 'The Queen is most anxious to enlist every one who can speak or write to join in checking this mad, wicked folly of 'Women's Rights' . . . It is a subject which makes the Queen so furious that she cannot contain herself. God created men and women different – then let them remain each in their own position' (quoted in Kamm, 1977, p. 179).

3

The contribution of Marx and Engels

It is at first sight odd to include in a work on feminist political theory a section on classic Marxism, because Karl Marx was not a feminist. This does not mean that he was hostile to female liberation but simply that, unlike Mill or Thompson, he did not see issues of sexual oppression as interesting or important in their own right, and he never made them the subject of detailed empirical or theoretical investigation. It is true that he several times stated that the condition of women can be taken as an index of social progress; however by the mid-nineteenth century this idea was commonplace (see Mill's *Subjection*, p. 38), and it certainly cannot be taken as evidence of feminist insight. Indeed recent writers have suggested that, far from providing a feminist view of history, it gave women an essentially *passive* role, seeing them as the sufferers or beneficiaries from man-made history (Coole, 1988; Barrett, 1987); cynics might also draw support from Marx's least frequently quoted formulation of the approach: 'Social progress can be measured exactly by the social position of the fair sex (the ugly ones included)' (1868 letter, quoted in Draper, 1972, p. 88). Nevertheless, although Marx himself had little to say directly about women, his theory does claim to provide a comprehensive analysis of human history and society, and later writers have attempted to apply it to feminist issues. This means that to understand much modern feminist debate, it is necessary to have some knowledge of Marx's original ideas, for his theory provides a perspective completely different from the feminist ideas we have discussed so far; it is to a brief account of his theory that we must therefore now turn.

Classic Marxist theory

The ideas that Marx and Engels developed were of course extremely complex, and they have been interpreted in very many different ways. However, at their core was a view of history and society that saw the world as constantly changing and progressing, and that insisted that liberal ideas of individual rights, justice and human nature were not universal principles, but the product of a particular period of human history. The key to understanding the process of historical development lay, they argued, not in the ideas that people may hold, but in their physical productive activity; it was the first co-operative act of production that formed the basis of the earliest primitive society and the beginnings of human history, for

> life involves before everything else eating and drinking, a habitation, clothing and many other things. The first historical act is thus the production of the means to satisfy these needs, the production of material life itself (*German Ideology*, p. 48).

As methods of production gradually became more complex, so too did the division of labour and the form of social organisation based upon it; with the production of a surplus came the institution of private property and the division of society into classes and, corresponding to and reinforcing these, the development of laws, states and systems of belief, for 'The mode of production of material life conditions the social, political and intellectual life process in general. It is not the consciousness of men that determine their being, but, on the contrary, their social being that determines their consciousness' (*Preface to the Critique of Political Economy*, Selected Works, p. 182). The process of historical development was neither random nor smooth, but was expressed through class conflict and revolution, for although human history was the study of man's progressive mastery over nature, so far this had taken place within a framework of ever-increasing alienation and exploitation. Nineteenth-century capitalism was not however the final form of human society, for the conditions were developing within it that would give birth to the final proletarian revolution; it was only through this that man could gain full control over the whole productive process, and only then that a classless communist society could develop in which full human freedom could eventually be achieved and 'the narrow horizon of bourgeois right be crossed in its entirety and society inscribe on its banners: From each according to his ability, to each according to his needs!' (*Critique of the Gotha Programme*, p. 17). The extent to which all this implies a theory of technological or economic determinism is a matter of intense political and scholarly debate, but it seems clear that in seeking to understand social, political and legal systems and the beliefs that people have about them, Marx said that we must look first at the economic system on which they rest. It also means that the possibilities for change will be fairly strictly limited by socio-economic conditions, rather than being a simple product of people's intentions – for 'Men make their own history, but they do not make it just as they please; they do not make it under circumstances chosen by themselves, but under circumstances directly encountered, given and transmitted from the past' (*The Eighteenth Brumaire of Louis Bonaparte*, in *Selected Works*, p. 97).

The implications of this whole approach for feminist theory are profound. In the first place, the family and sexual relationships are, like other forms of social organisation, placed in a historical context; neither eternally given nor consciously planned, they are the product of a particular historical situation and therefore open to change in the future. Secondly, however, this change will not be brought about by appeals to reason or to principles of justice, but only as part of changes in conditions of production; unlike the utopian socialists, Marx and Engels believed that the 'good society' could not be achieved at will, but only as a result of a particular stage of historical development.

Engels' The Origin of the Family, Private Property and the State

It was essentially these ideas that formed the basis of Engels' analysis in *The Origin of the Family, Private Property and the State*. Here he drew heavily on the work of the nineteenth-century anthropologist Lewis Morgan to trace the supposed evolution of the family from the earliest savage society to the present day. He totally rejected the claim that the modern family is somehow 'natural'; indeed, he argued that in the earliest societies sexual relationships had been totally promiscuous and unregulated, and that they gradually evolved to take the form of the 'pairing family' which characterised later forms of primitive society. The force behind this evolution was in the first instance natural selection (which ensured that those tribes prohibiting incest were stronger), and then the wishes of women, who increasingly found group marriage 'oppressive and humiliating' and longed for 'the right of chastity, of temporary or permanent marriage with one man only as a way of release' (*Origin*, p. 60). Primitive societies also differed from modern society in that relations between the sexes were based on *equality*; there was a sexual division of labour whereby women were responsible for domestic work and men for agriculture and husbandry, but even in the pairing family (which was not the same as strict monogamy), this did not involve subordination; the women reigned supreme in the home, and descent was calculated through the female line (Engels called this 'mother right').

This egalitarian situation was changed by the development of a new source of wealth in the male sphere of activity, through the domestication of animals and the breeding of herds. As some men gained property and power over others their position within the family was strengthened, and they wanted to pass their property to their children; to do this they had to overthrow the traditional order of inheritance and ensure strict monogamy on the part of each woman, who became the mere possession of her husband, the means of producing heirs. In Engels' vivid phase, 'The overthrow of mother right was the *world historical defeat of the female sex*. The man took command in the home also; the woman was degraded and reduced to servitude; she became the slave of his lust and a mere instrument for the production of children.' This means that the subordination of women coincided with the first private property and class society, for it was then that women lost control in the home and became economically dependent upon men; it also means that female oppression has no other material cause – it is a part of class society, but not a necessary or permanent feature of human relationships. From this it follows that the abolition of private property will mean an end to sex oppression, for men will no longer have any motive to exploit women: 'The supremacy of the man in marriage is the simple consequence of his economic supremacy, and with the abolition of the latter will disappear of itself' (*Origin*, pp. 65 and 95).

The basis for new and equal relations between the sexes was, Engels argued, already developing within capitalist society, for modern industry's increasing reliance on the labour of women and children in factory production was having a profound effect upon the balance of power within the family. Nearly forty years earlier in his *The Condition of the Working Class in England* (1845) he had been greatly concerned about such employment, noting the appalling effects upon family life and describing as an 'insane state of things' the not infrequent situation in which a woman was in paid employment and her husband 'condemned to domestic occupations' – this, he argued, 'unsexes the man and takes from the woman all true womanliness', and he commented that 'It is easy to imagine the wrath aroused among the working men by this reversal of all relations within the family . . .' (*Conditions*, p. 184). However, his concern that working women were neglecting their home and children takes on a new dimension when we remember the condition and nature of early factory employment and the particular problems faced by women, who had to work throughout pregnancy (even on occasion giving birth amongst the factory machines), and who often had to return to work less than a week after giving birth; they also faced problems of sexual harassment and exploitation by the male factory-owner. Engels' descriptions were largely based on analysis of government reports and official statistics, and they remain a searing indictment of mid-nineteenth-century conditions: 'Women made unfit for childbearing, children deformed, men enfeebled, limbs crushed, whole generations wrecked, afflicted with disease and infirmity, purely to fill the purses of the bourgeoisie' (*Conditions*, pp. 198, 187 and 203).

Although of course he retained his opposition to capitalist exploitation, by 1884 Engels saw female paid employment as a progressive force. The bourgeois woman was, he argued, still a mere breeding machine and provider of sexual services who 'only differs from the ordinary courtesan in that she does not let out her body on piece-work as a wage earner, but sells it once and for all into slavery'; her economic dependence on her husband meant that 'within the family he is the bourgeois and the wife represents the proletariat'. However, the proletarian marriage was not based on property, and because the wife was frequently a wage earner 'the last remnants of male supremacy in the proletarian household are deprived of all foundation'. This meant that, paradoxically, the proletarian wife was less oppressed as a woman than her bourgeois counterpart (although she remained oppressed as a worker), and that 'the first condition for the liberation of women is to bring the whole female sex back into public industry' (*Origin*, pp. 82, 85 and 86).

The second condition for liberation was the social revolution that Engels believed would soon occur, and which would replace the capitalist economic system with one based on common ownership. As private property disappeared so too would men's motive to produce heirs and their ability to 'buy' women, whether as wives or prostitutes. At the same time, women's productive labour would no longer involve neglect of home and family, for 'Private housekeeping is transformed into a social industry. The care and education of the children becomes a public affair; society looks after all children alike, whether they are born of wedlock or not.' Marriage ('that compound of sentimentality and domestic strife') and sexual relations would also be transformed as they ceased to be based on economic needs. Engels claimed that present arrangements were characterised above all by hypocrisy; enforced monogamy for women was accompanied by sexual licence for men, while adultery and prostitution rather than fidelity and love were the basis of modern bourgeois marriage. He thought that this would be replaced not by promiscuity but by 'individual sex love', which he believed already characterised relationships amongst the proletariat; however, he refused to speculate in detail about future sexual relations, arguing that these will only be known

> when a new generation has grown up; a generation of men who never in their lives have known what it is to buy a woman's surrender with money or any other social instrument of power; a generation of women who have never known what it is to give themselves to a man from any other consideration than real love, or to refuse to give themselves to their lover from fear of the economic consequences (*Origin*, pp. 87, 87–8, 66 and 96).

All this gives us a theory that sees the changing condition of women as a product of economic processes: the subordination of women began with private property and class society; amongst the propertyless classes it has already lost its economic foundations; with the impending socialist revolution it will disappear in its entirety. For non-Marxists the apparent reduction of all social questions to an economic cause makes Engels's approach unacceptable, as does his belief in the imminent replacement of capitalism by socialism; modern Marxists have however also been highly critical of Engels's ideas, and he has been attacked at a number of levels.

Modern criticisms of Engels

Obvious problems arise from his reliance of anthropological findings that are at best highly dubious (for discussion of this, see for example Lane, 1976; Maconachie, 1987). The assumption that there was a universal pattern of family development from the first human societies is questionable, as is the claim that there was an original condition of sex equality; early man's desire to leave property to his heirs was also assumed rather than explained. Engels' belief that it must have been men who created the first wealth has also been challenged, for it seems likely that women were the first cultivators who both provided subsistence and produced the first surplus: this has led some writers to suggest that for men to assert control over this wealth, sexual oppression must have *pre-dated* class society (Humphries, 1987). More serious in its implications for future developments is Engels' assumption that there was an original and natural division of labour between the sexes, an assumption that is also to be found in his and Marx's early writings (see *The German Ideology*, pp. 44 and 51). This meant that although he said that in socialist society housework and childcare would be collectivised, he never thought it necessary to discuss which sex should perform these tasks; given his other remarks, the implication is that they would be done by women, an interpretation that was certainly assumed by many later Marxists.

The assumption that women are naturally responsible for home and family also obscured Engels' understanding of contemporary society and led him to ignore the labour performed by women in pre-capitalist economies. He saw the problems a woman faced in trying to combine paid work with domestic responsibility, but he never really analysed the implications of this 'dual oppression', or suggested that it could be alleviated with male help; the long-term solution was collectivisation of domestic work, and he never considered that the proletarian husband might be exploiting his wife by refusing to share her household tasks. Similarly, his approach allowed little room for understanding the sex-specific oppression of women *as workers*; in particular, he failed to show why women were paid so much less than men. He also failed to explore the implications of male opposition to female labour; his belief that capitalist development would continue to draw more women into employment ignored the success of some parts of the workforce in achieving the 'family wage' (that is, a wage sufficiently high to maintain a dependent wife and children).

Engels has been further criticised for his views on human sexuality (see Evans, 1987; Jaggar, 1983; Millett, 1985). Like the mainstream feminists discussed earlier, he rejected the hypocrisy of the double standard of morality that praised chastity in women while condoning widespread prostitution, and his suggestion that morality may be dependent on economic needs offers an advance on earlier analyses. However, he consistently assumed that men's sexual needs are *naturally* greater than women's, without questioning whether this too might be a reflection of social and economic conditions: thus he assumed that it was women and not men who originally found group marriage 'degrading', and he consistently wrote of a woman 'giving herself' or 'surrendering' to a man – a use of language that would seem to exclude the idea of sexual activity based on equality and reciprocal enjoyment. He also assumed that sexual activity is naturally heterosexual; he described homosexuality as an 'abominable practice', and it is clear that it would have no place in socialist society. At the same time, his stress on economic motivation often led to an over-simplification of sexual morality and behaviour. For example, he thought that in socialist society, when children are the responsibility of the whole community, there will no longer be 'the anxiety about the "consequences" which today prevents a girl from giving herself completely to the man she loves' (*Origin*, p. 88); the possibility that effective contraception might also remove this anxiety, or that a girl might simply not wish to become pregnant, seems not to have crossed his mind. Similarly, while the family may serve an important economic function, to *reduce* it to this function is highly dubious; at the very least, it ignores important psychological functions, and, as we have seen, it denies the possibility of oppression within the proletarian family. This economic reductionism also ignores the enduring results of the different sexual needs that Engels assumed to be 'natural'. He described how girls were abducted and 'sexually used' in the later stages of primitive society (*Origin*, p. 51), but he did not see that this contradicted his claim that such societies were based on equality between the sexes, nor did he question its implications for the future; the possibility that male sexuality might continue to pose a threat to women in socialist society was never raised; unlike many modern feminists, neither Engels nor Marx ever saw rape as a source of men's power over women.

This point is related to Engel's failure to acknowledge that the proletarian family might also be a source of oppression and sexual exploitation rather than equality. He had remarkably little to say on the problem of domestic violence which received widespread publicity in the nineteenth century and which, as we saw, was a central concern of many feminists in both Britain and America; his only comment on the issue is a half-sentence that refers to 'a leftover piece of the brutality towards women that has become deep-rooted since the introduction of monogamy' (*Origin*, p. 83). In general he held a very romanticised view of proletarian marriage which he saw as the freely chosen result of love and sexual attraction; here male brutality could not last long as it no longer had an economic foundation, and the wife was free to leave. This rosy view ignored the reality of many women's lives and the fact that they were often *not* free to leave a violent marriage; quite apart from the fear of violent revenge, many women were unwilling to abandon their children, and few could earn enough to support themselves, let alone their children too; as we have seen, Engels ignored the causes and implications of women's low pay, and he also ignored the benefits that a husband might gain from his wife's sexual and domestic services, irrespective of whether his marriage continued to be based on love.

The relevance of Marxist concepts

To some extent these problems may be relatively superficial, a product of Engels' personal limitations and prejudices rather than the underlying methodology. However, there remains the problem of whether Marxism is really able to see or understand any non-economic sources of oppression, and this is related to its underlying theory of history. In the *German Ideology* Marx and Engels saw both production and reproduction as the basis of society: 'The production of life, both of one's own in labour and of fresh life in procreation, now appears as a double relationship: on the one hand as a natural, on the other as a social relationship' (p. 50). Engels expanded this position in a frequently quoted passage from his Preface to *The Origin*:

> According to the materialist conception, the determining factor in history is, in the final instance, the production and reproduction of immediate life. This, again, is of a twofold character. On the one side, the production of the means of subsistence, of food, clothing and shelter and the tools necessary for that production; on the other side, the production of human beings themselves, the propagation of the species. The social institutions under which the people of a particular historical epoch and a particular country live are conditioned by both kinds of production: by the stage of development of labour on the one hand and of the family on the other (*The Origin*, p. 4).

Despite these formulations, neither Marx nor Engels gave production and reproduction equal roles in the productive process. As we have seen, Engels did say that the family developed autonomously in the earliest human societies, but he argued that this independent development ceased when it reached the stage of the 'pairing marriage', and that 'Unless new *social* forces came into play, there was no reason why a new form of family should arise from the single pair' (*The Origin*, p. 60); here he argued that such social forces did arise in Europe, with the introduction of private property, but that in America they did not, so that the indigenous American family remained in its early form. This means that it was only in pre-class societies that the family and sexual relationships developed under their own momentum; for most of recorded history their form was dependent upon the development of production. Marx never said anything so specific, but it is quite clear that although he saw reproduction as a part of the material basis of society, it was in no way an independent source of change; in general, therefore, he found the oppression of women to be theoretically uninteresting, a product of class society rather than something worth understanding in its own right.

This theoretical perspective meant that Marx and Engels never explored in any detail the ways in which sexual relationships and family organisation have changed over time. It also meant that in terms of practical politics the whole question of women's oppression tended to disappear. Marx did say that 'of course' women could join the First International Workingmen's Association and he proposed the establishment of women's branches within it (see Vogel, 1983, p. 71); however, the idea that women as a group might have shared interests, and that these might be in opposition to men's interests, never arose. For some later Marxists, this approach has been explicitly interpreted as meaning that all problems of relations between the sexes can be postponed until 'after the revolution', and that any attempts to improve the situation of women in the short term are at best a bourgeois irrelevance and at worst a ploy to divide the working class and distract it from the class struggle. As we shall see in later chapters, this kind of assumption that if we 'take care of the class struggle then feminism will take care of itself' has been attacked by some modern feminists, who reject the idea that Marxism involves a crude reductionism whereby there is a one-to-one causal relationship between economic organisation and the situation of women. For such marxist feminists, reproduction is a key part of the material base which must be incorporated into a correct understanding of society; this opens up the possibility of a causal interaction between production and reproduction, which in turn implies the interaction of class and sex struggles – and in practical terms this means that the sexism of men in left-wing organisations or the working class can legitimately be challenged.

Despite this kind of attempt to 'rescue' Marxism for feminism, some critics have argued that the key concepts of Marxist theory are not gender-neutral ones which Marx happened not to apply to women, but that (like liberal ideas of reason, autonomy and competition) they are based on a male view of the world that excludes women's needs and experiences. Thus the concept of 'productive labour' is said to be based on a paradigm of male activity that ignores the domestic work performed by women, while insistence on the overwhelming importance of economic class interests and conflict ignores the common ties that may unite all women irrespective of their economic situation (and also ignores racial divisions in society). Others claim that the whole view of history as a process through which men increase their mastery over nature reflects an essentially male view that is responsible for our current ecological crisis; the drive to subdue or conquer nature is contrasted with the female method of working with and understanding it. Defenders of Marxism, however, argue that despite their apparent limitations its concepts do offer genuine insights. Thus Vogel has claimed that although of course Marx never developed their feminist implications, his economic categories *do* point the way to an understanding of domestic labour and of the role of women in the capitalist economy. She argues that, properly applied, they allow us to develop an understanding of how the proletarian family and the sexual divisions within it serve the needs of capitalism by 'reproducing the labour force'; this means that although Engels may have been wrong in seeing the transfer of property as the prime economic function of the family, and in failing to see sexual oppression within the working class, the form of the family and sexual oppression can still be seen as rooted in material conditions (Vogel, 1983; for further discussion of these complex ideas see Chapter 13 below).

Barrett has identified a similarly embryonic feminist theory in Marx's concepts of ideology and alienation, and in ideas put forward in an early essay (*On the Jewish Question*, 1843). For Marx and Engels, ideas were not unchanging or ahistorical, but the product of men's actual lives and experiences; an ideology is a set of such beliefs that purports to explain the world but which, because it is rooted in particular class relationships, offers only a partial understanding of reality. As it is based in real, productive life, an ideology will contain an element of truth, but at the same time this is distorted by narrow class interests and perceptions. In general, the dominant economic class will be able to impose its view of reality upon the whole society; ideology therefore becomes an important means by which the dominant class maintains its power, and 'The ideas of the ruling class are in every epoch the ruling ideas' (*German Ideology*, p. 64). As Barrett says, the implications of this for the ways in which men have maintained control over women through their control over ideas are very interesting; however she warns against a too easy transfer of the concept to the realm of sexual politics, which may not be based on economic relationships in the same way; as she says, Marx offers only 'an insight, a suggestive or illuminating metaphor, but scarcely a body of concepts or a theoretical account of gender ideology' (Barrett, 1987, p. 53).

The concept of alienation, which was particularly important in Marx's early writings, may similarly provide potential feminist insights, but certainly not a ready-made feminist theory. Originating in Hegelian philosophy, the concept is a very complex one, centering upon the idea of man's *loss of control* over what he himself has created. As we have seen, Marx saw man's productive life as a driving force in human history; however, as man's productive powers have increased, his ability to control or understand the whole process has become lost, and what was an expression of human creativity has become a mere means to the end of making money. This means that production has become an alien imposed activity, and the worker has lost all control over the products of his own labour; moreover, the more he produces the more his own poverty is increased. This process has reached its final form under capitalist production, under which the extreme division of labour removes all vestiges of creativity or job satisfaction, and poverty becomes absolute while wealth is vastly increased. At the same time, however, the process of alienation also creates the conditions for a new and higher form of society, in which men will enjoy all the benefits of technological advance and co-operative production: thus 'Communism is the *positive* abolition of *private property*, of *human self-alienation*, and thus the real *appropriation* of *human* nature through and for man' (*Economic and Philosophical Manuscripts*, p. 155).

Although this concept is clearly based on an idea of productive activity which, as we have already seen, is itself based on a male paradigm, some modern writers have argued that it provides an important basis for feminist understanding (see Jaggar, 1983, and Foreman, 1978). At a rather superficial level it may provide insights into women's parallel loss of control over the *reproductive* process, whereby developments in contraception and reproductive technology have become a means of controlling rather than liberating women; some have also argued that woman has become a packaged, feminised, marketable commodity, and has thus become alienated from her own self and her own sexuality. Perhaps more importantly, the concept is also bound up with the division of labour in society: this has reached an extreme form under capitalism, but Marx believed that it would be ended or greatly reduced in future communist society, in which work could be freely chosen and fulfilling. Although he was not concerned with the sexual division of labour, many modern feminists see this as a central issue and argue that men and women can only realise their full humanity when domestic responsibilities as well as productive work are shared by all. Here, however, although the concept of alienation seems relevant, no modern writer has applied it systematically. Barrett has developed a rather different argument to claim that the concept helps us to understand how people can create the conditions of their own oppression, seen 'not as an arbitrary imposition, but as a process involving the oppressed' (Barrett, 1987, p. 51). Again, the implications for women's role in maintaining their own oppression, particularly through the family and the socialisation of children, are interesting but remain unexplored.

As Barrett has further pointed out, some of the ideas expressed in Marx's early essay *On the Jewish Question* also offer insights that may be useful to feminist theory; the essay also helps pinpoint the ways in which a Marxist feminist analysis could differ from a liberal feminist one. In it Marx made a clear distinction between political emancipation and human emancipation: the former declared that all men are equal as citizens, but it left untouched the real inequalities existing in society; thus the state 'decrees that birth, social rank, education, occupation are non-political distinctions', but 'Far from *abolishing* these *effective* differences, it only exists in so far as they are presupposed' (*On the Jewish Question*, p. 12). Formal equality for all men as citizens therefore only disguises the real inequalities on which the state is based; real human emancipation requires a transformation of society so that such differences are denied their material basis, and the artificial distinction between state and society, citizen and private individual, disappears. Marx applied these ideas specifically to the Jews, whom he thought could not be emancipated simply by abolishing religion as a basis for political rights; in the same way, they imply that women's subordination will not be ended when sex ceases to be a political and legal distinction – from this perspective it is not equal rights that are important, so much as the transformation of the economic and social conditions upon which subordination is based. This gives us the crucial distinction between Marxist and liberal feminism, and anticipates the 'mature' Marxist theory which sees political power as a product of economic conditions, rather than as an independent cause of social transformation; it also has affinities with the radical feminist idea of the ubiquity of power, and the artificiality of the public/private distinction. However, the extent to which the state may have a degree of autonomy or may itself be an 'arena of conflict' has been fiercely debated by later Marxist theoreticians, so that the theory does not necessarily imply that the struggle for political and legal rights is without importance. Thus although these are only likely to be achieved at particular historical periods and they are not the final goal, they may both represent significant stages in reaching that goal and valuable gains in their own right – so that few women today would wish to return to the legal enslavement of Victorian times, however far present society may be from true sex equality.

A further distinction between a feminist theory based on Marxism and one based on liberalism arises from their different underlying ideas about human nature. Here the liberal idea that it is men's rationality that is the defining characteristic of humanity and therefore the basis of political right, is set aside for a view of man as *creator*, whose purposeful and planned productive activity differentiates him from the animals, for unlike them 'man produces when he is free from physical need, and only truly produces in freedom from such need' (*Economic and Philosophical Manuscripts*, p. 128). It is true that in Marx's later writings he rejected the idea that there is any kind of eternally given 'human essence', for man is, he said, simply the product of society, and the 'human essence is no abstraction inherent in each individual. In reality it is the ensemble of the social relations' (*Sixth Thesis on Feuerbach*, 1846). However, as we have seen, it is man's productive activity that in turn creates his society, so that he becomes in effect his own self-creator; therefore although men may exhibit different characteristics at different historical periods, the centrality of productive activity remains constant. This idea of conscious creativity gets away from the kind of dualism that pervades much of liberal thought and which elevates mental above physical activity; indeed Marx believed that this is an artificial separation that will be overcome in future communist society (*Critique of the Gotha Programme*, 1875, p. 17). This meant that women's reproductive and domestic work is not inherently inferior to men's intellectual activities, as it was for many liberals. Although Marx and Engels did tend to devalue women's work, this was because of the way it was organised as a personal service and not because of its essential attributes, so that Marxism as a theory is able to encompass a very positive view of the labour that has traditionally been performed by women. It also meant that sexuality could be recognised as a fully human activity, something which as we saw earlier John Stuart Mill and other liberal feminists had denied. Thus in 1844 Marx wrote that although for the alienated worker sex had been reduced to an animal function, 'Eating, drinking and procreating are of course also genuine human functions' (*Economic and Philosophical Manuscripts*, p. 125); while Engels, despite his questionable ideas about sex difference, saw 'individual sex love' rather than Mill's 'marriage of minds' as the highest form of relationship between man and woman. Unlike liberalism, Marxism therefore provides no theoretical basis for fear of sexuality or suspicion of sensual pleasure.

Marxism is an extremely complex theory, and although it offers feminists a number of suggestive insights, it is not some kind of 'lucky dip' from which concepts can be extracted at will; ideas that Marx developed in relation to class and economic processes *may* be applicable to an analysis of relations between the sexes, but they cannot be automatically transferred. Nevertheless it does claim to be a comprehensive theory, and a number of key points emerge which must form the basis of any coherent Marxist feminist position. In the first place, it is quite clear that for Marxists questions of sex equality cannot be understood in terms of abstract principles, but only in a historical context. Secondly, opposition to women's emancipation is not simply a result of injustice; rather it reflects material interests and the structured economic needs of society. Thirdly, for women as for any other oppressed group, emancipation is not equated with political and legal rights, but can only be won by restructuring the whole of society to give full economic equality. Fourthly, the material conditions for such changes are already developing within existing society; successful change requires both these objective circumstances and self-conscious revolutionary will and organisation. Fifthly, the struggle for sex equality is integrally connected to the economic class struggle; full freedom for women, as for men, requires the replacement of capitalism by communism. Finally, and more specifically, if women are to become equal to men they must achieve full economic independence; for this to be a source of liberation, housework and childcare must be reorganised on a collective basis.

These are the 'positive' ways in which Marxism may contribute to feminist theory. On the 'negative' side, it cannot allow for the possibility of oppression without an economic foundation, and this means that the very possibility of a non-economic conflict of interests between the sexes is denied, as is the possibility that patriarchy could exist outside of class society. Modern feminists who wish to use Marxist theory in a less reductionist way are therefore left with the problem of how to understand the inter-relationships of sex and class, patriarchy and capitalism; as we shall see in subsequent chapters, this is an area that has generated much debate.

4

Mainstream feminism: the vote and after, 1880s–1939

The situation of women in the late nineteenth century

By the end of the nineteenth century, many of the demands made by earlier feminists had been met in both Britain and America. In particular, although opportunities were still far from equal, education for girls and women had expanded at all levels; this in turn generated a demand for teachers that gave middle-class women a new source of employment, as did the 'typewriter revolution' and the great expansion of office work that had taken place by the 1890s. However, improved education for women did not in itself challenge their traditional role in society, for the elementary education that was all most girls received stressed domestic skills rather than attempting to broaden their horizons, and the women's colleges sought to produce educated wives and mothers rather than independent women. Similarly, new forms of employment did not necessarily mean female liberation, but frequently involved new forms of exploitation. Few women succeeded in the professions, and for most of those who entered paid work, economic independence meant bare survival rather than fulfilment; in general, new opportunities arose 'less because of the demands of feminists . . . than in response to the needs of business, the professions and government for docile, well-educated and cheap labour' (Rubinstein, 1986, p. x). It is also important to remember that at this point the single largest occupation for women in both countries remained domestic service, and that in America a majority of black women still worked in the fields. Nevertheless, it could be argued that the key demands of Mary Wollstonecraft and other early feminists had been achieved: the world of learning was no longer an exclusively male monopoly, education was seen as a requisite for responsible motherhood, and middle-class women who could not or would not marry at last had some respectable alternatives. Moreover, once women's rationality and capacity for learning had been conceded in principle, an important argument against giving them full legal and political rights had been removed; and improved education increasingly gave women the skills and confidence with which to demand and campaign for these rights.

In the legal sphere too, many feminist demands had met with success. By the end of the century, women in both Britain and America had won a significant degree of legal independence: a married woman could now own her own property and keep her own earnings, she had new rights concerning the custody and welfare of her children, and she had some degree of protection against physical abuse from her husband. The divorce laws still enshrined the 'double standard' of morality (so that 'simple' adultery was grounds for divorcing a wife but not a husband), but a woman now had the legal right to leave her husband. Similarly, although a husband still had sexual rights over his wife in the sense that rape within marriage was not a crime, he had lost the legal means of enforcing these rights. Men's sexual rights over women were also challenged by the repeal of the Contagious Diseases Acts (see Chapter 2 above), and by the raising of the age of consent for girls (to 16 in England and 18 in some American states). In general therefore, although women by 1900 certainly did not enjoy full legal equality with men, the most glaring legal violations of their rights as individuals had been removed; as in the field of education, the principle had been conceded that women could be treated as rational and autonomous individuals, albeit as individuals who might on occasion need protection from men.

These formal changes were accompanied by changes in social behaviour and expectations, particularly on the part of middle-class women, and the 'new woman' of the 1890s was portrayed in the press and novels of the time as the free-thinking, economically independent product of higher education. Although she was usually presented as a pathetic creature, losing her femininity in a ridiculous attempt to ape the achievements of men, she could also be seen as a heroine by those who sought some role in society beyond the capture of a husband, and who believed themselves, like Mary Astell two centuries earlier, to be 'capable of More Things than the pitiful Conquest of some Wretched Heart' (see Chapter 1 above). Parallel to the emergence of this 'new woman' was the much discussed 'revolt of the daughters', whereby young women increasingly refused to abide by the rigid social constraints that custom and their parents decreed. This was epitomised by the cycling craze of the 1890s which gave such young women an unprecedented freedom; as Rubinstein comments: 'It is unlikely that the Chaperone Cyclists' Association formed in 1896 had many clients' (Rubinstein, 1986, p. 216). This increased freedom was not accompanied by any general move towards sexual permissiveness, for 'free love' and birth control were largely seen as sources of sexual exploitation rather than liberation for women. However there was a greater degree of openness in discussion of sexual matters, and although many young women were still quite unaware of the 'facts of life', ignorance was less total than hitherto. Josephine Butler's campaign against the Contagious Diseases Acts and Ibsen's play *Ghosts* (1881), which dealt with the effects of congenital syphilis, represented a gradual shift to a society in which 'respectable' women were allowed to know that such things as prostitution, venereal disease and indeed sex itself did exist (see Kent, 1990).

At the same time, women were entering public life on an unprecedented scale. For some middle-class women, this public activity was an extension of traditional charitable work: in both Britain and America there was a growth of the 'settlement' movement whereby middle-class women sought to reform and improve the conditions of the working class by living amongst them; in England women were from the 1870s active on School Boards and in administering the Poor Law; in general there was an increase in movements for social reform led by or involving women. Working women themselves were also beginning to organise both independently and in mixed organisations – for example, in England the Women's Co-operative Guild had over 14,000 members by the early twentieth century. Women's trade unionism still involved only a minority of women, as it faced not only the hostility of employers, but often that of working men as well; domestic responsibilities also obviously made active participation by women very difficult. Nevertheless, with the gradual growth of organised labour, some women were involved in strikes and trade union activity, and the needs of women workers were finding a place on the political agenda.

All this means that by the end of the century women were no longer totally excluded from public life and political debate, and many were not only demanding but also achieving a role outside the home. Most of the clubs and organisations that had grown up were not self-consciously feminist, but they produced a generation of women with experience in campaigning, organising, fund-raising and public speaking. For such women, the right to vote, which Mary Wollstonecraft had only hinted at, and which had seemed such a revolutionary demand at Seneca Falls in 1848, now appeared both as an obvious entitlement and the one key right they lacked; in this context, the suffrage campaigns came to dominate the women's movement in both Britain and America 'not as their dominant concern, but as the demand which men were not willing to concede' (Levine, 1987, p. 57).

The suffrage campaign

The concentration of feminist energies on the campaign for the vote in the early years of the twentieth century has often been seen as a narrowing of feminist interests, a distraction from more serious issues, that mistook the formal trappings of political power for its reality and ignored the economic, ideological and sexual domination of women by men. This chapter will, however, argue that, far from being a straightforward liberal feminist demand as such comment suggests, the suffrage campaign meant very different things to different people, and that it could be based on a number of frequently contradictory assumptions. This means that although for some women the suffrage campaign was an end in itself, for others it was but a means, or part of a wider goal, so that 'In fighting for enfranchisement, suffragists sought no less than the total transformation of the lives of women' (Kent, 1990, p. 3). 'Votes for women' was therefore a deceptively simple slogan that concealed a number of very different political perspectives. It is to the disentangling of these that we must now turn.

Equality or difference?

Most obviously, as earlier chapters have shown, the demand for the vote could clearly be derived from liberal principles: thus it had been argued by such as Mary Wollstonecraft, Elizabeth Cady Stanton and John Stuart Mill that women are, like men, rational and autonomous individuals, and that they are therefore entitled to full and equal political rights. At the same time, these early writers had also allowed for the possibility of natural difference between the sexes, and the claim that men and women are morally and intellectually equal had coexisted with the idea that women were the custodians of sexual purity, temperance and traditional values. By the end of the century, particularly in America, the idea that women were the potential saviours of the nation, who must be given political rights to reform and purify the conduct of public affairs, had come to dominate some sections of the suffrage movement; from this perspective it was not women's rationality but their sex-specific virtues that were seen as important. An important aspect of this sex difference was said to lie in women's inherent pacifism, which was contrasted to men's predisposition to war, and strong links developed between feminist and pacifist analyses, with militarism being seen as both cause and consequence of women's oppression; the image of woman the nurturer and giver of life opposing man the destroyer is one that remains powerful today (see Bussey and Tims, 1980; Cambridge Women's Peace Collective, 1984; Evans, 1987; Florence *et al.*, 1987; Strange, 1983; Ruddick, 1990; Thompson, 1983; Wiltsher, 1985). Underlying this kind of analysis is a view of woman that stresses her activities as mother and nurturer and insists on the value of her traditional role; from this perspective women should not try to 'be like men', but must preserve their own values and virtues. In practice, many suffrage campaigners attempted to combine this position with liberal ideas of natural rights and sex equality; however, once the vote was won, the incompatibility between a position that asserted the equal worth of men and women and one that stressed their essential difference was to become apparent in practice, and to split the feminist movement in two.

The retreat from liberal arguments also involved a shift away from the idea that the vote was an individual entitlement, and towards utilitarian arguments about its beneficial social consequences. Mill himself had earlier argued that men and society, as well as women, stood to gain from women's enfranchisement, and a very similar position was later held by Millicent Garrett Fawcett (1847–1929), the leader of the main constitutional suffragist organisation in England until 1919. Like Mill, she combined equal rights and utilitarian arguments, and she called her suffragist paper the *Common Cause* because 'It was the cause of men, women and children. We believe that men cannot be truly free so long as women are held in political subjection' (quoted in Oakley, 1983, p. 191). In America however, the natural rights arguments that had been so prominent half a century before at Seneca Falls had by 1900 been largely dropped, to be replaced rather than combined with claims about the desirable consequences of enfranchising women. This new approach meant that, increasingly, 'Expediency and interest replaced right and justice in the feminist vocabulary' (Evans, 1977, p. 204; see also Kraditor, 1965). It also meant that utilitarian arguments could be used not only to claim political rights for women, but also to deny them to other groups in society.

Anti-democratic strands in the suffrage campaign

The shift away from liberal 'equal rights' arguments came therefore to be linked with a profoundly anti-democratic strand in the ideas of the suffrage movements; although particularly strong in America, this was also important in England. It seems at first sight surprising that a movement to extend political rights could be seen as anti-democratic; but whereas a strict and consistent application of equal rights arguments would seem irrevocably linked to ideas of political equality, utilitarian arguments could be used to justify the exclusion of 'unfit' groups from political power at the same time as enfranchising women – thus Carrie Chapman Catt (1858–1947), the leader of the American suffragist movement, demanded: 'Cut off the vote from the slums, and give it to women' (quoted in Evans, 1977, p. 204). The germ of this idea had already been present in earlier writers, for Mill expressed fear of tyranny by the ignorant majority, and shared with Stanton the view that the vote should be confined to those who could read and write; by the end of the century a much more overt elitism found powerful expression within the suffrage movement.

In England, the campaign for women's suffrage had begun at a time when most men were still denied the vote, and although of course many rejected a property-based franchise for women as an unacceptable betrayal of the working class, and others accepted it only as a staging post on the road to full adult suffrage, some middle-class women saw a limited franchise as desirable precisely *because* of its class basis – as such, it was seen as a way of defending property and conservative values against the ignorant masses. By the end of the century, the vote had been won by many more working-class men, so that women's enfranchisement on the same terms would in fact have increased the voting strength of the working class; nevertheless the demand for anything less than full universal suffrage was still frequently seen by both opponents and proponents as a class-based claim for the 'ladies' vote'. This view was reinforced by the largely middle-class background of both the constitutional suffragists and the militant suffragettes in the Women's Social and Political Union (WSPU). (The terms 'suffragist' and 'suffragette' are often confused or used interchangeably; it was however only the latter who used militant and illegal campaigning methods.) Although the WSPU, under the leadership of Emmeline Pankhurst (1858–1929) and her daughter Christabel (1880–1958), began in 1903 as a democratic and pro-labour campaign based in the north-west of England, it rapidly jettisoned attempts to win the support of working-class women in favour of attracting wealthy and hopefully influential patrons, and it became a highly autocratic and undemocratic organisation. For some suffragettes, hostility towards men merged with a more general hostility towards the working class, so that the suspicion of many within the labour movement that the suffrage campaign was simply a movement of middle-class ladies indifferent to other social needs, was not entirely without foundation.

In America, this anti-democratic strand was far more dominant, and here race took the place of property as the key issue. As we saw in the previous chapter, although the American women's movement had been born out of the campaign against slavery, even its founders were not averse to harnessing racist prejudices to their cause. Kraditor has argued that 'The suffrage movement was essentially from beginning to end a struggle of white, native born, middle-class women for the right to participate more fully in the public affairs of a society the basic structures of which they accepted' (Kraditor, 1965, p. x), and certainly as the campaign for women's suffrage became a mass movement and a mainstream rather than a radical fringe demand, it inevitably attracted the support of women who were in all other respects highly conservative. By the end of the century, the situation of many former slaves had sharply deteriorated, and racist violence against them had reached new heights; not only did the leaders of the suffrage movement 'abandon the entire Black people at the time of their most intense suffering since emancipation' (Davis, 1982, p. 118), but women's suffrage was increasingly promoted as a means of *maintaining* white supremacy. This was indeed to become the main argument for the women's cause in the southern states. From 1903 the demand for the 'educated vote' dominated the campaign; this sought to combine the enfranchisement of most women with the disenfranchisement of 'unfit' working men and negroes, thus shifting the balance of voting power away from blacks and immigrants and in favour of the respectable middle classes; it meant in effect that 'votes for women, which had once been an expression of equal rights, became an issue of social privilege' (Banks, 1986, p. 1410).

Socialists and the suffrage campaign

Of course, not all suffrage campaigners accepted this kind of conservative and racist position, nor did they all see the vote as a goal in itself, a means of slotting women into a system which remained itself unchallenged. In America, some sections of the suffrage campaign did attempt to involve working-class, black and immigrant women. Although the main leadership did not take this line, and retreated from the broader issues that Stanton had earlier espoused, others continued to insist that feminism could be a source of wider social change, and argued that to succeed it must be linked to socialist goals (see Cott, 1987). In England, concentration on the London leadership has tended to obscure the extent of working-class involvement in the suffrage campaigns, particularly in the north-west; here women did not prioritise the vote for their own sex, but were more concerned with achieving full adult suffrage for all, seeing this as a means to social and economic reform (Liddington and Norris, 1978; Mitchell, 1977). Sylvia Pankhurst (1882–1960) also refused to toe the 'party line' laid down by her mother and sister, and concentrated her efforts on campaigning with working-class men and women in the East End of London; she worked closely with the male-led labour movement, and saw feminism as part of a wider movement for socialist change. Elsewhere in Europe, the fight for the vote was spearheaded by the new mass socialist parties rather than the middle-class feminist organisations. In Germany in particular, a Marxist feminist analysis was developed which saw political rights for women as an important weapon in the revolutionary struggle and which, in contrast to the 'bourgeois feminist' position, insisted that women's oppression would only be ended with the overthrow of capitalism. The whole question of the relationship between socialism and feminism is of course a highly complex one which will be explored further in the next chapters; here it is sufficient to note that any kind of socialist feminist position within the suffrage movement tended to see the vote in utilitarian terms, that is, as a means to a social goal rather than an individual right; it also refused to accept that the suffrage issue transcended all others, or that divisions of class or race could be dismissed as insignificant squabbles amongst men. This position was diametrically opposed to the radical feminist analysis that was developing within some sections of the movement, and which is particularly explicit in the ideas of Christabel Pankhurst, to which we now turn.

Christabel Pankhurst

The political involvement of all the Pankhursts began well to the left of British politics, and Sylvia Pankhurst described her childhood home as 'a centre for many gatherings of Socialists, Fabians, Anarchists, Suffragists, Free Thinkers, Radicals and Humanitarians of all schools' (Pankhurst, 1977, p. 90). It was both their own observation of the situation of working-class women and the male chauvinism and selfishness of many men within supposedly 'progressive' groups that led the Pankhursts to see feminism as a key issue. For Christabel Pankhurst this developed into an analysis that saw women's oppression as basic to the whole of society, underlying and determining all other aspects of life. Like modern radical feminists she thought that 'the subjection of women as a group, to men as a group, was the fundamental determinant of all other aspects of social life' (Sarah, 1983, p. 270); and like them she saw this subjection as all-pervasive, involving not just political power, but also ideological, economic and sexual control. This meant that the struggle for the vote was part of a struggle against all forms of male control, while the *methods* she chose could be seen as liberating in themselves, quite apart from their likelihood of success. Hitherto the suffragists had played according to the rules of the game, conforming to received notions of respectable womanhood and ladylike behaviour; when the suffragettes began to march, to demonstrate, to interrupt, to storm the Houses of Parliament and to court arrest and imprisonment, they were challenging basic assumptions about gender roles and attributes, and, according to a recent commentator, they were 'taking one of the most important steps in the history of women' which 'split assunder patriarchal cultural hegemony by interrupting men's discourse with each other' (Marcus, 1987, p. 9). The courage of the suffragettes in facing the dangers of hunger-strikes and force-feeding (experienced by over a thousand women; see Marcus, 1987, and Morrell, 1980) meant that they could certainly not be seen as frail and timid creatures in need of male protection. Moreover, the tactics used by their opponents, particularly the explicitly sexual violence sometimes used by the police, exposed the reality of this 'protection' in practice (see Rosen, 1974, pp. 158–60). The challenge to conventional views was completed by the brief but famous period of active militancy in the years immediately before the First World War, when an outright war on property (but not on life) was declared: arson and window-breaking are hardly the traditional activities of 'ladies', and so 'The suffragettes smashed the image of woman as a passive, dependent creature as effectively as they smashed the plate-glass windows of Regent Street' (Rover, 1967, p. 20). Although such militant tactics were not widely used in other countries, they attracted world wide publicity, and there were limited attempts to emulate the methods of the suffragettes in Germany, Hungary and France. In America, the main suffrage organisation stressed respectability above all else; however, even here large public demonstrations and parades came to be a widely accepted form of political protest, and the smaller Women's Party adopted a policy of deliberate confrontation, leading to arrests and hunger strikes, although on a much smaller scale than in Britain (see Evans, 1977, pp. 192–7). Here again, as Christabel Pankhurst saw, the knowledge that women could act in such ways was significant not only for its direct effect on the franchise campaign, but for its impact on the prevailing ideology.

For Christabel Pankhurst, as for earlier feminists, another important aspect of women's subordination was their economic dependence upon men; she therefore insisted that all women be enabled to compete freely and equally on the labour market, and 'Equal Pay for Equal Work' became a slogan of the Women's Party which she co-founded in 1917. Although she advocated increased involvement by fathers in child-rearing, she did not seriously challenge women's responsibility for domestic work; unlike most earlier feminists, however, she did not ignore the implications of this for women's economic situation. Housekeeping as it was currently organised was, she argued, an intolerable burden on married women, and a waste of their time and economic energies; it was also unpaid and largely unrecognised. If, however, it were organised on a more efficient and co-operative basis, then productivity would be increased as women were freed from unnecessary labour. She therefore advocated 'Co-operative Housekeeping' (in particular, the central production and distribution of food by expert cooks and nutritionists, and the provision of laundries) as a more rational and equitable use of resources, which would also recognise the value of domestic work. This has some affinities with Engels' ideas on the collectivisation of housework as discussed in the previous chapter, but unlike Engels she did not see it as dependent on wider socio-economic changes, and she never really explored the economic basis of her proposed reforms, or explained in any detail how they could be financed. Despite her early involvement with the Independent Labour Party, she refused to see socialism as the solution to women's problems, and she insisted that sex interests transcend those of class: 'Why are women expected to have such confidence in the Labour Party? Working men are just as unjust to women as are those of other classes' (quoted in Rosen, 1974, p. 29); in general her politics moved steadily in a conservative direction.

Women's lack of political and economic rights were not for Christabel Pankhurst simply facets of female subordination, but were causally related to what she increasingly saw as the central aspect of oppression – their sexual exploitation by men. Here she argued that if a woman is unable to sell her labour to earn a living then she is forced to sell her body (either temporarily as a prostitute or permanently as a wife), and that men denied women the vote primarily as a means of covering up sexual vice. As we saw in the previous chapter, fear of male sexuality was a dominant strand in nineteenth-century feminism in both Britain and America, and this fear found its most powerful expression in Pankhurst's pamphlet *The Great Scourge and How to End It* (first published in 1913). In this she claimed that 75–80 per cent of men were infected with gonorrhoea and many others with syphilis, that marriage was therefore 'a matter of appalling danger to women' and that venereal disease was so rampant that 'race suicide' was imminent (in Marcus, 1987, p. 210, and *passim*). Men *can*, she argued, be as pure as women, but they will never be so voluntarily; the cure was therefore 'Votes for Women; Chastity for Men', as the former would give women the power to enforce the latter. Much subsequent commentary has dismissed this as the irrational and hysterical outburst of a frigid, man-hating virago, and has tended to concentrate on Pankhurst's exaggerated statistics rather than on the arguments behind them. However the problem with which she was concerned was very real, even if less acute than she supposed, and some modern radical feminists have hailed her pamphlet as an important step forward for feminist theory. In particular, it is claimed that in seeing sexuality as an arena of struggle, where subordination can be both reinforced and challenged, Pankhurst expanded our perception of sexual politics to the private and personal, so that *The Great Scourge* represents 'a sustained challenge to the organisation of sexuality in the interests of men and a cogent analysis of the relationship between male control of sexuality and the subjection of women in general' (Sarah, 1983, p. 260; see also Jeffries, 1982, and Kent, 1990).

In fact, Pankhurst's analysis was less original than such comment suggests, for, as we saw in the last chapter, the oppressive effects of male sexual behaviour had been of major concern to earlier nineteenth-century feminists, who similarly saw chastity for both sexes as the solution; it was also widely discussed in popular novels of the day (Bland, 1987). Nevertheless it does mean that the campaign for the vote could have far wider implications than the 'liberal feminist' label so often attached to it suggests, and that for some it was a radical feminist demand that certainly did not see women's subordination as beginning and ending with their lack of political rights. However, Pankhurst's analysis remains unsatisfactory for those who deny that political change can bring about a transformation of private, sexual relationships (for Eisenstein's similar criticisms of Stanton see Chapter 2 above), and many modern radical feminists would consider her concentration on public political rights to be a distraction from more fundamental inequalities, rather than a means of ending them.

A further implication of Pankhurst's analysis, and one shared by some modern radical feminists, is that the struggle for women's rights is part of a sex war in which, unless they offer total and unconditional support, all men are to be considered the enemy. Alliance with existing parties was therefore rejected, and although she suspended all suffragette activity in 1914 to work with men in support of the war effort, the 1917 manifesto of her short-lived Women's Party stated that 'it is felt that women can best serve the nation by keeping clear of men's party machinery and traditions, which, by universal consent, leave so much to be desired' (*The Britannia*, 2 November 1917). However, unlike some modern radical feminists, Pankhurst did not extend her hostility to male sexuality, politics and institutions to advocate extreme separatism or lesbianism as a solution; commentators have speculated about her own sexual orientation, but it is probable that she accepted the widespread view that any form of sexual activity is an inferior form of human behaviour which, in the interests of both mental and physical health, should as far as possible be avoided by both men and women.

All this gives us an analysis of women's oppression and the role of the vote in ending it that is very different from the conventional view of the suffrage campaign, and which encompassed not only formal rights but the whole of political, economic and personal life. It is also an analysis that denies the liberal premise that reform can be achieved through reason and persuasion; for Christabel Pankhurst and the militant suffragettes, it was less the justice of their cause than the demonstrable strength of women that would ensure their victory. Although much less clearly formulated than in modern theories, this position may have links with those feminists who have recently questioned the whole concept of 'rationality' as a part of male ideology that denies or denigrates other forms of knowledge such as intuition or empathy (Lloyd, 1984; Braidotti, 1986; see also Gilligan, 1982). It has also led some commentators to suggest that the militant suffrage campaign became an increasingly irrational movement devoted to 'the politics of the apocalypse' (Rosen, 1974), and that as it became characterised by authoritarianism, anti-socialism, hysteria and a cult of violence it was in fact moving in the direction of fascism (Evans, 1977). Such analysis is of course anathema to many modern feminists, but in later years supposedly feminist groups were to support both Hitler and Mussolini, whose ideas on women's role and virtues could be reconciled with some aspects of a feminism based on belief in essential sex difference; as we have seen, some feminists also held profoundly anti-democratic and racist views. The analysis also gains some support from Christabel Pankhurst's own later activities (which have been ignored by admirers such as Sarah, 1983, and Spender, 1983a). Earlier, she had condemned war as a senseless manifestation of male aggression, 'the tragic result of the unnatural system of government by men only' (quoted in Sarah, 1983, p. 279), but in late 1914 this pacifism was transformed overnight into a nationalistic militarism. Rejecting any idea of a negotiated peace, she and her mother changed the name of their newspaper from *The Suffragette* to *The Britannia*, and suffragettes were the first to hand out white feathers (the symbol of cowardice) to men in civilian clothing. In 1919 (the first election in which women were able to stand or vote), she unsuccessfully opposed labour on a nationalistic and anti-Bolshevik platform; following a religious conversion she later abandoned politics, and from 1921 she devoted her life to preaching the imminence of Christ's Second Coming. Of course, such facts do not mean that either radical feminism or the broader suffrage campaign can be dismissed as essentially irrational or inherently fascistic; however, they illustrate well the very different directions in which feminist beliefs can lead, and the conclusions to which individual feminists may be drawn. They therefore show the dangers of assuming that any movement, individual or idea that has been labelled 'feminist' can automatically be seen as 'progressive'; historically, feminism has most often been associated with humanitarian, liberal or socialist beliefs, but in some forms it has the potential for development in a right-wing direction.

Subsequent commentary has on the whole failed to recognise the diversity of beliefs underlying the suffrage campaigns. It should, however, now be clear that, contrary to popular belief, this was not a quintessentially 'liberal feminist' demand, for apparent unity as to the goal obscured the very different assumptions and values held by different sections of the movement. At the same time, there were frequent disagreements over methods and tactics, and the clash between Marxist and 'bourgeois' analyses was already clear in many European countries; when the vote was finally won, the practical irreconcilability of the various positions became apparent, and mainstream feminism dissolved more clearly into its constituent parts.

After the vote: the re-emergence of contradictions

The first country in the world to give women the vote was New Zealand in 1894, shortly followed by Australia; in Europe, Finland and Norway both enfranchised women before 1914, and most other countries did so shortly after the war (here France provided a notable exception). In Britain, the suffrage campaigns finally met with limited success in 1918, when the vote was given to women over 30 who were also local government ratepayers, wives of local ratepayers, or university graduates. This had the effect of enfranchising slightly over 50 per cent of the adult female population in a year in which virtually all men were given the vote; it was not until 1928 that it was granted to women on the same terms as men. In America, women had won the vote as early as 1869 and 1870 in the states of Wyoming and Utah; in 1920 the Nineteenth Amendment to the American Constitution, enfranchising all adult American women, was finally ratified.

The reasons for this enfranchisement were extremely complex, and varied from country to country; they frequently owed more to political expediency than to any mass conversion of politicians to the feminist cause. Thus in Britain, the issue became entangled

in the convoluted logic of party politics and politicians' manoeu-
verings for position over the question of Irish independence.
Increasingly too, ruling groups came to see women as a stabilising
force that could be used against the threat of unrest and disruption; in this sense, therefore, their enfranchisement was a conservative rather than a radical step, designed to counteract the
potential power of new immigrant groups in Australasia, immigrants and blacks in America, and the working class in Europe
(see Evans, 1977). Fear of renewed suffragette militancy (which
had been suspended for the duration) was also important, as
were the changes in social attitudes, behaviour and expectations
generated during the war years.

Whatever the mix of reasons, in many nations a seemingly
critical feminist battle had now been won; this victory was not,
however, followed by steady advance, but by intense disagreements amongst feminist in the inter-war years. Certainly, any
hopes or fears that women would vote as a united group proved
unfounded; like men, women voted according to their class,
religion and family traditions rather than on feminist issues. The
hope that politics would be morally transformed by the enfranchisement of women was also to be disappointed. Despite the
fears of the liquor industry (which had vehemently opposed
women's suffrage in America), many women actively opposed
prohibition (see Cott, 1987, pp. 263–4), and female enfranchisement seems to have had little overall effect on the issue. Inter-
nationally, some feminists opposed militarism in 1914, and in 1915
the Women's International League for Peace and Freedom, a
pacifist organisation that still exists today, was founded with the
support of women from both sides of the war (see Bussey and
Tims, 1980; Evans, 1987; Florence *et al.*, 1987; Wiltsher, 1985).
However most suffrage leaders, like most women, supported the
war effort, and although some continued to be active in pacifist
organisations after the war, they remained a minority with little
significant effect on government policies. There was, moreover,
no great rush of women waiting to stand for public office; a
small number of women were elected to both local and national
governments, but they did not act as a united group and their
numbers remained very low. It is true that in the years immediately after they won the vote, women made some further legal
gains (mainly concerning marriage, child custody and entry into

the professions), and some concessions were made on women's welfare issues; however the nervousness that induced politicians to make such changes soon evaporated, and in general it seemed that 'In Britain as in America, the torch which the suffragettes had laid down was simply not picked up' (Bouchier, 1983, p. 16).

Equal rights v. welfare feminism in America

In fact, the problem was not so much lack of will, as profound ideological disagreements amongst feminists, who had been united only in their demand for the vote; far from being the 'silent years' of feminism, the inter-war period was therefore a time of highly significant debate, in which the contradictory nature of the assumptions behind the suffrage campaign became apparent. In particular, liberal assumptions that women should be seen primarily as individuals rather than as members of a sex group, that they should be free to compete with men in whatever sphere they chose and that state intervention is to be avoided wherever possible, clashed head-on with those that stressed women's sex-specific needs and attributes, that insisted on the primacy of their role as wives and mothers, and that sought collective interventionist solutions to the problems of women's welfare.

A key issue at the time was the question of protective legislation, which was aimed at protecting women from the worst effects of dangerous and unhealthy occupations and long working hours (see Crystal Eastman in Cook (ed.), 1978, for an excellent contemporary account of the debate, and Cott, 1987, for a recent analysis). Some saw protection simply as a desirable first step towards improving working hours and conditions for both men and women rather than as a specifically women's issue: in general, however, feminist opinion was divided between the majority who advocated protection as a real and necessary improvement to the lives of working women and a minority who argued that it would only confirm women's subordinate situation and perpetuate the traditional division of labour.

In America, this minority position was defended by the small *Women's Party* which every year from 1923 managed to secure the introduction of an Equal Rights Amendment before Congress. The approach of this group was based on a fierce rejection of traditional ideas of sex difference and women's role, and in insisting on a married woman's right to a career and economic independence it pushed liberal feminism to the logical conclusion that J. S. Mill and most nineteenth-century American feminists had avoided. However, in seeing a career as a source of fulfilment it ignored the fact that for the vast majority of women paid employment was an added burden rather than a source of liberation. As Cott says, this kind of feminism appealed primarily to those 'who belonged to and were privileged by the dominant culture in every way except that they were female' (Cott, 1987, p. 76), and it contributed to the widespread perception of American feminism as a movement of and for the white middle classes.

Another problem with this kind of feminism arose from its attempt to combine liberal principles with a much more radical analysis of women's oppression. Here it was claimed that artificially-created sexual division is the 'primary antagonism' in society which towers above 'the petty quarrels of religious creeds, above the rivalries of class, above the slaughterings of nations, above the sinister enmity of races' (quoted in Cott, 1987, p. 76). Not only do the proposed legal solutions seem inadequate, given the immensity of the problem that has been identified, but as Eisenstein has pointed out, the perception of women as a sex-class, united in their struggle against men, runs counter to the liberal insistence that, once they are given equal political and legal rights, it is up to *individuals* to change their situation (Eisenstein, 1981). Cott has therefore argued that those few women who in inter-war America achieved success in the male world were unable to work for the wider interests of their sex, for to succeed they had to accept the existing rules of the game, and if they were to draw attention to the disadvantages faced by other women they would in effect be drawing attention to their own inferiority:

> The resort to individualism took the feminist standpoint that women's freedoms and opportunities should be no less than men's, but individualism offered no way to achieve the goal except by acting as though it had already been obtained. Although it produced outstanding models of individual accomplishment, it could not engender a programme for change in the position of women as a group (Cott, 1987, p. 281).

In general, the feminist label in America in the inter-war years tended to become restricted to these equal rights campaigners, whose position was increasingly seen as both old-fashioned and narrowly elitist. Thus Cott reports that whereas in 1913 an enthusiastic proponent could describe feminism as 'something so new it isn't in the dictionaries', by 1919 some 'progressive' women were referring to their position as 'post-feminist' (Cott, 1987, pp. 13 and 282). Nevertheless many other groups continued to work for the needs and interests of women as they saw them. This involved both charitable work by and for women, and political campaigns to improve their living conditions; the main suffrage organisation became the *League of Women Voters*, and although as we saw women did not tend to vote on sex lines, this acted as a pressure group, particularly concerned with the welfare of children and their mothers. Here it enjoyed some early successes when politicians were still nervous of women's supposed political power, although the 'Red Scare' that followed the 1917 Bolshevik revolution meant that collectivist or interventionist policies had no hope of reaching the statute book, while the (unfounded) accusation that many of the leading women's organisations were part of an international Bolshevik conspiracy further discredited their cause (see Cott, 1987, p. 242 for the 'Spider Web Chart' of 1924 that purported to show these links).

To a large extent, this kind of 'welfare feminism' stemmed from nineteenth-century ideas about women's moral superiority as carers and nurturers, and it certainly did not involve any challenge to traditional sex roles; critics of this approach accuse it of equating motherhood with the condition of *all* females and, by stressing biological difference, of denying freedom of choice to both men and women. During the Depression this attitude led many women to agree that the preservation of jobs for male breadwinners should be a priority, and demands for equal pay and opportunity were replaced by campaigns to allow women to perform their traditional roles under the best possible conditions. Nevertheless, it was such groups that were largely responsible for keeping the whole idea of state responsibility for the welfare of its citizens on the political agenda at a time when this was rejected not only by business interests and the main political parties, but also by organised labour; they were also subsequently able to ensure that there was some acknowledgement of the needs of women in the New Deal (see Chapter 8 below).

Equal rights v. welfare feminism in Britain

The split between equal rights and welfare feminists became explicit rather later in Britain than in America, partly because the struggle for equal voting rights was not finally won until 1928. The situation in Britain was also very different because welfare feminists were not politically isolated as in America, but could frequently make common cause with the new Labour Party.

As we have seen, women had long been involved in charitable work, and a number of studies carried out in the first decades of the century increased public awareness of the particular problems faced by women, revealing an appalling catalogue of chronic poor health, bad housing and malnutrition (Davies, 1978; Reeves, 1979). Organisations such as the Women's Co-operative Guild argued that these problems were the products of poverty rather than of ignorance or bad housekeeping, and they insisted that the solution lay in state provision rather than individual self-help or charity. The inter-war years were therefore characterised by campaigns for improved maternal and infant health provision, for the inclusion of women in the developing system of national insurance, and for economic assistance to women through maternity benefits or child allowances (Dale and Foster, 1986). All this was a far cry from the laissez-faire individualism of earlier feminists such as Fawcett, and meant that 'the notion of the feminist as a middle class women in pursuit of a job was radically overturned', so that 'feminism's identification with middle-class professional women had been shattered, and the working-class mother had emerged as the new symbol of oppressed womanhood' (Phillips, 1987, pp. 98 and 102). This change was in line with the general trend in British politics away from liberal ideas of laissez-faire and towards a greater degree of state intervention that was eventually to produce the Welfare State; thus Banks has claimed that 'to a large extent we may see the Welfare State in Britain as a product of an alliance between welfare feminism and the Labour Party' (Banks, 1986, p. 174).

As in America, welfare feminism had the advantage of addressing the real needs of large numbers of women, and in this it contrasted favourably with the equal rights feminists who seemed largely concerned with the needs of middle-class women. It was also seen by some as a step towards improved conditions for all.

However, again as in America, in stressing the needs of women as wives and mothers, it sometimes seemed to deny them the option of being anything else, and in concentrating on the welfare of women in the home it tended to ignore the exploitation of those in paid employment – and in the aftermath of the First World War the number of 'surplus women' rose dramatically, so that nearly one third of women had no choice but to be economically self-supporting. With the ending of the war, the large numbers of women who had been substituting for men in all kinds of occupations were replaced by returning soldiers; for welfare feminists this was a welcome return to the natural order of things, rather than a blow to their cause, but for many individual women it meant extreme hardship.

Eleanor Rathbone and the family allowance campaign

Perhaps paradoxically, the one campaign that might have served the needs of both single women and mothers was the demand for family allowances, associated with the name of Eleanor Rathbone, a long-time suffrage campaigner and social reformer who was elected as an Independent member of parliament in 1929. Rathbone claimed to represent a 'new feminism' based on women's real and specific needs and differences from men, rather than on the abstract rights claimed by older liberal feminists; nevertheless she was also concerned with questions of equal pay and freedom of choice, and aimed at economic independence for all women.

Her main demand was for a policy of 'family endowments' to be paid directly to women, for she insisted that the task of bringing up children must receive financial recognition in order to alleviate poverty, to give women financial independence, and to recognise the importance of their maternal role – and here she was scathing about those who claimed to revere motherhood while refusing to act to alleviate the squalor and poverty it so often involved:

> the sentimentalist, who has taken motherhood under his special protection, is shocked at the base suggestion that anything so sordid as remuneration, anything so prosaic as the adjustment of means to ends, should be introduced into the sacred institution of the family and applied to the profession of motherhood (Rathbone, 1927, p. 66).

This was clearly in line with the ideas of welfare feminism, but anathema to liberal feminists like Fawcett, who believed that parents should take responsibility for their own children, rather than relying on the state. However, although her prime concern was with the welfare of mothers and children and she did not challenge the traditional division of labour, Rathbone was not attempting to 'force women back into the home', as some critics have suggested, but to give *all* women a *choice*: women would no longer be forced into the labour market through financial necessity, but if they wished to pursue a career they could use their family endowment to purchase domestic help. She also believed that her proposals could lead to equal pay for men and women. At present, she argued, a man's wages were based on the assumption that he had a non-earning wife and children to support, whereas in fact over half of working men over the age of 20 had no dependent children at all; once mothers and children were provided for by the state, a man's pay could, like a woman's, reflect the work which he as an individual had performed, rather that covering frequently non-existent family responsibilities; with this removal of the 'family wage', the need for wage differentials between men and women would disappear. In practice, when family allowances were introduced after the Second World War (for second and subsequent children), they were at a level far below that which would give women financial independence or undermind the idea of the male breadwinner. In this sense they had become a means of alleviating poverty and encouraging population growth rather than of shifting social and economic power in the direction of women; nevertheless it was feminists such as Rathbone who ensured that the allowance was paid directly to mothers, and who insisted that the needs of women and children be incorporated in the new Welfare State. Modern feminists have therefore seen the defence of family allowances as both an important practical issue and a part of an ideological struggle to have women's work fully recognised; the Wages for Housework group has recently attempted to fuse earlier arguments with a Marxist analysis of women's domestic labour, and has resurrected Rathbone as a heroine for its cause (see Chapter 13 below).

Birth control

Another area which spanned the concerns of both equal rights and welfare feminists was the issue of birth control. This had formerly been largely regarded as a source of sexual enslavement rather than liberation, and nineteenth-century proponents such as Annie Besant had received little support from the suffrage leaders. There was, however, a gradual change in attitudes towards sexuality, which came to be seen as an important source of human pleasure rather than a sin or a purely animal activity: as the American activist Crystal Eastman said, 'Feminists are not nuns' (in Cook, 1978, p. 47). In both Britain and America after the First World War, some women took freedom of choice to mean sexual permissiveness and to advocate 'bachelor motherhood'; nevertheless such deliberate flouting of convention, although widely reported, was still rare, and as Rowbotham comments 'In the 1920s sexual defiance was a style . . . a release for a privileged minority, not a new way of living for the majority' (Rowbotham, 1973a, p. 124). More important for the acceptance of birth control was the recognition by social reformers of the appalling effects on women's health of repeated pregnancies; this led to the demand that contraceptive knowledge be made available to working-class women; in Britain this involved not only the establishment of charitable clinics to provide such information, but also a demand for state funding. Here, although there was much support for such welfare feminist measures within the Labour party, there was also a sometimes well-founded suspicion of the motives of reformers; for example, Marie Stopes, the author of *Married Love* (1928), was motivated not only by compassion for the plight of working-class women, but by fears that unchecked breeding by the impoverished working class would lead to 'race deterioration'. For some working-class men and women, therefore, the birth control movement was seen as a sinister move towards controlling the working class rather than a means of liberating women; it was also seen as a way of blaming poverty on feckless over-breeding rather than on capitalist exploitation. Nevertheless, a woman's ability to control her own fertility came to be a key feminist demand which could be advocated both by equal rights campaigners and by those welfare feminists who saw family planning as an essential prerequisite for responsible motherhood. During this inter-war period, feminists concentrated largely on contraception (Banks, 1986, pp. 192–4; but see also Rowbotham on the pro-abortionist Stella Browne [Rowbotham, 1977]); their arguments recur, however, in modern debates about abortion and reproductive technology, which many modern feminists see as a key issue (see Chapter 11 below).

In general, welfare feminism clearly represented a shift away from liberal individualism and laissez-faire, and towards more collectivist and interventionist solutions. It also tended to concentrate on the short-term interests of women and to aim at improving the conditions under which they performed their traditional roles, rather than challenging the traditional division of labour and the confinement of women to the private sphere; this approach was often based on an insistence on the high value of domestic work and the belief that although men and women might differ in their natural attributes, women were in no way inferior. However, as the family allowance arguments show, to 'envalue' women's traditional activities is not necessarily to deny them the right to choose an alternative role; as J. S. Mill said in 1881, it is only when women have freedom of choice that we can know what their 'natural' abilities are. It may be, therefore, that the conflict between 'equal rights' and 'welfare' feminism is less absolute than it at first sight appears, so that acceptance of the proposals of one need not involve rejection of all the principles of the other.

For some critics, a problem with both equal rights and welfare feminism is their relationship to other forms of social change. Thus it is argued that the former ignores oppression within the home, and that although it advocates equal rights for men and women in the public sphere, this is within an unequal and hierarchal society in which most must be losers. The latter, on the other hand, tends to assume that state machinery can be used benevolently to redistribute resources and improve the situation of women, whereas, critics say, the state is not some neutral tool, but a reflection or instrument of prevailing patriarchal or capitalist class interests. From the perspective of such radical, socialist or Marxist critics, real change must involve more fundamental social transformation.

During the inter-war years there was little development of radical feminist theory, indeed much earlier analysis of the all-pervasive nature of male power seems to have become forgotten, not to be rediscovered until the 1960s. The entire 'middle years' were, however, a time when socialist and Marxist feminist ideas were being developed and, some believed, being put into practice. It is with these developments that the next chapters are concerned.

5

Socialist feminism in Britain and America

In many European countries there seemed by the end of the nineteenth century to be a sharp split between 'mainstream feminists' with their demands for equal political and legal rights, and Marxist socialists with their talk of class war and revolution. In both Britain and America, however, there was much more of a continuum, as the social concerns that had long characterised sections of the women's movement merged with a more radical critique of existing society which led some to socialism as well as feminism. For most, this socialism was based on humanitarian ideals or a pragmatic response to poverty and the conditions of working-class life, and owed little to Marxist ideology. As such, it favoured gradual and piecemeal reform rather than revolution, and it could seem readily compatible with a feminism based on ideas of social justice rather than on an analysis of patriarchy; from this perspective, socialism and feminism could be seen as complementary, promising equality and an end to exploitation for all.

Women and feminism in socialist organisations

Although many male socialists may have shared this perspective in theory, in practice socialist organisations in both countries tended to combine formal commitment to a degree of sex equality with a marginalisation of 'women's issues', discriminatory practice and a frequently unthinking sexism that permeated all levels of political and personal life. Thus in England, Hannah Mitchell, a

109

working-class socialist and suffrage campaigner from the north of the country complained:

> I soon found that a lot of the Socialist talk about freedom was only talk, and these Socialist young men expected Sunday dinners and huge teas with home-made cakes, potted meat and pies, exactly like their reactionary fellows

and

> Most of us who were married found that 'Votes for Women' were of less interest to our husbands than their own dinners (Mitchell, 1977, pp. 96 and 149).

At times, these different priorities resulted in a clear clash between the methods and aspirations of socialists and feminists. Most famously, the British Labour party refused to support the suffrage campaign for women's enfranchisement on the terms that already existed for men, on the grounds that this would only strengthen the voting power of the middle class; the response of some women to this 'betrayal' was to follow Emmeline and Christabel Pankhurst out of the party, and to form their own militant and independent organisation (see Chapter 4 above). However, as Rowbotham has shown, such polarisation at the level of national organisation concealed a widespread continuity at the grass roots, as women continued to campaign both in women's sections and in the mainstream of trade unions and such organisations as the Labour party, the Fabian Society and the Co-operative Guild (Rowbotham, 1977; see also Walker, 1984, ch. 3; and Rowan, 1982). Far from rejecting socialism as inherently patriarchal or hostile to the interests of women, there seems to have been a widespread feeling that the shortcomings of socialist organisations were merely contingent; this meant that there was within the mainstream of the British socialist movement no theoretical confrontation of the 'divided loyalties', the 'dilemmas of sex and class' (Phillips, 1987a, her book title) that might be faced by socialist feminists; as we saw in the previous section, the Labour Party's programme generally meshed well with the demands of a welfare feminism that preferred reformism to either sex or class warfare.

Perhaps surprisingly, major theoretical analysis of the relationships between socialism and feminism was also absent in Britain's first Marxist party, the small Social Democratic Federation. As Hunt has shown, the official party line that only economic issues are directly relevant to socialist politics, so that other matters are a question of individual conscience, enabled it to avoid confrontation by adopting a 'no policy' position on women's issues. In practice, this meant that although feminist views were expressed in the party press, anti-feminist and misogynist views were seen as equally legitimate, and indeed set the tone for the debate. Therefore, although many women did see themselves as facing sex-specific problems, and tensions became acute over such issues as the vote and women's work, in principle feminism 'remained an optional extra for socialists' which the male leadership could ignore (Hunt, 1988, p. 475).

In America, there was a complex and often uneasy intermingling of the 'orthodox Marxism' imported by German refugees facing Bismarck's anti-socialist laws in the 1880s, and a home-grown socialism (see Buhle, 1981). This latter form of socialism was essentially a moral movement which owed much of its inspiration to Edward Bellamy's *Looking Backward* (1888) and led to a form of socialist feminism that was in the tradition of earlier abolitionist, temperance and anti-prostitution campaigns. Frances Willard, the temperance leader, came to embody this approach, as she increasingly saw drunkenness as a product not a cause of poverty, and the solution as lying in Christian socialism rather than individual restraint or class conflict; similarly, the anti-prostitution campaign had by the early twentieth century developed a distinctive socialist dimension: 'If the mainstream woman's movement of the nineteenth century had named man as the potential debaucher, socialists had substituted capitalism and its masters as the curse of maidenly virtue' (Buhle, 1981, p. 253). Such socialist feminists based their arguments on the ideas of woman's moral superiority and her potential role as regenerator and reformer of a corrupt society that, as we saw, had come to dominate mainstream campaigns in America; for many, this was accompanied by the sanctification of traditional family life and a commitment to the ideal of woman as homemaker rather than producer in the public sphere.

Charlotte Perkins Gilman

The idea of female superiority was also important for the woman who has been described as 'the leading intellectual' in the women's movement in the United States at the beginning of the century: Charlotte Perkins Gilman (1860–1935) (see Rossi, 1973, p. 568); in her theory, however, it gained a new significance and led to very different conclusions. Although she was not really involved with the organised feminist movement, Gilman enjoyed widespread if temporary fame in the years before the First World War, and her views were expounded in fiction, journalism and highly popular public lectures, as well as in theoretical works. In all of these she developed a woman-centred view of the world that linked female values with human progress and socialism, which she saw as the inevitable product of a particular stage of human history. Although she said she disagreed 'with both theory and method as advanced by the followers of Marx' (quoted in Hill, 1980, p. 283), this last point has clear affinities with a basic tenet of Marxism, as has Gilman's insistence that economic conditions are basic to human development, that human nature is not fixed but the constantly evolving product of society, and that work is a basic human need which in future society can be liberated from economic compulsion and freely performed for the general good. Like Marx, she saw society's economic development leading it beyond selfish individualism, exploitation and the profit motive and towards human freedom, co-operation and equality. Unlike him, she did not think this would come about through class conflict and revolution, but by the gradual and peaceful continuation of tendencies already present in modern society: 'The change . . . is not one merely to be prophesied and recommended: it is already taking place under the forces of social evolution; and only needs to be made clear to our conscious thought, that we may withdraw the futile but irritating resistance of our misguided will' (*Women and Economics*, p. 122).

This kind of analysis was by the end of the nineteenth century not strikingly original; what gave Gilman's ideas a dramatic novelty was her combination of such socialism with a wholeheartedly woman-centred approach to history and society. According to Gilman, sex relations are not simply a by-product of economic development but a basic force. Originally, she argued, women were the first producers, for while man was 'gallantly pursuing the buffalo, . . . acting merely as an animal under direct stimulation of hunger and the visible beast before him', women were thinking ahead and sowing grain for themselves and their children (*Human Work*, p. 207). They were, moreover, the first educators, and 'the woman, the mother, is the first co-ordinator, legislator, administrator and executive' (*the Man Made World*, p. 198). These and the essentially human attributes of caring, loving and protecting, stemmed originally from women's maternal role, but have to be *learned* by men who have no such natural virtues, for 'To violently oppose, to fight, to trample to the earth, to triumph in loud bellowings of savage joy – these are the primitive male instincts' (*World*, p. 189). History was therefore the process by which men became fully human and developed production and other originally maternal functions such as legislation to their highest form. In the past, men's strength had enabled them to subordinate and exclude women, but now increased specialisation and the division of labour were enabling women to enter industrial production. These economic developments were also increasing the organic nature of society, so that selfishness, competitiveness and individualism ('the spirit of the predacious male', *World*, p. 197) would soon become outmoded in a new era which would be characterised by such 'womanly' qualities as collectivism and socialist co-operation in the interests of all.

All this gives a history of sexual relations and a promise of their transformation in the future which, however shaky its anthropological foundation, gave women a sense of power and optimism; this was accompanied by trenchant condemnation of the present, increasingly outmoded, arrangements. Central to this was Gilman's insistence that woman must become economically independent from man; far from being 'natural', her present dependency meant that she was the only animal for whom the sexual relationship was also an economic one, for her exclusion from production meant that her survival depended upon her ability to attract a mate. This meant that not only were women denied expression of their productive nature, but they were forced to compete with each other in the marriage market, a particularly demeaning state of affairs as women are both compelled to marry, but also obliged to pretend indifference rather than actively pursuing a man: 'Although marriage is a means of livelihood, it is not honest employment where one can offer one's labour without shame' (*Economics*, p. 89). Like earlier writers, she also claimed that this marketing of women in marriage meant that it was essentially the same as prostitution: 'The transient trade we think evil. The bargain for life we think good.' She added that the revulsion that 'respectable' women felt for prostitution was therefore simply 'the hatred of the trade-unionist for scab labour' (*Economics*, pp. 64 and 100). Not only did this universal commercialism of sex demean women, but it led to an exaggeration of sexual differences and the encouragement in women of inferior qualities such as frailty and weakness; these qualities would, she believed, be passed on to children, both boys and girls, leading to a decline in the quality of the whole human race.

Women must therefore be given economic independence both for their own sake and for the benefit of humanity; this independence would also transform the existing oppressive family structure, leading to a higher form of relationship that was not based on economic need. Here Gilman parted company with most feminists of her day, and forcefully attacked the traditional family: far from being the cosy world of popular sentiment, she saw it as a place of degrading toil and exploitation, where women slaved for no reward, and where their unnatural confinement led to frustration, anger and, all too often, madness. It was, moreover, an exceptionally inefficient way of performing functions essential for society's survival: she argued that cooking, cleaning and child-rearing were complex skills requiring expert and scientific knowledge; the present system whereby they were performed by all women inevitably meant unhealthy, malnourished and ignorant children growing up in tension-ridden homes. Professionalisation of such tasks was therefore for Gilman the key to both the liberation of women and a better society; it was also a process that was already underway, as laundry, cooking and much of childcare were passing out of the home and into the hands of infinitely more efficient specialists. Against those who attempted to resist this trend, and who claimed that it would destroy the family and monogamous marriage, she argued that it was only the oppressive aspects of these that would disappear. Thus the relentlessly hard work now involved in motherhood would be removed, and parent-child relations would be based on genuine love rather than jealous exclusivity and possessiveness, and the home would become a place of love and rest for women and men alike.

These ideas clearly owed much to Gilman's own unhappy experiences of domestic life; she suffered acute depression after the birth of her daughter, and she was widely vilified when she entrusted the child to the care of her former husband and his second wife, who was and remained her own good friend. They meant that for her, the worlds of private and public oppression and liberation were inextricably linked, and that the key to liberation lay in a general move to a society in which 'womanly values' of peace, love and co-operation were no longer confined to the home, but the basis of the whole social order. In this context the differences between men and women would become less important than their potential shared humanity (she therefore described herself as a humanist rather than a feminist), and men too would benefit immeasurably from the ending of female subordination. Like class exploitation, sex oppression could therefore be ended in the interests of all, without the need for conflict, revolution or revenge.

Although Gilman's period of popularity and influence was short-lived and it is only recently that her ideas have been rediscovered, she provided an important and pioneering analysis of the inter-relations of the political, cultural, economic and personal dimensions of life that anticipates some key strands in the modern women's movement. Unlike much modern feminism, however, her analysis of personal life remained within relatively conventional bounds, and she had little to say about sexuality; in this she was quite unlike her infinitely less respectable contemporary, the anarchist Emma Goldman (1869–1940).

Emma Goldman's anarchist feminism

As Marsh has pointed out (Marsh, 1981), although most anarchists were not feminists, anarchism's insistence on human individuality and freedom can readily be given a feminist dimension, while the idea of a society based on trust and co-operation rather than exploitation and force finds echoes in many sections of the women's movement. In the hands of Emma Goldman, the most prominent of the anarchist feminists in America in the early twentieth century, it led to an analysis of the sexual and familial bases of women's oppression that, as many writers have commented, is in many ways remarkably close to modern radical feminism. According to Goldman it was not women's right to vote or to work that was liberating, but personal autonomy expressed through free love and psychological independence: 'True emancipation begins neither at the polls nor in the courts. It begins in woman's soul' (quoted in Shulman, 1983, p. 227).

'Democracy' was, she argued, a facade that left the structures of oppression standing, while employment was simply a new form of exploitation; for a minority of 'emancipated women' it might appear liberating, but such women lost more than they gained: sacrificing all to their careers, fearful of love and childbirth, they had become 'professional automatons' cut off from 'life's essence' (in Shulman, 1979, p. 137). The state, private property and the wage system were therefore for Goldman all interrelated systems of oppression that must be destroyed, not negotiated with; and this familiar anarchist critique was extended to attack the home, motherhood, the family and conventional morality as the core oppressors of women.

Although the utopian socialists had attacked the traditional family and sexual morality, nearly all later feminists had abjured free love and embraced respectability; for 'Red Emma', however, the free expression of sexuality became a dramatically central issue. At present, she argued, a woman is condemned to be 'a celibate, a prostitute, or a reckless, incessant breeder of hapless children', and of these three the celibate is the most unfortunate: 'There is nothing more pathetic, nothing more terrible, than this grey-grown victim of a grey-grown Morality' (in Shulman, 1979, pp. 129 and 132). Sexual liberation is not, however, simply a means of individual fulfilment, critically important though this is, but it is connected to the wider social morality to which exploitation and private property are central, and women are but one form of possession. Love and passion must therefore, she argued, be freed from ideas of ownership, fidelity and control; however, like Mary Wollstonecraft, with whom she identified (see Chapter 1 above), she often found that her heart could not always follow where reason led, and that jealousy and possessiveness were more easily eradicated in theory than in practice. Her letters show her love affairs to have brought her agonies of jealousy as well as ecstasy, as she found that 'sex is like a double-edged sword, it releases our spirit and binds it with a thousand threads' (quoted in Wexler, 1984, pp. 278–9).

Goldman's sexual radicalism and her active involvement in revolutionary politics both gained her extreme notoriety and meant that she had little influence outside the narrow circle of anarchist politics. However, Marsh argues that she faced up to fundamental issues ignored by the mainstream women's movement: 'In the short run, the organized suffragists seemed to have been following the most assured path to equality. In the long run, however, American society still struggles with the issues abandoned by them but kept alive by the unsuccessful, unpragmatic anarchist feminists' (Marsh, 1981, p. 64). Spender, however, suggests that Goldman's analysis failed because although she pinpointed the elements of personal oppression being explored by feminists today, she lacked any awareness of sex oppression or patriarchy: 'For one who is against everything, she is significantly silent on the abuse of women by men'; this failure to analyse or indict male power is combined, Spender says, with a failure to identify the potential collective power of women, so that 'sisterhood' is a concept absent from Goldman's political vocabulary, and it is left to the individual woman to assert her will against the forces of oppression (Spender, 1983a, p. 504). Nevertheless, unlike some radical feminists today, Goldman did not isolate personal change from wider social transformation or ignore the realities of class oppression; she did not believe that true freedom for men or women would be achieved within capitalist society, but only under socialism.

Mary Inman and American communism

Orthodox Marxists of course agreed with the last part of this analysis, while rejecting the anarchists' belief that revolution could be the product of a spontaneous act of will rather than of objective economic circumstances, long-term political organisation and class struggle. Feminism was certainly never central to the small Communist party that survived in America after the First World War, and which increasingly followed the 'official line' emanating from Moscow. The party was, predictably, characterised by sexism and discrimination and a general perception of 'women's issues' as trivial, diversionary and almost infinitely postponable. Nevertheless, during the 1930s a handful of women did reach relatively high positions in the organisation, and debates in the party press at times 'gave a legitimacy and a focus to women's problems and concerns' (Shaffer, 1979, p. 96). More importantly, they gave rise to a theoretical contribution that anticipates much modern Marxist feminist analysis in the work of Mary Inman.

Although Inman rejected the 'socialist feminist' label and claimed to be writing in the Marxist-Leninist tradition, the ideas expressed in her book *In Woman's Defence* (1936) go well beyond the usual orthodoxies, as she extended her analysis beyond the conventionally defined boundaries of the economic and political to examine women's oppression in the home, in education, in the media, in the manufacture of femininity and in the sexual double standard (which she referred to as 'fascism in the bedroom'; quoted in Shaffer, 1979, p. 292). She claimed, too, that *all* women are oppressed in these areas of life, and insisted that the working-class man could himself be an oppressor of his wife – she called this 'male domination under class rule' (Shaffer, 1979, p. 85). Like some modern Marxist feminists, she also attempted to extend Marxist economic categories to include women's domestic labour and to show the functional necessity of housework for capitalism as the process by which labour power is reproduced and maintained; this enabled her to argue that women as housewives could agitate and organise for changes in their working conditions rather than seeing trade union activity as the only valid form of struggle. However, although she therefore called for unity between *all* women, she was enough of a Marxist to claim that this could only be as part of the class struggle, and that the real interests of working-class men are also served by sex equality, rather than the illusory domination that is all they can enjoy under capitalism. Inman's views were vehemently denounced by the communist leadership (see Landy, 1943), and she herself left the party. Her ideas have until recently been lost to history; they have, however, a startling modernity, and anticipate modern debates on domestic labour, and on the interconnections of patriarchy and capitalism.

No doubt during this period there were also many unsung heroines who 'washed up for socialism' (Walker, 1984, p. 71) while thinking subversive feminist thoughts; there were, too, many other socialist feminist women famous at the time such as Crystal Eastman (Spender, 1983a, Cook, 1978), Olive Schreiner (Spender, 1983a; First and Scott, 1980; Stanley, 1983), Sylvia Pankhurst (Edmondson, 1981) and Dora Russell (Spender, 1983a), and others who played an important role at grass-roots level but who are only now being rescued from oblivion, such as Selina Cooper (Liddington, 1984), Stella Browne (Rowbotham, 1977) and Hannah Mitchell (Mitchell, 1977). The insights of these women were often important; at the time, however, the marginalisation of women's issues within socialism meant that their ideas seemed to die with them, and socialist feminism has lacked a cumulative body of ideas, an ongoing debate; in reclaiming their ideas, modern feminist research can enrich contemporary understanding and provide it with a history.

For Marxist feminism, the process has been rather different, as organised Marxism's tendency to insist that there must be a 'correct' position on all issues has meant that there has been no shortage of 'classic texts' and 'party lines'; emphasis on these, however, obscures the debates that took place, and ignores those contributions that were not officially sanctioned. In fact the 'Woman Question' forced itself onto the agenda, and became an important theoretical and practical issue for European Marxism in the late nineteenth and early twentieth centuries, where debate centred first upon the German Social Democratic party, and then upon events in Russia.

6

Marxist feminism in Germany

Before the First World War, the German socialist movement was the largest and most successful in the world; as such, it had a dominating position with the Second International (1889–1914), and debates within the German Social Democratic party (SPD) had a far-reaching influence. The SPD itself was formed in 1875 as the result of an uneasy coalition between reformist and Marxist socialists, but by the time of the Erfurt Programme in 1891 it was, under the leadership of August Bebel, fully committed, in theory at least, to a thoroughgoing Marxist position, complete with the rhetoric of class war, revolution and the inevitable victory of socialism; it was also, despite anti-socialist legislation during the 1880s, now the largest party in the German parliament. This shift in a Marxist direction was accompanied by a shift in attitudes over the role of women, as the debate between those traditionalists who thought woman's destiny lay in the home and those who welcomed her entry into the labour force was resolved in favour of the latter. However, both at the level of general politics and on women's issues, there appeared to be growing contradictions between the party's formal commitment to the long-term goals decreed by Marxist orthodoxy and its more pragmatic pursuit of short-term reforms and parliamentary success. The ensuing debate between 'orthodox Marxists', 'radicals' and 'revisionists' was reflected in arguments over the so-called 'Woman Question' which were never really resolved.

Bebel's contribution

The single most important work in establishing the official party line on this question was Bebel's *Woman Under Socialism* (also published as *Woman in the Past, Present and Future*), which Evans has described as 'The seminal book in the formation of socialist attitudes towards women' (Evans, 1977, p. 156). First published in 1878, it went into numerous editions and was rapidly translated into many languages. As the book most frequently borrowed from workers' libraries in Germany, it was enormously popular, and it had a much wider and more immediate impact than Engels' *The Origins of the Family, Private Property and the State* (1884), although it is the latter that is now generally regarded as the classic Marxist text on women.

Bebel's analysis had much in common with Engels', and they shared the basic position that women's oppression is a product of class society that will only be ended when proletarian revolution brings about a socialist society in which women will have full economic independence, and domestic work and childcare will be collectivised. Bebel, however, went beyond Engels in a number of ways, and he gave women's issues a centrality quite lacking in Marx's own writings, insisting that socialism could not succeed without the active participation of women and that 'there can be no emancipation of humanity without the social independence and equality of the sexes' (*Woman*, p. 6). Unlike Engels, he saw that the working-class woman in paid employment is oppressed as a woman as well as exploited as a worker. He argued that under conditions of capitalist competition she cannot earn as much as a man and that she is additionally worn down by domestic toil: while her husband 'avails himself of the freedom that accident gives him of having been born a man' and seeks refuge in drink and gambling, the wife 'sits up, and sews and patches deep into the night . . . she must work like a dray-horse; for her there is no rest or recreation' (*Woman*, p. 103). He also identified non-economic sources of oppression such as the double standard of sexual morality and the restrictive effects of conventional female dress. This led him to argue that all women, regardless of class, have some interests in common and might unite on some demands; he therefore saw female suffrage not only as a means of furthering the class struggle but as an individual entitlement based on women's contribution to society and a weapon needed by women *as a group* to defend their interests.

Despite all this, Bebel's analysis has found little favour with modern feminists (see Vogel, 1983; Coole, 1988; Hunt, 1986 and 1988; Boxer and Quataert, 1978; but see also Draper and Lipow, 1976, for a more positive view). In particular, it is argued that, although he was very aware of non-economic issues, his over-rigid loyalty to the Marxist tradition meant that he could not really confront or explain them. As Hunt has said, in Bebel's work 'the Woman Question has found a socialist answer by disappearing into the class or Social Question . . . There is therefore no theoretical space to develop an understanding of patriarchy, as either a separate or a related system, for sex oppression has in effect been rendered invisible' (Hunt, 1986, p. 53). The solution for women could ultimately only be to join the fight against capitalism; the proletarian man and woman must realise that they were both 'tugging at the same rope' and there would be no need for an autonomous struggle against patriarchy, for this would necessarily disappear under socialism. As we shall see in Chapter 13, the problem of whether patriarchy has an independent existence and how it can be confronted within left-wing movements is one that Marxist feminists are struggling with today; it was also one faced but never really acknowledged by those women in the Second International who attempted to put Bebel's ideas into practice.

Clara Zetkin

The foremost of these was Clara Zetkin (1857–1933). Her name has since been eclipsed by that of her contemporary Rosa Luxemburg (1871–1919) and to a lesser extent by Eleanor Marx Aveling, Karl Marx's daughter; at the time, however, she was effectively 'the leading woman of European socialism' (Foner, 1984, p. 42). Unlike Luxemburg, she concentrated her energies on women's issues, and as editor of the SPD's women's journal *Die Gleichheit* ('Equality') she addressed the theoretical and practical problems involved in recruiting women to the socialist cause. She had a considerable measure of success in ensuring that the 'Woman Question' remained on the agenda of international socialism (even if official policy was not always matched by genuine commitment), and it was largely due to her efforts that Germany had by 1900 'a large, well-organised, and extremely militant socialist women's movement' (Vogel, 1983, p. 107). However, although by the mid–1890s she held a leading position in the SPD, she increasingly found herself in conflict with the other party leaders both on women's issues and on the whole question of whether socialism could be brought about by piecemeal reform and parliamentary methods. Here Zetkin's determinedly radical position isolated her not only from the party leadership, but from a new generation of women party members who were concerned more with welfare and children than with challenging the power structure or achieving wider social change, for 'The transformation of Social Democracy into a state-supportive reform party had its parallel in the metamorphosis of the proletarian women's movement into a training ground for social angels' (Thonnessen, 1973, p. 9). In 1917 she left the party, in 1919 she was elected to the German parliament as a member of the newly-formed Communist party and she spent most of her later years in the Soviet Union. Although, as Evans has pointed out (Evans, 1987), Zetkin was a figure of opposition rather than orthodoxy within the international communist movement, the expression of any views contrary to the Stalinist party line became increasingly difficult, and any independent discussion of the Women's Question was effectively silenced.

Hostility to bourgeois feminism

For Zetkin, as for many other socialist women, Bebel's book had been an inspirational starting-point: 'It was more than a book, it was an event, a great deed' (quoted in Foner, 1984, p. 22). She accepted wholeheartedly his central thesis of the necessary interconnections between the aspirations of women and the achievement of socialism; indeed, she went even further than Bebel in her insistence on the primacy of class over gender interests and her denial that middle-class and proletarian women could ever share a common goal. This meant that in practice she was extremely hostile to 'bourgeois feminists' with their demands for improved education, employment prospects and legal status, and she refused point-blank to co-operate with them in their campaigns for the vote. This position was backed up by a materialist analysis of the modern women's movement which argued that it was composed of three separate strands based on three opposing class positions: the 'Upper Ten Thousand' were concerned with freeing property rights from their last feudal restrictions by granting them to women; women of the petty bourgeoisie and intelligentsia needed economic independence at a time of capitalist crisis when many men could no longer afford to maintain a wife; and working-class women were struggling alongside their men to bring about an end to capitalism. Like Luxemburg, whose diatribes against bourgeois women were even more vitriolic (she called them 'parasites of the parasites of the social body'), she believed therefore that there could be no common ground, and that class loyalties would reassert themselves as soon as legal and political rights were won. Proletarian women therefore needed political and legal rights only as part of their fight against capitalism, and there could be no common front with 'bourgeois feminists' involved in a superficial struggle against men.

Her analysis also meant that the very possibility of sex oppression within the working class was ruled out of order. Like Engels and Bebel, she argued that the lack of property in the working class and the entry of proletarian women into industry meant that there was no material basis or motivation for the continuation of gender inequality. Proletarian men and women must see each other not as oppressors and oppressed, but as comrades, fighting together for the common good. In practice, of course, she was well aware that all was not rosy in the proletarian garden, and that even in the SPD the most old-fashioned chauvinism still flourished. Not only was there still a strong strand that believed that the role of a socialist woman could only lie in providing a secure domestic base for her husband, while others were able to concede the principle of more active participation only if this were not at the expense of their own hot dinners, but women's issues were repeatedly marginalised, trivialised and removed from the mainstream agenda; like other women leaders, she was also the subject of cruel sexist jokes. Until 1908, women could not join the SPD officially, as the law in many Germany states still forbade women to join political organisations or to attend public meetings; they could therefore become involved only by joining the semi-autonomous women's section. Although Zetkin opposed separatism, she came to see the advantages of such a distinct women's group within the party where, in a supportive atmosphere, women could develop the skills that would enable them to participate in the wider movement and, by building up a firm understanding of their own interests, maximise their influence and ensure that their needs were not swept aside. Zetkin's views were not, however, acceptable to the party leadership, and the resulting integration of women into the mainstream after 1908 effectively meant the marginalisation of radical women such as herself and the silencing of an independent women's voice.

Zetkin's methodological framework did not, however, enable her to confront such problems theoretically, nor did she expand her analysis to explore the problems of sexuality and domestic responsibility that had been raised by Bebel. Here again she was certainly not unaware of the issues involved. In her speeches she could easily draw applause by references to the problem of husbands who expect to be waited upon by their wives, and in conversation with Lenin in 1920 (recalled by Zetkin in 1924) she acknowledged his complaint that 'at the meetings arranged for reading and discussion with working women, sex and marriage problems come first. They are said to be the main objects of interest in your political instruction and educational work'. She attempted to justify herself by claiming that such discussions could lead to an understanding of the different historical forms of the family and their dependence on economics: 'All roads lead to Rome. Every truly Marxist analysis of an important part of the ideological superstructure of society . . . had to lead to an analysis of bourgeois society and its foundations, private property.' However, when Lenin expressed doubts as to whether such analysis actually occurred, she agreed and said that she had therefore ensured that personal matters were no longer the focal point of discussion (in Lenin, 1977, pp. 102–3). The problem here was that for Zetkin such issues could only be seen as part of the ideological superstructure rather than as subjects in their own right. This reduction of the most intimate problems to an economic basis is one which many modern feminists find unsatisfactory, for removing male oppression from the political agenda did not mean that it disappeared in the home, the party or in society as a whole; it means, however, that it could not be confronted, and that while patriarchy remained unnamed by Marxist feminists it could not effectively be challenged.

Although the 'bourgeois feminists' (or 'women's righters' as they were often called) were sometimes more able to identify instances of sex oppression, their liberal individualist perspective did not allow for the possibility of the systematic domination of women by men, or for the ways in which such oppression might serve the needs of capitalism. Some of course did criticise social inequality, but many were in most respects highly conservative, and few were prepared to work with or join a party which was still formally committed to class war and revolution and which refused to allow the reality of any cross-class gender interests. Therefore although by 1900 Marxists and feminists shared common demands, the women's movement remained irretrievably split at the level of both theory and practical political activity. Many commentators have suggested that this split was responsible for German women's lack of success in achieving the legal rights won earlier in many other European countries, but this failure has to be seen in the more general context of the weakness of liberalism in the German political system (see Evans, 1980).

Lily Braun and the revisionist debate

Nevertheless a few feminists did join the SPD. Of these, the most notable was Lily Braun (1865–1916), and the ensuing battle between her and Zetkin over the correct socialist solution to the Woman Question reflected a wider debate over the future direction of the party and the nature of socialism itself. By the end of the century, it seemed to many that the electoral success of the SPD meant that it was becoming a part of the very system it was dedicated to overthrowing, and that its increasing preoccupation with short-term goals and attracting votes meant that it was no longer a revolutionary party. For the 'revisionists' led by Eduard Bernstein, these changes were to be welcomed. In *Evolutionary Socialism* (1899) he argued against an approach to socialism based on economic determinism, and he demanded that the party's official ideology be revised to accept that capitalism was neither on the point of collapse nor leading to the impoverishment of the working class. On the contrary, he claimed, gradual reform was leading to a general improvement in living conditions and class conflict was losing its significance; from this perspective, achievable short-term gains were more important than a mythical predetermined goal, and socialism was transformed from the inevitable product of economic forces to an ethical ideal, for which all men of goodwill could work. Such an approach was much more attractive to feminists like Braun than the radical insistence that political activity must be aimed at the total transformation of society and that it must be accompanied both by trade union activity and by a revolutionary mass movement. It opened the door to co-operation across class lines, and it meant that feminist goals, like other benefits of socialism, need not be postponed until 'after the revolution' but could be achieved as part of the gradual process of social change; in this context, legal and political rights were not to be seen as weapons enabling proletarian women to participate more fully in the class struggle, but as valuable ends in themselves. It also meant, Braun argued, that the establishment of co-operative living arrangements could be seen as an important step forward; here she claimed that such domestic co-ops would both relieve women of the burden of household toil and encourage the growth of the co-operative feelings that would be required in a socialist society. Luxemburg had long rejected co-operatives as a misguided attempt to return to a pre-capitalist lifestyle that could never lead to socialism, and Zetkin condemned Braun's ideas 'the last blossoming of utopianism in its most dangerous, opportunistic form' (quoted in Quataert, 1978, p. 130). She argued that such experiments would be a diversionary luxury affordable only by the affluent, and that because they concerned only patterns of consumption, leaving production quite unchallenged, they could never become an agent of social transformation. She also rejected Braun's interest in birth control and the call by some socialists for a 'birth strike' which it was said would both ease the burdens of working-class women and deprive capitalism of its next generation of soldiers. This, Zetkin argued, was a dangerous distraction from the real problems that falsely blamed poverty on over-breeding rather than capitalist exploitation; it might help individual women, but by reducing the size of the working class it could only harm its long-term class prospects.

Although the ideas of the revisionists were never formally accepted by the party, the 'orthodox' line became increasingly out of kilter with political reality, as the SPD combined formal loyalty to Marxist dogma with increasingly reformist practice; this rightward move was symbolised when in 1914 all but one of the SPD members of parliament voted to support Germany's war effort. Like Luxemburg, Zetkin vigorously opposed the war, and in 1915 she organised an international conference of socialist women to campaign against it. Whereas some mainstream feminists also attempted to co-ordinate international activity against the war, they tended to see it as a manifestation of male aggression that must be countered by female pacifism (see Chapter 4 above). Zetkin, however, true to her materialist approach, saw it as a product of capitalist imperialism; the campaign against the war was therefore part of the international socialist attack on capitalism in which women, because they did not face conscription, were able to play a major role.

Modification of Zetkin's position

Although Zetkin frequently opposed the SPD's drift to reformism and its prioritisation of electoral popularity, she herself may not have been immune to such pressures, and some of her ideas were significantly modified over time. In particular, her early analysis of the family as an oppressive institution and her insistence on the importance of women's participation in trade union and political activity were replaced by the reassurance that under socialism the family would remain as a moral unit, that 'It is out of the question that the task of socialist women's activity should be to alienate proletarian women from their duties as wives and mothers' and that 'Many a wife and many a mother who imbues her husband and children with class-consciousness accomplishes just as much as the women comrades whom we see at our meetings' (Draper and Lipow, 1976, pp. 199 and 120). This shift was reflected in Zetkin's editorship of the SPD women's journal *Die Gleichheit*. She originally saw this as an important theoretical publication, providing information on trade unions, strikes, wage levels and working conditions and aimed at the most 'advanced' women workers. In practice, however, although female party membership grew rapidly (to reach over 16 per cent of total membership by 1914), most of the new recruits were not as had been expected factory workers, but the non-working wives of male party members. Zetkin was therefore persuaded to aim much more of her material at these new members, and *Die Gleichheit* came to include practical household tips as well as ideas on how to instill socialist values in children and a general reassurance that in keeping the home fires burning, women were making an important contribution to the socialist cause. Evans has defended this move: 'Zetkin's increasing tendency to appeal to the proletarian women as wives and mothers rather than as workers was no more than a gradual recognition that this was what, in their own consciousness and that of their husbands, they were' (Evans, 1987, p. 26). However, while failure to challenge this consciousness might lead to political popularity in the short run, in the long run it could only mean that women were marginalised in the decision-making processes and that power relationships between men and women remained unexamined.

In 1903 Zetkin wrote: '[Marx's] materialist concept of history has not supplied us with any ready-made formulas concerning the women's question, yet it has done something much more important: it has given us the correct unerring method to comprehend that question' (in Foner, 1984, p. 93). Her own attempts to put this method into practice gave her a new perspective on the women's movement by enabling her to disentangle some of the class interests involved, but it led her to a too-easy rejection of any idea of shared gender interests across class lines and it prevented her from identifying or challenging patriarchial practices and beliefs at a theoretical level. It also meant that she came to defend a position whereby women played an essentially supportive role in a socialist movement dominated by men and in which their concerns were seen as trivial or diversionary; despite her own undoubted commitment to sex equality, it seems therefore that her methods could not lead her to her goal.

Some critics of Marxism would argue that such shortcomings are the inevitable product of an inadequate theory which, in seeking to reduce everything to an economic cause, is quite unable to grasp the all-encompassing nature of patriarchal power and its manifestation in personal as well as public life. Certainly, for some later Marxists the legacy of Zetkin and the Second International has been a crude economic determinism and a hostility to feminism as a diversionary and divisive movement of middle-class women. Modern Marxist feminists are however attempting to show that Marxism can provide the basis for a more sophisticated approach. The adequacy of the Marxist approach to the Woman Question was also of course explored in Russia, where from late 1917 state power was in the hands of Marxists; although all kinds of problems arose in putting theory into practice and many gains were lost with Stalinist repression, it was here that the first serious attempt to extend Marxist analysis to questions of sex, morality and family life was made by Alexandra Kollontai.

7

Marxist feminism in Russia

Although the Russian revolution has often been seen as a testing-ground for Marxist theory, it must be stressed that for Marx himself communism was essentially the product of industrial capitalism, in which technology could be used to liberate men from drudgery, and problems of scarcity would be ended; as capitalism was becoming a worldwide system, he also believed that communism would replace it on a world scale. All this was very different from the situation facing the Russian Bolsheviks when they seized power at the end of 1917, for although Russia had been industrialising rapidly it was still basically a peasant society, and the war with Germany had had a devastating effect on the economy. Moreover, contrary to the expectations of its leaders, events in Russia did not spark off successful proletarian revolutions in the more advanced European nations, but were followed by both civil war and foreign invasion. Many Western defenders of Marxism would therefore argue that the material preconditions for a successful communist revolution simply did not exist in Russia in the early twentieth century, and that failure was inevitable. From the point of view of the Woman Question, the resources needed to liberate women were not available: Engels, Bebel and Zetkin had all argued that women in communist society would be freed from domestic toil, but the provision of adequate public facilities was a luxury unattainable in a society fighting for its very survival. Nevertheless, the issue was not simply set aside in the immediate aftermath of revolution. Indeed the resulting social dislocation and questioning of all traditional arrangements and values meant that relationships between men and women were fiercely debated and some serious attempts were made to put Marxist theory into practice; although of course the Soviet Union did not solve the Woman Question, the ideas and experiences of these early years may still have relevance for feminists today.

Early Russian feminism

The earlier history of feminism in Russia was in some ways similar to that in Western Europe, as from the mid-nineteenth century middle-class women increasingly demanded the right to education, to a career, to full legal equality and the vote. As in Germany, this was in the context of a society in which liberalism was weak and only left-wing organisations seemed prepared to treat women's issues seriously; therefore although many feminists remained true to their class, others came to link feminist concerns with ideas of wider political, economic and social change. Unlike Germany, however, the parliamentary road to socialism was firmly closed, and significant numbers of women therefore came to be involved in more radical and revolutionary political movements – indeed, as Stites ironically comments: 'the vocation of revolutionary was the only one open to women which would greet her as an equal, allow her talents freely to unfold, and permit her to rise to the top' (Stites, 1978, p. 153).

Radical involvement ranged from outright terrorism (it was a woman who assassinated the Tsar in 1881) to the mass Populist movement 'to the people' in the 1870s, when thousands of young people attempted to bring ideas of socialist revolution to the peasants; female involvement in subversive movements was by the early twentieth century so great that the authorities had to build a new women's prison. The early revolutionaries were generally intellectuals rather than peasants or workers; as such they were able to support feminist ideals at an abstract level 'unencumbered by the need to compromise with political reality or take account of the anti-feminist prejudices of a working-class following' (Evans, 1977, p. 179), and in some circles quite radical notions of gender identity and the need for female autonomy were discussed (see Engel, 1978). From the 1850s some were also influenced by the nihilist idea of immediate personal liberation through total moral, sexual and intellectual freedom. This left Russia with a heritage of sexual radicalism and experimentation which had been quite lacking in German left-wing culture, and which was to surface in the years following the revolution. Such individualistic solutions were, however, anathema to orthodox Marxist analysis, and as the influence of Marxism increased towards the end of the nineteenth century, any idea that sexual questions might be seen as an autonomous problem disappeared; as in Germany the Woman Question came to be seen as an aspect of the wider Social Question which would automatically be resolved in future socialist society.

The first serious attempt to apply orthodox Marxism to the situation of Russian women was made in 1900 by Nadezhda Krupskaya (Lenin's wife). In her pamphlet *The Woman Worker* she described the appalling conditions of work facing Russian women in both town and country, but she followed the line already laid down by Engels, Bebel and Zetkin in arguing that women's participation in the labour force was ultimately progressive and that liberation could only come about through participation in the class struggle. Although her analysis was not original, her pamphlet enjoyed considerable popularity and helped ensure that women's demands for full legal and political equality were from 1903 included in the party programme (see Stites, 1978, pp. 239–43).

Lenin himself did not display the indifference or hostility to women's demands that Krupskaya complained of in other men. In particular, he went beyond the usual platitudes about legal rights and future equality to an insistence on the need to liberate women from domestic drudgery which Vogel claims was 'unique in the Marxist literature' (Vogel, 1983, p. 121). Not only did he argue that women would be liberated by technology and public provision, but he demanded that the old male 'slave-owners point of view' be rooted out, and he roundly condemned 'the common sight of a man calmly watching a woman wear herself out with trivial, monotonous, strength- and time-consuming work . . . and watching her spirit shrinking, her mind growing dull, her heartbeat growing fainter, and her will growing slack' (in Lenin, 1977, pp. 115 and 111). He also agreed that because of their specific needs and problems, separate organisations and methods might be needed to recruit women and involve them in revolutionary politics; he therefore supported the establishment of a special women's department (the Genotdel) in 1919.

Women's issues were not, however, a political priority for Lenin. Despite the frequently quoted comments on housework, he never really questioned whether or how men could be persuaded to change their attitudes; he also refused to treat problems of sex and marriage as serious political issues, regarding them as a frivolous distraction at a time of revolutionary crisis. Trotsky claimed that such neglect of the social and personal dimensions of women's oppression led to a too-narrow concept of liberation. He argued that equality within the family was infinitely harder to achieve than political or workplace equality, he saw male attitudes as a major problem and he saw changes within the home as central for the success of communism: 'From the enslavement of women grew prejudices and superstitions which shaped the children of the new generation . . . Freeing the mother means cutting the last umbilical cord linking the people with the dark and superstitious past' (*Women and the Family*, 1970, pp. 34–5, written 1924–5; see also *Problems of Life*, 1924). However, although he identified areas of concern, Trotsky too failed to give such ideas more than lip service or to make them the focus of his political activity. In general, therefore, although their sympathies may have been genuine, the male communist leaders failed to take on board the serious practical and theoretical issues involved if women were to achieve full equality with men; from their perspective, it was an issue for which Marxism already provided clear answers, and which therefore need not involve any questioning of orthodox theory or political priorities. It was left to a handful of women activists, of whom Alexandra Kollontai (1873–1952) was the most significant, to explore the implications of the quest for equality, and to discover that the solution of the Woman Question was perhaps more complex than orthodox theory suggested.

The ideas of Alexandra Kollontai

Kollontai once claimed that 'Women, and their fate, have occupied my whole life. It was their lot which pushed me into socialism' (quoted in Stites, 1978, p. 250). In fact, however, the reverse appears to have been true, as Kollontai's early commitment to socialism showed no awareness of the special needs of women; on the contrary, it was what she saw as the feminist threat to the socialist movement that first drew her attention to women's issues. At first she simply upheld Marxist orthodoxy as interpreted by Zetkin, and campaigned vigorously against what she saw as a selfish, egotistic bourgeois women's movement, demanding that this be replaced by the class-based solidarity of proletarian men and women. Soon, however, she became much more critical of socialist practice, and aware of the ways in which women's needs were marginalised by the male-dominated party hierarchy; she therefore demanded that separate women's organisations be established within the party, and fought vigorously for women's issues to be kept to the forefront of the political agenda.

Practical achievements

The provisional government set up after the February revolution had given women civil and political rights, and when in October 1917 Kollontai became the first woman in modern history to hold Cabinet office as Commissar (Minister) of Social Welfare, her first task was to complete the process by giving women full legal independence and equality within marriage, legalising abortion, ending illegitimacy as a legal category and establishing the principle of equal pay. She also laid the legal foundations for state provision of maternity and child health care and succeeded in committing the party to the principle of communal housework, childcare and eating facilities (a pledge withdrawn by the party in the early 1920s). Although lack of resources often meant that such decrees could only represent statements of intent, they were quite an extraordinary achievement given the chaotic conditions and demands being made on the new government. They reflected both the determination of individual women like Kollontai and a more general shift in attitudes that had taken place since Marx's time; this in turn was a result both of the impact of feminism and of the increased strength and organisation of the female workforce.

However, the Marxist solution to the Woman Question had promised more than legal equality and welfare rights, for these were already being won in capitalist societies; rather it claimed that women's economic independence, based on full participation in production and liberation from domestic toil, would transform the whole of private life, as morality, the family and relationships between men and women would be based on free choice and equality rather than dependence and exploitation. As we have seen, Engels, Bebel and Zetkin interpreted all this in a fairly conservative way, for they saw freely-chosen monogamy as the likely form of future sexual relationships, and Zetkin in particular came to stress that the family would continue as a social and moral unit even when it ceased to serve an economic function. Kollontai however, was much more radical; she was also much less prepared to agree that the attitudes underlying existing gender relations would automatically change with economic progress. Rather, she argued that they must be tackled in their own right, and that the ideological superstructure is not *only* a reflection of the economic base but can also itself play a role in social transformation.

In practical terms, this meant that the situation of women could not simply be changed by state enactment or provision, but must also involve a change of consciousness; this in turn would be both cause and result of changing circumstances and women's full participation in the building of socialism. It was this principle that Kollontai tried to put into practice in her brief period as head of the women's department (Genotdel) in 1920–1. Activity within the Genotdel was seen as a two-way process, by which women would be educated and informed of their rights and also enabled to bring their needs to the attention of the party; it also sought to combine practical help with theoretical discussion and challenges to traditional patriarchal attitudes. Organisationally it operated both nationally and at grass-roots level, where there was a loose federation of discussion and self-help groups. The idea was that women should be involved in their own emancipation and therefore that they themselves should, with state help, organise the nurseries, laundries and educational campaigns that would liberate them. It was also intended that experience in separate groups would give women the skill and confidence to assert their own interests and to work together with men in mixed trade union and party organisations. Certainly women's political participation did increase, particularly at local level, and the Genotdel penetrated even the distant Muslim areas of the Soviet Union. This was, however, the period of 'war communism', when the country was fighting for its very survival: with widespread famine, the economy in ruins, transport almost non-existent and steel production less than 5 per cent of the pre-war level, nursery provision and women's education were hardly going to be seen as priorities, and in practice material conditions for most women – as for most men – deteriorated sharply. It was also a period in which the whole idea of the kind of 'revolution from below' favoured by Kollontai was viewed with increasing suspicion by the party leaders; indeed her support for an opposition group and her attack on what she saw as increased centralisation and bureaucratisation within the party were seen by Lenin as a threat to party discipline and unity. At a secret session of the 10th Party Congress in 1921 a resolution was passed banning factions, and in 1922 Kollontai was effectively removed from the centre of political debate and influence by being sent on a minor diplomatic mission to Norway. With her fall from power, the officially sanctioned attack on patriarchy ended, and the Genotdel concentrated on more low-key welfare issues; in 1929 it was abolished by Stalin on the grounds that the Woman Question had been solved.

Sexual morality and communism

Despite her failure to achieve the kind of radical transformation for which she hoped, Kollontai's work remains of major theoretical importance. She is best remembered (and frequently misunderstood) for her views on sexuality, but these can only be understood in the wider context of her vision of communism as a form of society developed by the people themselves and in which selfish competition and individualism are replaced by loving comradeship and co-operation. Communism for Kollontai was therefore not simply about redistribution of economic resources or public ownership of the means of production, but about changing the very nature of men and women. Such changed people would relate to each other in ways very different from those which we know today, and their behaviour would be based on a new higher form of morality; this morality however would not simply be the automatic by-product of economic change, for struggles in the ideological superstructure would themselves help bring about material change: 'The new morality is created by a new economy, but we will not build a new economy without the support of a new moral-ity' (in Holt, 1977, p. 270). From this perspective, changes in sexual morality were not simply important in their own right, but part of the process of creating good socialist men and women. They were also central to challenging men's power over women, and here Kollontai made an important step in identifying the political significance of areas of life conventionally defined as 'private', and in attempting to extend Marxist analysis to morality, sexuality and the family without simply reducing these to passive reflectors of the economic base.

Like the earlier Marxist writers, Kollontai agreed that bourgeois morality was based on hypocrisy, inequality and possession, but she extended this to argue that no one in capitalist society could escape its effects and that it generated unequal power relations in the most intimate areas of life, even when these were not based upon economic dependence. 'True love' in capitalist society was therefore an impossibility for the working proletarian woman and the 'career girl' as much for the dependent bourgeois wife, for sex and marriage had come to be based upon emotional and psychological as well as economic inequality. This meant that Engels' solution of economic independence for women could not on its own lead to true sexual equality, which requires a 'radical reform of the human psyche'; this in turn, however, could only come about as part of the general communist transformation of society.

It was on the nature of the desirable form of future proletarian morality that Kollontai parted company with earlier writers most decisively, for while they tended to see genuine monogamy as the ideal form of sexual relationship, she was much more concerned with the *dangers* of sexual exclusiveness, which she suggested might be contrary both to the interests of women and to the welfare of society as a whole. On this she has been much misrep-resented and misunderstood, as her enemies portrayed her as both preacher and practitioner of casual promiscuity and the 'glass of water' theory of sex that saw it as a simple physical need that should be satisfied as readily as thirst. In fact, her own sexual activities would probably have passed unnoticed in a man (she married twice and had two other recorded affairs), and she cer-tainly never advocated promiscuity. She did however hold the view, then thought shocking in a woman, that sex was neither sinful nor shameful, but that it could be a high form of human activity, and she showed sympathetic tolerance for the sexual experimentation that characterised the chaotic post-revolutionary years, in which rejection of bourgeois values was equated by some with rejection of all sexual restraint. Here she differed markedly from Lenin, who spoke with contempt and disgust of those 'yellow-beaked fledglings newly hatched from their bourgeois-tainted eggs' who preached casual sexual gratification: 'To be sure, thirst has to be quenched. But would a normal person lie down in the gutter and drink from a puddle? Or even from a glass whose edge has been greased by many lips?' (Lenin, 1977, pp. 104–5). However, although she saw such excesses as excusable or even inevitable at a time of social upheaval, when more serious relationships could hardly hope to succeed, Kollontai did not think them desirable. She saw that for women, sexual 'liberation' all too often meant 'liberty, equality and maternity' (Stites, 1978, p. 360); she also objected to the reduction of human sexuality to an animal activity, and saw promiscuity as an anti-social form of behaviour that both endangered the health of the workers and distracted them from more serious tasks.

Nevertheless, the solution for Kollontai could not be as simple as Engels' basically monogamous 'individual sex love'. Earlier in her life she had believed in the possibility of one 'great love' (and the permissibility of other relationships before this was found), but by the 1920s she believed such all-consuming passion should have no place in communist society: 'proletarian ideology cannot accept exclusiveness and "all-embracing love" ' (in Holt, 1977, p. 288). It was not simply the idea of ownership involved, or the fact that the woman in such a relationship would still inevitably give more of herself than the man; rather she believed that such intense love between two individuals was essentially anti-social, isolating the couple from the wider community and reducing their interest in the general social good. Such relationships would, she believed, in fact become *unnecessary*, for they were a response to the isolation engendered by capitalist society, in which love and closeness could be experienced in no other way. Communist society would, however, be based on companionship and solidarity, so that intimacy and emotional comfort would not be confined to the family or sexual relationships, and sexual love (Eros) would become part of an expanded human capacity for love: 'In the new and collective society, where interpersonal relations develop against a background of joyful unity and companionship, Eros will develop an honourable place as an emotional experience multiplying human happiness' (in Holt, 1977, p. 290).

For some critics, this seems a rather cold-blooded insistence on the joys of collective solidarity rather than individual love and passion ('The old idea was "all for the loved one", communist morality demands all for the collective', in Holt, 1977, p. 231), but Kollontai, who had by the 1920s read Western writers on sexuality such as Havelock Ellis and probably Freud, was seeking to transform rather than to deny the role of the erotic in future society. In this context, she argued that sexual love would not be a simple animal activity based on physical attraction alone (which she called 'Wingless Eros'), but would also involve the sensitive and comradely love of equals, in which the partners would retain both their personal integrity (there would be no 'slavish dissolution of personality') and their commitment to the collective. It is here, when she expands on the joys of 'Winged Eros' that other critics have accused her of flowery romanticism and a woolly utopianism that could have little basis in reality; from a radical feminist perspective, her failure to consider the possibility of homosexuality as a valid form of relationship or strategy for change might also be a problem. However, the importance of Kollontai's ideas perhaps lay less in the precise nature of her views on future relationships than in her perception of how such apparently private matters intersect with wider questions of social morality. The 'correct' form of interpersonal relationships was not for her something that would be automatically discovered in the future, but was an issue that must be fought for as part of the class struggle. Ideology was therefore not a straightforward reflection of class interests, but itself an arena of conflict; here Kollontai's ideas anticipate those of the Italian Marxist Antonio Gramsci and those modern marxists who argue for a degree of 'superstructural autonomy'.

The family, childcare and motherhood

Changes in the nature and role of the family were for Kollontai similarly both effect and cause of wider social change. As we have seen, Engels thought that collective housekeeping and childcare were essential for the liberation of women, and although Zetkin downplayed the latter, public provision of such services as laundry, cooking and cleaning were by the early twentieth century clearly-established Marxist principles, which were firmly endorsed by both Lenin and Kollontai. In practice, of course, such provisions were not forthcoming on anything like the scale required, and the standard of collective facilities was appalling; as Trotsky reported, many early experiments ended in dirt and chaos, and 'the communal houses were often grim and depressing, the shared kitchens chaotic and the creches makeshift' (quoted in Rowbotham, 1972, p. 148). Kollontai never abandoned the goal of good public services based on the perceived needs and co-operation of those who used them, while Trotsky came to favour small-scale experiments in collective housekeeping until such time as mass public provision could be afforded; however, as Stalin consolidated his power during the 1920s such views were effectively silenced.

Childcare was a much more complex and emotive issue than housework, and here again Kollontai was more radical than some more cautious Marxists, stressing the anti-social aspects of the traditional family which, she claimed, was not only inefficient and oppressive but an important means of transmitting and perpetuating old bourgeois values. She therefore argued strongly in favour of communal child-rearing, through which 'the new generation will, from the earliest years, learn to value the beauties of solidarity and sociability, and become accustomed to looking at the world through the prism of the collective and not through his own selfish ego' (quoted in Stites, 1978, p. 267). Communal child-rearing would also mean that women would no longer have to sacrifice everything for motherhood, and would never have to make the kind of agonising decision that Kollontai herself made when she chose to leave her young daughter in the care of her former husband in order to dedicate herself to revolutionary activity. Her proposals did not mean, she insisted, that children would be forcibly removed from their mothers. Indeed she stressed the importance of the maternal instinct and the joys of motherhood that could be experienced once the drudgery, poverty and ill-health that surrounded it were removed; the mother would be 'relieved of the cross of motherhood and be left with the smile of joy which arises from the contact of the woman with her child' (in Holt, 1977, p. 143). However, in the context of a caring communist society, the maternal instinct would have a wider meaning and higher social value than at present: 'Of course the maternal instinct is strong, and there is no need to stifle it. But why should this instinct be narrowly limited to the love and care of one's own child? . . . [in communist society] the woman not only cares for her own children, but has a genuine affection for all children' (in Holt, 1977, p. 144). Here again we have the idea of a reciprocal interaction between economic base and superstructure: communism provides both the material conditions and the sense of shared responsibility and affection that make collective childcare possible; collective childcare promotes the values that will enable communist economic relations to work, and it also allows women to enter social production, where they learn the good socialist values that they can feed back to their children. From this perspective, the question of childcare was not simply a woman's issue, a kind of 'optional extra' to be provided when times were good, but an integral part of the process of establishing a communist society.

Modern feminists have not found all this entirely satisfactory. Thus Diana Coole is highly suspicious of her idea that elements of personal life should be assessed in terms of their social consequences, for she sees this as opening the door to a Stalinist type manipulation of ideas, the family and sexuality. However, Kollontai was not saying that sexual and familial relationships *should* not be seen as purely private, but that they *cannot* be, for the attitudes and experiences they engender inevitably have an influence beyond the individuals immediately involved. The desirability of particular forms of manipulation (or, from a more benign point of view, education) may therefore be questioned, but this does not in itself invalidate her analysis. Other critics dislike Kollontai's stress on the maternal instinct and her glorification of the potential joys of motherhood. Such emphasis on sexual difference inevitably falls foul of the liberal feminist stress on equality; although others would welcome her attempt to 'envalue' the role of motherhood (which has interesting affinities with Mary Wollstonecroft's idea that good citizens require good mothering, see Chapter 1 above), they criticise her failure to examine the role of fathers, or to question the sexual division of labour in any kind of detail. It seems that while women are to be enabled to be both mothers and producers, men are to be only producers; the idea that men might, through parenting, increase their capacity for sensitivity, caring and co-operation (values which Kollontai saw as central in a communist society) is never explored. Moreover, while women were mothering, collectively or otherwise, they could not be contributing equally to decision-making in the public arena; it would therefore tend to be men who would decide on political and economic priorities – including, presumably, the level of provision for childcare facilities.

It is, however, Kollontai's views on the social responsibilities attached to motherhood that are most out of line with modern feminist thought. Here she argued that in communist society, where the community cares for the pregnant mother and her child, maternity is no longer a matter of individual choice but a question of social duty: 'Soviet power sees maternity as a social task' (in Holt, 1977, p. 143). This meant that in communist society there would be no need for abortion and that a pregnant woman must, as a responsible member of society, care for her foetus by looking after her own health, for 'in these months she no longer belongs to herself; she is serving the collective, "producing" from her own flesh and blood a new social unit of labor, a new member of the labor republic' (in Holt, 1977, p. 144); it also meant that she had a duty to breast-feed her baby as long as this might be necessary. Kollontai therefore totally denied women any abstract or absolute right to control their own reproduction and treat their bodies as they pleased. Reproduction was as much a social matter as production was; it was therefore an area of legitimate social concern that could be subject to collective planning rather than individual choice. For a generation of feminists for whom 'a woman's right to choose' is often a cardinal principle of faith, such views seem startlingly retrogressive and dangerously close to the forced motherhood policies of Stalin and, more recently, Ceausescu of Romania. Kollontai did not, however, argue that such responsibilities should be forced on women in an unequal, oppressive or selfish society, but saw them as arising naturally out of the wider and more generous social relationships that she thought would characterise mature communist society. In this context the idea that childbearing might involve duties as well as rights takes on a very different significance; until such time, however, women could not be expected to see motherhood as a social responsibility rather than an individual burden, and Kollontai therefore supported the legalisation of abortion in 1917 (a right revoked by Stalin in 1936).

After 1923 Kollontai had no real influence on events in the Soviet Union. The remainder of her political life was largely spent outside the country in a series of diplomatic posts, and she kept silent on Stalin's policies, although these were the antithesis of everything she had ever worked for; her views on the family were officially pronounced erroneous and her ideas soon ceased to be remembered. Alix Holt has however recently argued that her work 'represents the most important contribution of the period to the development of the relationship between the women's movement and the socialist programme, and her contribution to this long-neglected area of Marxist theory deserves to be more widely known and appreciated' (Holt, 1977, p. 27). As we have seen, she attempted to extend Marxist analysis to areas of life that had previously been seen as theoretically uninteresting and practically unimportant. She developed a looser form of Marxism that was very different from the simplistic determinism that too often characterised debates within the Second International and that enabled her to allow some autonomy and reciprocal causality to elements of the superstructure. This meant that although she did not really have a systematic theory of patriarchy as a unifying system of domination, she was able to identify power relations in morality, sexuality and the family, and to insist that these, as well as the economic world, be seen as key areas of struggle for communist men and women. Although at the time her ideas were not developed and they did not become part of any ongoing Marxist or feminist debate, they raised issues that are only seriously being tackled today; despite some of her theoretical shortcomings and confusions her work therefore represents a significant advance on earlier Marxist attempts to conceptualise women's subordination and suggests ways in which this might be ended.

Part II

Modern feminist thought

8

The background to modern feminism

Women after the Second World War

By 1945, women in most of Europe and America had won a high degree of political and legal equality with men. No longer were they excluded from political participation, education and employment and no longer did they lose all autonomy upon marriage; even in France, where the earlier feminist movement had been particularly unsuccessful, women were finally enfranchised in 1944, and the Code Napoleon, which explicitly subordinated women to their husbands, was gradually modified. In America, the traditions of welfare feminism had been continued in the 1930s when a network of influential women led by Eleanor Roosevelt, the President's wife, were able to make an important contribution to the planning and administration of the New Deal; although women did not receive state aid to anything like the same extent as men, their needs could no longer be ignored, and Ware claims therefore that 'It is in the 1930s that many of women's expectations beyond suffrage finally found fulfilment' (Ware, 1981, p. 2). In England, the new welfare provision based on the 1942 Beveridge Report included the payment of state allowances to mothers for their second and subsequent children; although they fell far short of full economic independence, such measures did much to ease the burdens of ill-health and poverty. In the field of employment too, important gains had been made. During the war, women had not only worked outside the home in unprecedented numbers (in Britain in 1943, 80 per cent of married women were involved in some kind of war work; see Carter,

147

1988), but they had worked in skilled and high status jobs for which they had previously been thought unfit. Although many returned home in 1945, the shortage of manpower and the need to restructure the economy ensured that the upward trend continued, so that in both Britain and America the 1950s saw an increase in the numbers of women in paid employment. By this time many of the women who stayed at home were benefiting from a general rise in living standards and a greater availability of consumer goods: the combination of increasingly sophisticated household appliances with a long-term decline in family size meant that domestic work no longer needed to involve ceaseless toil and that the housewife could devote herself more to the needs of her children. It seemed therefore to many that a new age had begun, and that most women could find true fulfilment in a domesticity from which drudgery had been removed, while the minority that preferred to follow a career could do so freely.

In this context feminism had little appeal, for it was associated with battles long-won or with values that found little support in the pro-family and increasingly hedonistic atmosphere of the post-war years. Thus Sheila Rowbotham recalls that to her feminism 'was all very prim and stiff and mainly concerned with keeping you away from boys', while 'emancipated women' were 'frightening people in tweed suits and horn-rimmed glasses with stern buns at the backs of their heads' (Rowbotham, 1973b, p. 12). In contrast to earlier years, no significant group was interested in challenging male power within the home, or in questioning the idealised version of family life that was assumed to be the norm. Those who insisted on a woman's right to a career saw this as an alternative to marriage and motherhood rather than something that could be combined with it, while communists followed the Stalinist line that earlier socialist attacks on the family had been mistaken, and that women's true fulfilment lay in motherhood.

However although there was no significant feminist movement, some campaigns continued, for women's formal equality masked a high degree of inequality in practice. Women remained a minority at all levels of political life, they were grossly under-represented in high professional positions, they were discriminated against in all areas of employment, they were paid less than men, welfare provisions assumed and encouraged dependence on a husband, and many women certainly did not share the benefits of their newly affluent society. As Banks says, 'there were . . . even in the uncompromising 1950s, signs that equal rights feminism was not only alive but struggling to make itself heard' (Banks, 1986, p. 221), and in both Britain and the United States there were increasing pressures, particularly from professional women, for equal pay and an end to discrimination in employment. There were also less readily articulated problems and discontents. Many working-class women had always been in paid employment, but the growing numbers of 'working wives' were increasingly burdened with guilt as economic necessity and the demand for their labour clashed head on with the cult of domesticity, the belief that the husband should be the sole breadwinner and the discovery of the supposedly harmful effects of 'maternal deprivation' on young children. On the domestic front, liberation from housework was an ever-receding mirage, as standards and expectations seemed to rise as fast as household gadgets multiplied; later events were to show that many suburban housewives living the 'American dream' were in fact far from happy, but the idealisation of their role precluded the idea of a career as an alternative form of fulfilment.

Wilson has therefore argued that the harmony and consensus of the period were in fact deceptive, that discontents and protests were isolated and silenced rather than eliminated and that 'women's liberation has been in part a reaction against that silence' (Wilson, 1980, p. 187). As with earlier feminism, the movement that was to erupt in the 1960s had no single cause and drew on a number of existing political traditions as well as developing radically new theory. For young women growing up after the war there was, however, no ready access to the rich heritage of feminist thought and history, for many of the ideas that have been discussed in this volume have only been rediscovered in the last twenty years. It is in this context that we must understand the importance of the book to be considered in the next section, for Simone de Beauvoir's *The Second Sex*, first published in 1949, was for a generation of women the only available feminist text.

Simone de Beauvoir and *The Second Sex*

France in the mid-twentieth century was in many ways a particularly unlikely source of new feminist theory. Women had been slow to gain the legal and political rights won earlier in America and much of Europe, and the entire political culture was dominated by strong patriarchal assumptions; from anti-Republican Catholics on the right to socialists on the left, the consensus was that women's place lay strictly in the home. There was no strong tradition of 'mainstream feminism', which was by 1945 'the monopoly of a handful of upper class women' (McMillan, 1981, p. 187). Although the socialist party had long been theoretically committed to women's rights, it remained influenced by the anti-feminist ideas of the nineteenth century anarchist writer Proudhon (who said the women could have only two possible roles – that of housewife or harlot; see McMillan, 1981), and it accepted the standard view that feminism was a middle-class distraction from more important class issues and that all women's problems would be solved under socialism; later there was little questioning on the left of Soviet claims that full equality for women had in fact been achieved in the Soviet Union (see Sowervine, 1982). Therefore although there had been exceptional women such as Madame Pelletier, who developed a far-reaching analysis of women's position and fought for the feminist cause within the socialist party (see Mitchell, 1989), or Viola Klein, who attempted a scientific investigation of 'The Feminine Character' (Klein, 1946), there was no significant women's movement or public discussion of women's issues; for a young Frenchwoman growing up between the wars, feminism was simply not on the available political or philosophical agenda.

Simone de Beauvoir (1908–86) has always insisted that she herself has never suffered because of her sex: 'Far from suffering from my femininity, I have, on the contrary, from the age of twenty on, accumulated the advantages of both sexes' (*Force of Circumstances*, 1968, p. 199). Born into a conservative petty-bourgeois family, she was able to escape her background through academic success, and she consistently rejected domesticity and conventional female roles. The central relationship of her life was with the philosopher Jean-Paul Sartre, but they never married or shared a home; their relationship was not based on sexual exclusiveness, and she had a number of other affairs (although significantly fewer than Sartre). She had no children, she lived most of her life in hotels, and in effect she lived very like a man in the male world of the French intelligentsia; it was not until she was nearly 40 and about to embark on her autobiography that, following a suggestion from Sartre, she decided that in order to understand herself she must also understand what it meant to be a woman. The result of her investigations was the massive *The Second Sex*, published in 1949. This drew upon a whole range of philosophical, psychological, anthropological, historical, literary and anecdotal material to argue that the most important obstacle to a woman's freedom was not her biology, or the political and legal constraints placed upon her, or even her economic situation; rather it was the whole process by which femininity is manufactured in society. In her celebrated phrase 'One is not born but rather becomes a woman' (*Second Sex*, p. 297), and her discussion of the ways in which girls are forced into certain paths and denied expression of their full humanity led her to an examination of the experiences of girls and women that included discussion of hitherto taboo areas of female life such as menstruation and sexuality, which she discussed with a frankness unprecedented in a serious academic work. This meant that like later radical feminists, de Beauvoir saw the ways in which apparently non-political areas of life such as the family tied in with the wider power structures. However, like Marxist feminists, she did not see the liberation of women as an ahistorical act, for it was only under modern conditions of production that women could realise their potential for free and autonomous action.

Existentialism applied to women

Here an understanding of what de Beauvoir meant by freedom requires some knowledge of her philosophical framework – the existentialist theory developed by Sartre and fully accepted by her. Central to existentialism was a questioning of existing customs, values and beliefs and a rejection of the idea that an individual's fate is irrevocably predetermined, whether this be by conventional expectations, early childhood experiences or economic conditions. It therefore opposed the assumptions of both

Freudian psychoanalysis and the kind of crude Marxism that characterised communist parties at the time, and stressed instead an individual's total freedom and responsibility for his own life. For Sartre, the only 'authentic' way of living was one that recognised this freedom; such freedom is not however easily accepted, for it involves an overwhelming responsibility and sense of aloneness. For many, the recognition of human freedom is quite simply unbearable and is therefore denied; the individual lapses into 'bad faith' and blames circumstances for his own actions and character rather than accepting responsibility. At the same time, the individual's freedom seems unacceptably limited by the very existence of other people, for whom he is but an object; here Sartre argued that there is a conflict at the most basic level of human consciousness, as each individual seeks domination by asserting himself as subject and the Other as object. Later he was to suggest that an individual's acceptance of freedom involved responsibility for the freedom of others also, and to see the exercise of freedom in terms of collective class action and conscious revolutionary activity; at the time of *The Second Sex*, however, he seemed to see this conflict as basic to the human condition, and solutions as basically individualistic; in this context the task of philosophy was essentially to reveal to people the possibility of freedom, and to show that man can freely choose and create his own future.

In *The Second Sex* de Beauvoir argued both that such freedom and responsibility could be achieved by women as well as men, and that historically it had been denied to them. Here it was the concept of the 'Other' that provided her with a starting-point. For Sartre, the sex of the potentially autonomous individual was not an issue, but de Beauvoir argued that it was all-important, as for most of human history man has successfully relegated woman to the status of permanent Other, excluded from the realm of true humanity, never an equal and so never a threat:

> She is defined and differentiated with reference to man and not he with reference to her; she is the incidental, the inessential as opposed to the essential. He is the Subject, he is the Absolute – she is the Other (*Second Sex*, p. 16).

This was originally possible, de Beauvoir argued, because women's lack of strength and childbearing role excluded them from the productive process; this did not, though, mean that a biological or materialist explanation on its own could account for women's subordination, for this required the original drive to dominate, the 'imperialism of human consciousness' posited by Sartre (*Second Sex*, p. 89). Now, however, modern technology and contraception meant that women's subordination was no longer based on physical necessity; the only thing preventing women from seeing themselves as subjects in their own right was the artificial idea of womanhood engendered by society, which still saw women as secondary objects, acquiring meaning only in relation to men. If women were to be free, they must therefore be freed from this prevailing idea, and persuaded to take responsibility for their own lives, rather than accepting the security of dependence or the 'bad faith' represented by conformity to the feminine ideal. The aim of *The Second Sex* was therefore to reveal the artificial nature of womanhood, in order that this might be rejected, for

> No biological, psychological or economic fate determines the figure that the human female presents in society; it is civilisation as a whole that produces this creation, intermediate between male and eunuch who is described as female (*Second Sex*, p. 295).

A negative view of women?

In the course of discussing what it means to be a woman, however, de Beauvoir provided a detailed account of women's biology that critics have seen as entirely negative. Ignoring any possibility that some aspects of male biology might also be unpleasant or problematic, and rejecting the idea that maternity might be a source of pleasure and fulfilment, she described the processes of menstruation, pregnancy, childbirth and lactation with extreme disgust, seeing women trapped in their bodies, victims of the reproductive needs of the species. She did not accept that these biological handicaps need any longer determine woman's position in society or 'her ovaries condemn her to live for ever on her knees' (*Second Sex*, p. 736), but argued that it is only by *overcoming* their biology that women can become 'fully human'. Here she argued that modern machines mean that their lack of strength need no longer exclude them from production; like men, women

could therefore lead independent, rationally ordered and autonomous lives once they were freed from artificially restricting myths
and cultural assumptions.

Although this analysis shares the Marxist belief that women's
liberation was becoming possible because of modern methods of
production – and in later writings she placed even more stress
on a materialist explanation of women's situation (see *Force of
Circumstances*, p. 197; *All Said and Done*, p. 449) – de Beauvoir's
whole stress on rationality, autonomy and self-affirmation is far
closer to the liberal than the Marxist tradition. Here she has
been accused of uncritically accepting a male paradigm that places
reason above emotion, mind above body and culture above
nature, and which equates man with the former and women with
the latter; this paradigm implies that it is only by *denying* her
female-ness that a woman can achieve humanity, and devalues
traditionally female qualities such as nurturing and co-operation
(see Evans, 1985; Heath, 1989; Moi, 1987 and 1990; Leighton,
1975; Walters, 1979; Lloyd, 1984). In later interviews de Beauvoir
did concede that it was good that women were ceasing to be
ashamed of their bodies, but she continued to deny that female
biology could be a cause for celebration or a source of innate
qualities such as pacifism:

> One should not believe that the female body gives one a new view of
> the world. That would be ridiculous and absurd. That would mean
> turning it into a counter-penis (quoted in Schwarzer, 1984, p. 79).

The problem here is not so much that she rejected the idea of
female superiority, but that in stressing men and women's
common humanity, de Beauvoir does not seem to consider the
idea that this humanity could incorporate the values that have
traditionally been associated with women. Similarly, although her
descriptions of the trials and tribulations of marriage and
maternity were in part a much needed corrective to the prevailing
syrupy view of domestic bliss, her denial that motherhood (or
fatherhood) could be a source of positive values seems a too-easy
rejection of a whole area of human experience. In both cases, her
perceptions were perhaps limited by her own experiences as a
token woman who functioned as an honorary man, and by the
individualistic assumptions of existentialist philosophy, in which

the drive to dominate is assumed, and the possibility of an equivalent drive to co-operation, nurturing, mutuality or sharing is ruled out of order.

Sex and class

De Beauvoir has also been accused of providing individualistic solutions to collective problems, ignoring the needs and problems of working-class or peasant women, and effectively blaming the victims of patriarchy for their own oppression. Certainly in 1949 she never considered the possibility of united action by women to improve their position, but stressed that it was up to individual women to take control over their own lives. However when the women's movement developed in France after 1968, she was an active participant and convert to the idea of female solidarity; for the first time she started to call herself a feminist, she was to the forefront of campaigns to legalise abortion, she defended the need for separate women's organisations free from the threat of male domination, and her earlier apparent contempt for women was replaced by a new stress on sisterhood and the value of female friendship (see Schwarzer, 1984). It is true that in her descriptions in 1949 of how femininity is constructed and maintained she drew largely on the experiences of middle-class French women, and her proposed solution, which saw women as independent, fulfilled and liberated through their careers, could have little meaning outside her own class. However she herself recognised this limitation, and saw that for the working-class woman faced with domestic responsibilities, paid labour could only be an additional source of drudgery and exploitation; for such women, the price of independence would at present simply be too high. Like Marxist feminists, she certainly saw women's entry into the paid labour force and their achievement of economic independence as far more important than legal or political rights. She also seems consistently to have assumed that true freedom for all women would be impossible without socialism (which she said had *not* yet been achieved in the USSR, although she was for a time enthusiastic about China). Late in life she admitted that she did not know the exact connection between capitalist and patriarchal oppressions, but argued that for feminism to succeed it must be part of the class struggle (Schwarzer, 1984). Meanwhile, she argued that even for the professional woman there would be all kinds of problems from which her male counterpart would be immune; as the demands of her career clashed with traditional assumptions about her domestic and sexual life, she too would be tempted to abandon the struggle and sacrifice her autonomy for the sake of security. Here de Beauvoir was not so much blaming women for lapsing into 'bad faith' as seeking to understand the temptations and pressures that might be involved. Her purpose, moreover, was to expose the socialisation processes in order that they could be identified and challenged; by revealing femininity to be a social construct it could be demystified and subverted. Unlike some modern writers who seem to describe patriarchy only in order to bewail the lot of women, de Beauvoir therefore described it in order to refute it; in this context it was up to individual women to act, but she never saw this as an easy option. She was, however, an optimist (she said later that she had underestimated the problems still facing women in 1949); she believed that circumstances were changing and with them the expectations of both men and women. For individual pioneers things might be hard, but this was only to be expected at a time when 'The free woman is just being born' (*Second Sex*, p. 723), and she believed that changes in education, culture and morality were all working in women's favour. This led her to conclude, in terms strikingly similar to John Stuart Mill nearly a century before, that although we cannot be sure what differences will remain between men and women in the future,

What is certain is that hitherto woman's possibilities have been suppressed and lost to humanity, and that it is high time she be permitted to take her chances in her own interest and in the interest of all (*Second Sex*, p. 724).

Many modern radical feminists would argue that this conclusion ignores the very real emotional, psychological, sexual, domestic and economic interests that men have in maintaining women's subordination and the resistance which they are therefore likely to offer to women's liberation; by the 1970s de Beauvoir had come to agree that men should be treated 'with suspicion', but she certainly never accepted an analysis of patriarchy that saw them as 'the enemy' (Schwarzer, 1984).

Her life and influence

Although de Beauvoir's own life has often been portrayed as the ideal of independent womanhood, some radical feminists reject this as a model because, like her theory, it seems to be based on a rejection of traditional female qualities. Her relationship with Jean-Paul Sartre has also been criticised; she claimed that her love for Sartre was based on absolute trust and equality, although not on exclusiveness, but recent critics have seen this central relationship as encapsulating the inequality and female dependency she was supposed to have rejected. Despite the publication of recent early private correspondence which suggests that she engaged in quite widespread sexual experimentation (at times involving her own pupils), it seems clear both that Sartre took far more advantage of the 'open' nature of their relationship than she did, and that she suffered far more from jealousy; it is also likely that despite the alleged honesty of their relationship, Sartre did not scruple to lie to her about his affairs (see Winegarten, 1988, p. 30). Others attack not the sexual inequalities that may have been involved in the relationship, but the whole attempt to intellectualise and rationally plan sexual behaviour; this could give rise to a cold-blooded approach that, as de Beauvoir admitted, caused great pain to other people, and it reflects her general mistrust of passion and emotion and her over-enthusiasm for a life of reason. She is also said to have allowed herself to be intellectually dominated by Sartre (much less well known than the fact that she came second to him in their final philosophy examinations is the fact that he had failed them the year before); moreover, although she succeeded in liberating herself from most household tasks, she still performed more domestic duties than Sartre. Despite these limitations, however, de Beauvoir lived in a manner dramatically more independent than most women of her time. Today's changed circumstances present young women with a much wider range of alternatives, and the attractiveness of her life as a role model has diminished; for an earlier generation, however, it suggested exciting new possibilities. Above all, it showed that women *could* make choices, they *could* reject their traditional roles and they could, apparently, find happiness and fulfilment in so doing; as such, it was 'a symbol of the possibility, despite everything, of living one's life the way one wants to, for oneself, free from conventions and prejudices, even as a woman' (Schwarzer, 1984, p. 3).

It is therefore in the context of her time that the importance of de Beauvoir's life and work has to be understood, and most commentators combine their criticisms with praise for her pioneering role. Today existentialism has gone out of fashion, and much of *The Second Sex* appears inconsistent, overstated, selective or even commonplace; at the time, however, it was both shocking and inspiring, and de Beauvoir herself was amazed at both the hostility and the support it generated. Above all, it broke the silence that surrounded women's experiences, and it enabled some women to see the world in a different light. As such, 'In the darkness of the Fifties and Sixties, *The Second Sex* was like a secret code that we emerging women used to send messages to each other', so that 'The book is part of some women's personal history, and part of the history of feminism' (Schwarzer, 1984, p. 13; Okely, 1986, p. 70).

9

Modern liberal feminism and its critics

As we have seen in earlier chapters, liberal feminism has seldom been expressed in pure form, but has been entangled with other, sometimes contradictory, traditions and assumptions. Nevertheless it retains a clear central core of ideas based upon the belief that women are individuals possessed of reason, that as such they are entitled to full human rights, and that they should therefore be free to choose their role in life and explore their full potential in equal competition with men. In accordance with these principles, earlier liberal feminists demanded the right to education, employment, property and the vote; their goal became full legal and political equality with men, and they claimed that this would benefit not only women but also men and society as a whole. During the inter-war years, feminism based on such equal rights arguments had been in abeyance, as 'mainstream' feminist activities concentrated on supporting women in their traditional roles rather than on challenging their remaining legal inequalities.

However, as discussed in the previous chapter, the years after the Second World War contained the seeds of the discontents that were to erupt in the 1960s; this 'Second Wave' of feminism was to develop rapidly in all kinds of directions, but it began in America as an essentially liberal protest against the failure of that society to deliver to women the promises of independence, self-expression and fulfilment that seemed central to the American dream. As such, it has seldom been expressed as a self-conscious political theory, but more as a 'common sense' application of pre-existing values to women's situation; this has led in recent years to a decidedly one-sided theoretical debate, with critics of liberal feminism attacking positions that have never been fully articulated. A danger here is that a liberal feminist 'straw woman' may be created and demolished, without acknowledging the complexities of real political debates. However, the task of uncovering and examining the assumptions behind modern movements and campaigns is critical to the success of feminism; the fact that these assumptions are seldom consciously propounded or defended may indeed make the task more urgent.

Betty Friedan and the politics of NOW

The clearest and most famous expression of American liberal feminism is to be found in Betty Friedan's *The Feminine Mystique* (first published 1963; references to the 1986 edition). Although this cannot really be considered a work of political theory, it encapsulates the arguments and assumptions of the liberal approach; subsequent modifications that she has made to her original position also reveal particularly clearly some of the contradictions which this involved. In her book, Friedan argued that since the Second World War American women had been manipulated and persuaded into the belief that their only fulfilment lay in domesticity, and that earlier feminist dreams of education and independence had been displaced by an all-pervasive 'feminine mystique'. This mystique, which taught that 'the highest value and the only commitment for women is the fulfilment of their own femininity' was, she claimed, more dangerous and insidious than earlier traditional values, because it was supported by pseudo-scientific theories (particularly vulgarised Freudian analysis and functionalist sociology) and reinforced by women's magazines and the entire advertising industry. This meant that the whole of an American woman's life was geared towards attracting and keeping a husband, and serving the needs of him and his children; denied the expression of her own humanity, she was forced to live her life vicariously, parasitic upon the activities of her husband in the 'real world' outside her home. Such a life, Friedan claimed, could not lead to happiness, for no multiplicity of consumer goods could compensate for the inner emptiness involved; at best it could lead to passivity, at worst, bleak despair. This despair could not however be articulated, for its existence was denied by the feminine mystique, which interpreted women's unhappiness in terms of their own failure to 'adapt' to their sexual role; isolated in her 'comfortable concentration camp', each individual suburban housewife was therefore 'so ashamed to show her dissatisfaction that she never knew how many other women shared it'. The cause of this 'problem that has no name' was, Friedan said, simply the fact that American women were denied any opportunity for independence or self-development; its most dramatic effects were the rise in mental illness, alcoholism and suicide among women, but it also had a highly damaging effect upon the next generation, indeed:

> If we continue to produce millions of young mothers who stop their growth and education short of identity, without a strong core of human values to pass on to their children, we are committing, quite simply, genocide, starting with the mass burial of American women and ending with the progressive dehumanization of their sons and daughters (*Mystique*, pp. 38, 245, 17 and 318).

This meant that the interests of society and the needs of women demanded that women be freed from the feminine mystique and enabled to 'say "No" to the housewife image'. Like Simone de Beauvoir, Friedan believed that the crucial issue was to reveal to women the possibilities of freedom and fulfilment outside the home and the artificial nature of the restrictions that currently confined them; here she saw education as the key to widening women's horizons and therefore called for 'a national education programme, similar to the G.I. Bill' (which had been introduced for returning soldiers in 1945). Unlike de Beauvoir, however, she unequivocally rejected any attack on conventional morality and family life. With the help of maternity leave and workplace nurseries she believed that women could *combine* long-term career plans with their family responsibilities; like Margaret Thatcher, who wrote in 1954 that with efficient organisation 'as well as being a housewife it is possible to put in eight hours work a day besides', she said that women must 'see housework for what it is – not a career, but something that must be done as quickly and efficiently as possible'. Her goal therefore was to allow women to live for themselves as well as for others by being educated to their full potential and enabled to follow a career outside the home; she believed that this would also create new possibilities for love with men, which could now be based on shared work and values rather than inequality (*Mystique*, pp. 270, 323, 297).

Whatever its shortcomings and exaggerations, *The Feminine Mystique* clearly struck a chord with many women. By 1970 it had sold over a million copies in America and Britain, and it is often seen as the inspiration for the feminist activity that exploded upon the American political scene in the years after its publication. However, whereas in the 1950s de Beauvoir's *The Second Sex* had been a bolt from the blue, *The Feminine Mystique* crystallised ideas that were already in the air. Support for an Equal Rights Amendment to the constitution had been gradually growing for some years and was now backed by both the main political parties, and as women continued to enter paid work in increasing numbers, pressure for improved pay and conditions was building up. In 1963, the year *The Feminine Mystique* was published, the Kennedy Commission on the Status of Women produced a report which documented the discrimination faced by women in many areas of life; in the same year the Equal Pay Act was passed, and in 1964 a clause prohibiting discrimination by sex was added to the Civil Rights Act. The addition of this clause to an Act concerned with racial discrimination had in fact been a last-ditch attempt to block the whole issue, but it was the subsequent failure of the authorities to implement the sexual equality aspects of the Act that led many women to see the need for a national pressure group to promote their cause; the result was the formation of the National Organisation of Women (NOW), which was founded in 1966 with Friedan as its president, and which rapidly became the world's largest feminist organisation.

According to its founding statement, the aim of NOW was

> To take action to bring women into full participation in the mainstream of American society *now*, exercising all the privileges and responsibilities thereof in truly equal partnership with men.

Here we have the logical culmination of the demands that had been developing over the centuries and a total rejection of the 'separate spheres' argument: no longer confined to the home, women were to use their hard-won legal rights to join men in economic, social and political life, and Friedan's arguments about women's need for fulfilment outside the family were taken as a self-evident starting point. No further subversion or criticism of society was intended, for America's democratic institutions were seen as a means to the well-being of all its citizens, and the traditional family still seemed the lynchpin of the good society; the idea that a liberal democracy might contain structured inequalities and interests that would block the participation of particular groups was not even considered. It was agreed that, as argued in *The Feminine Mystique*, the long-term interests of men and society as a whole would be served by sexual equality; although it was assumed that women would be most active in pursuing their own interests, support from men was therefore welcomed, and about 10 per cent of NOW's members have always been men. The strategy was to establish a pressure group organised on conventionally hierarchical lines, that would use the law and existing political processes to seek an end to discrimination and to achieve full equality of opportunity in all areas of life; following Friedan's arguments about the artificial nature of conventional femininity, NOW also challenged the prevailing gender ideology, particularly by demanding changes in education and in the media portrayal of women.

At some levels, NOW has met with considerable success. It gained some legal victories and contributed to a significant shift in consciousness on women's issues, so that in education, politics and the workplace women's demands can no longer be entirely excluded from the agenda; no longer a fringe minority interest, feminism is part of the mainstream of American political and economic life. The impact of American feminist ideas has also been felt worldwide. For example, although it is often said that there has not been an equivalent growth of liberal feminism in Britain, it was similar 'common sense' ideas about justice and the needs of society that inspired the Equal Pay and Sex Discrimination Acts of the 1970s and the setting up of the Equal Opportunities Commission. In most industrial nations there are now far fewer formal barriers to full equality with men than in the 1960s, more women than ever before are in paid employment, some have broken into exclusively male preserves, some are in important positions of public power and increasing numbers are in well paid senior positions.

Criticisms of liberal feminism

Critics, however, argue that even within its own terms liberal
feminism has failed. They argue that women have manifestly failed
to gain real equality with men in the worlds of work and politics,
for the publicity received by a few token women conceals the
overwhelming predominance of men in positions of power and
authority, and women's earning power remains dramatically lower
than men's. Even the goal of full legal equality has not been met;
in particular, the successful passage of the ERA, which in the
early heady days of NOW had seemed a foregone conclusion,
was finally defeated by a loose populist coalition of conservative
business interests and the 'Moral Majority' (which claimed that
absolute legal equality represented an attack on family responsibilities and the American way of life, that it would absolve husbands from any responsibility to maintain their wives and children,
that it would involve the drafting of women into active military
service and that it would rob working-class women of protection
against bad conditions of employment; see Hewlett, 1988, and
Mansbridge, 1986).

For some critics, this failure is said to be an inevitable consequence of faulty premises and priorities. Many liberal feminists,
however, have not questioned their goals and methods, but argue
that these must be pursued and employed more vigorously. There
are therefore demands for the extension and more rigorous
enforcement of anti-discrimination and equal pay law, and for the
effectiveness of the latter to be increased by extending it to work
of equal value. Education continues to be seen as a priority, but
there has been a shift from the formal provision of educational
opportunities to more active attempts to counter traditional socialisation and gender stereotypes. Some argue further that because
of the degree of discrimination and disadvantage they face, true
equality for women must involve a temporary measure of 'affirm-
ative action' whereby women are appointed or promoted in
advance of equally qualified men, or even of 'reverse discrimination' whereby they are appointed before a *more* qualified man.
(For a summary of the arguments involved, see Jaggar, 1983, pp.
190 – 3, and Young, 1989; see also Richards, 1982.) Others claim
that it is the burden of childcare responsibilities that has prevented
women from competing and attaining equally with men, and they

therefore demand both that women's freedom of choice should be extended by giving them full control over their own fertility (in particular, the right to abortion) and that action be taken to make the rearing of children and the pursuit of a career more readily compatible. Although NOW has always included childcare provision and maternity leave in its list of demands, these were not originally prioritised, and Friedan herself has admitted that neglect of these issues has placed impossible demands upon women (*The Second Stage*, 1981). She is therefore now calling for increased nursery and childcare provision, greater involvement by men in child-rearing and for a basic restructuring of work patterns to enable both men and women to combine family responsibilities with a career. She has also written enthusiastically about the 'Swedish model', which involves the state promotion of gender equality through active intervention in education, provision of childcare and welfare facilities, positive attempts to change the attitudes of men, and extensive legislation for parental leave and flexibility in work arrangements (Friedan, 1970).

The state

At first sight, all this might seem a simple extension of liberal principles, and campaigners do not seem to think that any basic revision of theoretical assumptions is involved. Critics, however, argue not only that these principles are themselves inadequate, but that they are inevitably challenged and undermined by such feminist demands. In particular, these demands involve a use of the law and state power beyond that envisaged in classical liberal theory; no longer is the state simply to provide the equal legal framework that enables individuals to pursue their own ends, but it is being asked to intervene on behalf of a particular group which is seen as having particular needs and suffering from particular disadvantages. Of course there has been a long and gradual trend within much of liberal thought away from the classic laissez-faire position and towards a greater degree of state responsibility for the economy and general social welfare. This trend is, however, currently being opposed by the neo-liberals of the New Right, and in America it has never involved the degree of state intervention that seems to be implied by some recent feminist demands. From a liberal perspective, the danger is that such demands will prove incompatible with individual autonomy and self-determination, and that they may dangerously increase the power of the state; here some feminists have argued that while extensive state provision and intervention may free women from dependence on individual men, it increases their dependence on the patriarchal state (for discussion of this, see Borchorst and Siim, 1987; Smart, 1989; Hernes, 1988; Siim, 1991, and Chapter 11 below). Friedan, however, seems quite unaware that her proposals may involve any threat to freedom or liberal principles, or that the Swedish approach does not rest upon an American type liberal political system, but upon a social democratic one in which extensive state intervention to promote equality in all areas of life has long been seen as legitimate, and in which the public sector receives a higher percentage of the GNP than any other western society.

It seems therefore that the demands of 'mainstream' feminism may come into conflict with the assumptions of liberalism, involving a shift in perception whereby extensive state intervention is seen as a means rather than a threat to individual freedom. Radical and Marxist feminists argue, however, that this new view also rests upon a misunderstanding of the role of the state. It involves, they say, an uncritical acceptance of the pluralist assumption that all competing groups have potentially equal access to state power, and that this will be used impartially to promote justice and the general social good. In practice, mainstream feminist demands have frequently met with vigorous opposition, and legislation has often failed to produce the results its advocates intended. Thus even in Sweden, women remain concentrated in low paid, low status and part-time jobs, 'men still occupy practically all positions conferring power and influence in society' and 'many men still behave as if they were married to full-time housewives' (Ericson and Jacobsson, 1985, pp. 89 and 79; see also Scott, 1982). Liberal feminism, however, cannot anticipate or explain such opposition and failure, because it has no conception of the structural inequalities and vested interests that may block women's progress. For example, although Friedan has described the ways in which the cult of domesticity serves the needs of the capitalist economy (*Mystique*, p. 181), she seems to assume that once the injustices of women's position have been pointed out, then capitalists will make the necessary sacrifices and adjustments; similarly it does not seem to have occurred to her that many men might be reluctant to surrender public power and economic superiority in order to participate more fully in family life.

Equality

It is not only in terms of their attitude to the state that feminists have found themselves running up against key liberal assumptions. Existing ideas of equality, human nature, rationality and the very meaning of 'the political' have all been challenged or modified by feminist experiences, although once again the full implications of these have not always been taken on board. Thus the demand for full legal equality runs into immediate difficulties when it is extended to women, for it ignores not only existing differences in the social roles of the sexes, but the implications of basic biological differences. For example, as Vogel has pointed out, the right of a male citizen to pass property to his heir cannot simply be extended to women in a gender neutral fashion, for this male right involves a degree of control over a woman's body that would be undermined if she were given equal rights and independence (Vogel, 1989). The approach can also mean that feminists become entrapped in equal rights arguments which may in some situations be quite inappropriate: thus Sevenhuijsen (1991) argues that in child custody cases the discourse of equal parental rights is inappropriate, and should be replaced by one based on needs and welfare.

Critics have therefore attacked both the theoretical premises and the practical consequences of the liberal idea of equality and of 'sex blind' legislation which ignores biological differences and the social realities of a gendered society. They claim that an unmodified liberal feminism cannot meet its own stated goals, because it cannot acknowledge the fact that women's reproductive role handicaps them in a society in which the competitive terms have been laid down by men: aspiring to compete on strictly equal terms, it has tended to see any recognition of sexual difference as an admission of inferiority or as a reduction of women to a biological function. In practical terms this has meant, particularly in America, that many feminists have been reluctant to campaign for maternity rights and benefits; as a result, two decades of feminist activity have produced a society with the worst maternity and childcare provision in the Western world, in which 'career women' face enormous problems if they wish to have children, the wage and power gaps between men and women have not significantly altered and in which the situation of many women has in fact deteriorated (see Hewlett, 1988). There is therefore again pressure within liberal feminism for a modification of strict liberal principles. Tortuous arguments have been developed to justify giving maternity rights to 'pregnant persons', and some have argued that 'the equal right which women need to claim is the right to have their particular needs attended to' (Midgley and Hughes, 1983, p. 174; see also Wolgast, 1980). Such problems are, Carol Bacchi had recently claimed, the inevitable products of a value system which ignores human interdependence; here she argues that the whole difference/equality debate within feminism is a distraction from the need to develop a broader understanding of equality that can acknowledge the diversity of individual circumstances: 'if society catered appropriately for all human needs, men and women included, discussions about women's sameness to or difference from men would be of little significance' (Bacchi, 1990, p. xi). The problem remains, therefore, of whether the liberal idea of equal rights can overcome its limitations and whether it can reconcile the reality of different needs with the ideal of free and open competition.

The demand for equality raises the question of 'equality with whom?' Here liberal feminists are often accused of reflecting only the concerns of middle-class white women who are privileged in every way other than their sex, and of ignoring the inequalities amongst men and the realities of class and race oppression. The liberal approach is also said to accept the necessity of hierarchical competitive society in which most men and women can only be losers; such a view is decisively rejected by radical and Marxist feminists.

Human nature

For some critics, the problem goes even deeper, for liberalism is said to rest upon a partial understanding of human nature and motivation which involves a denial or devaluation of women's experiences and of society's reproductive needs. Jaggar has described the liberal idea of human nature as 'political solipsism': this sees each individual as essentially rational, independent, competitive and autonomous, a view which she says ignores the nurturing, co-operation and mutual support that are an essential basis for human society, and that have historically been central to women's lives. Jaggar therefore argues that 'the assumption of individual self-sufficiency is plausible only if one ignores human biology' and that it is 'hard to imagine women developing a political theory that presupposed political solipsism, ignoring human interdependence and especially the loving care of the young' (Jaggar, 1983, pp. 41 and 46; see also Pateman, 1986a and Wolgast, 1980).

This liberal paradigm produces a number of interrelated problems for feminists. In the first place, if it is based on an incomplete view of human nature, it cannot provide an adequate understanding of human motivation and behaviour; it will therefore be unable to predict political outcomes or provide a workable political strategy. Secondly, in treating men as the norm, it imposes particular goals and standards under a universal guise, requiring women to become 'like men' rather than envaluing traditionally female attributes and ways of thinking. Thirdly, even if liberal feminism's values and priorities are accepted, its failure to discuss society's reproductive and domestic needs has important practical consequences, for these needs will not simply 'go away' once it is recognised that women have a right to fulfil themselves in other roles. The liberal feminist promise of liberation from domesticity therefore begs the question of who is to care for children and the home; although as we have seen some writers now advocate flexible work arrangements and greater male involvement in the home, it is hard to see why capitalism should accommodate these changes or why a majority of men should willingly embrace activities which feminists have seen as inherently unfulfilling (Friedan cites as evidence of a change in male attitudes the fact that 'three out of four gourmet dinner parties suddenly seem to be cooked, soup to mousse, by men' [1981, p. 41]; sceptics might find a sudden male enthusiasm for cleaning the lavatory rather more convincing).

A final problem arising from the individualistic assumptions of liberalism is the difficulty these may pose for a feminist politics based on recognition of shared gender interests: the liberal belief that it is up to each person to make the best of his or her own life clashes with feminist awareness of group disadvantage and the need for collective action. Eisenstein has therefore argued that there is a contradiction at the heart of liberal feminism, which is constantly threatening to overstep the boundaries of liberalism itself, and that in thus revealing the limitations of liberal thought it has the potential for developing in a truly radical direction (Eisenstein, 1981; see also Cott, 1987, p. 6). In later writing, however, her views have been somewhat modified. She argues that feminism has indeed contributed to the modern 'crisis of liberalism', but that former liberal feminists like Friedan have become 'revisionist' rather than 'radical' feminists. There is therefore certainly no automatic increase in political awareness as she would understand it; liberal feminism has failed to evolve, and she believes that it remains the task of socialist feminists such as herself to provide feminism with a viable political theory (Eisenstein, 1984).

In practice, although liberal feminism remains based on the assumptions of competition, the pursuit of self-interest and the inherent 'fairness' of western democracies, not all liberal feminists are as rabidly individualistic as some of the above criticisms suggest. Moreover it is not self-evident that recognition of male or capitalist power, or the insistence on the importance of the values of co-operation, nurturing and love need preclude all ideas of individual responsibility and fulfilment. Such values need not be written off as 'male' or 'bourgeois', but can perhaps be rescued and reconciled with other values; the vision of the creative and fulfilled individual, whose needs and desires are bound up with those of the whole community is central to both Marx and Mill, and it is only a minority of radical feminists who wish to submerge women's personhood in their biological function. Nevertheless, for many critics the liberal feminist view of human nature remains a major theoretical problem; for some, this is also bound up with the liberal stress on *reason*, which has provided a focal point for much recent feminist debate.

Reason

The issues involved here are complex, but the arguments can be reduced to four main overlapping areas; the liberal concept of reason is said to involve false claims for objectivity and universality based on the limited experiences and perceptions of men; its insistence on the value of the mind over the body is said to be bound up with a rejection of all things female; it is said to ignore or devalue other forms of knowledge or modes of activity; finally, it is alleged that the uses of reason are far more limited than has been supposed, and that there are areas of life to which it is highly inappropriate.

First of all, it is said that in ignoring the experiences of half the human race, men have over the centuries produced only an incomplete form of knowledge and understanding; Braidotti for example sees this as leading to a binary logic which 'as a consequence of its phallocentric assumptions, produces faulty and incomplete notions, untruths, scientific judgements – it is just not good enough as a system of thought' (Braidotti, 1986, p. 48; see also Rose, 1986; McMillan, 1982). It is further argued that 'male knowledge' is based on a sexually particular way of thinking, which some feminists see as based in biology. Thus some radical feminists claim that women's reproductive role leads them to a way of apprehending the world that goes beyond the formalities of male logic and calculation, and that encompasses a different system of ethics. Some post-modernist feminists claim also that it is differences in sexuality that produce different modes of thought: they claim that men experience a simple and localised sensuality that leads them to develop simple, mono-causal theories, while women's diffuse sensuality leads them to more diffuse forms of knowing (for further discussion of these ideas, see Chapter 12). For others, it is women's typical experiences, rather than any innate biological differences, that are important. Thus Gilligan has argued that the former have led to empirically identifiable differences between men and women in the ways in which they think and moralise about the world. Here she claims that while male ethical systems are based on ideas of justice and right, female ones are based on caring and responsibility; she argues that these are 'two different modes of experience that are in the end connected' and that a mature theory and ethical standpoint must incorporate both (Gilligan, 1982, p. 174). Ruddick has also argued that the demands of child-rearing lead to the development of particular ways of thinking and to a moral standpoint opposed to militarism (Ruddick, 1980, 1984 and 1990; see also the excellent discussion in Grimshaw, 1986). Other writers, however, sound a note of caution. Dietz argues that 'maternal thinking' is inherently limited and cannot provide an adequate basis for political theory or citizenship (Dietz, 1985), while Grimshaw reminds those who wish to replace or supplement 'male philosophy' with one based on female experiences that there is no unity of experience shared by all men or by all women, so that the 'divergences in the lives of women and in feminist thinking, mean that there is no non-contested or isolable paradigm of female virtues or priorities which can be seen as a source for feminist philosophical thinking' (Grimshaw, 1986, p. 259); Sevenhuijson has further claimed that the kind of moral reasoning identified by Gilligan is not unique to women, but that it can be traced back to the moral theory of the Scottish Enlightenment (Sevenhuijson, 1991).

The second area of debate centres around the arguments put forward by Lloyd in *The Man of Reason* (1984). In this, Lloyd argued that 'Reason' in Western philosophy is not, as commonly supposed, sex neutral, because it has been defined in terms of overcoming nature, emotion and particularity, and these have been traditionally identified as essentially female: 'the feminine has been associated with what rational knowledge transcends, dominates or simply leaves behind' (Lloyd, 1984, p. 2). Women have therefore been traditionally excluded from the life of the mind, and it is only by *denying* their female-ness that they have been allowed to enter. Coole similarly argues that claims for equality based on an assertion of identity 'have often rested on a profound rejection of all things female' (Coole, 1988, p. 3), and she sees this as but one aspect of the 'fundamental dualism' of Western political thought, whereby such categories as reason, mind, the public and the universal are not only equated with the male, and opposed to the female categories of passion, body, the private and the particular, but seen as central and superior while the female categories are marginal and inferior. Unlike Pateman, who has argued that Reason cannot be sex-neutral or 'disembodied', and that the exclusion of women was *central* to the concerns of western philosophers (Pateman, 1986b), Lloyd does seem to think that in principle an objective and sex-neutral form of reason is possible; in practice, however, she warns that philosophy inevitably reflects the interests and perceptions of particular philosophers rather than timeless truths, and that it has through the centuries been systematically biased against women.

While it is now fairly obvious that the terms of political debate have been laid down by male theorists, it should be noted that it is not only the traditional activities of women but also those of working-class men that are perceived as inferior and less than truly 'human'. Moreover feminist acceptance of the view that women are somehow more entangled in their biological processes then men may itself rest upon uncritical acceptance of male norms; if these are rejected, it may be that menstruation and pregnancy can be seen as 'normal', while uncontrollable erections and nocturnal emission appear as evidence that it is *men* who are subject to uncontrollable bodily processes (for a similar shift in perspective, see Steinem's witty essay *If Men Could Menstruate*, in which she argues that if it were indeed men and not women who menstruated then this would be seen as a clear sign of male superiority, a monthly purification that meant men alone could enter the priesthood, a biological link to the cycles of the moon and planets that meant that they alone could be mathematicians or understand the patterns of the universe, a symbolic blood-letting that made them alone fit to be warriors [Steinem, 1984]. It may therefore be that the dichotomy between man and woman, mind and body, reason and nature may be less clear cut than both traditional theory and feminist criticism suggests; it may also be that the distinctions are not inherently hierarchical, but may in principle simply represent different and interrelated modes of knowledge and existence.

Arguments about the alleged superiority or inferiority of the 'male world' of reason is, however, central to the third area of debate. As we have seen, it is a basic tenet of liberal feminism that it is women's mental equality with men, their possession of reason, that entitles them to the rights of citizenship. Some critics however, argue that to accept this criterion is to devalue forms of knowledge based on emotion, intuition and empathy which have traditionally been associated with women and which some see as superior to 'male logic', which is rejected as a form of patriarchal domination. However as Richards has argued, in practice reason need not be in conflict with other modes of knowing, but is frequently based upon them, and although it may have been misused to dominate women, 'Reason is not the same thing as men's often questionable use of reasoning' (Richards, 1982, p. 41). Many feminists like Coole therefore reject the idea that 'reason and logic are inherently alien to a feminist epistemology and should therefore be abandoned' (Coole, 1988, p. 274), or that women have unique access to mysterious forms of understanding inaccessible to men. It is argued rather that different approaches may be complementary, so that once again the dichotomy between reason on the one hand and intuition and imagination on the other would seem to be a false one.

Related arguments have been used by some radical feminists to deny the superiority of mental over physical activities, or to challenge the kind of liberal view expressed by Richards, who claims that 'domestic work cannot make the best use of the abilities of any highly able woman, and few achievements of any housewife are comparable to what a gifted woman could achieve outside' (Richards, 1982, p. 204). Here it is often argued that domestic work and childcare should be 'envalued'; the priorities of a society in which 'producing a book on childcare earns more respect than producing a happy baby' (Jaggar, p. 188) are decisively rejected, and women are urged to find fulfilment in traditional activities rather than to ape the achievements of men. As we have seen, forms of this argument within feminism can be traced back to Mary Wollstonecraft (see Chapter 1 above), but the implications are rejected as reactionary by many other writers, who, while they may agree that domestic work and mothering are important and potentially fulfilling for some people, reject the implied confinement of women to a biological or familial role and the over-sentimentalisation of motherhood that may be involved. A further criticism of earlier liberal feminists was their denial of the role of sexual pleasure, which was seen as an essentially dangerous and animal-like experience. Modern liberals are much more likely to allow a role to the erotic, and to see free sexual expression as a valid aspect of individuality; the suspicion remains, however, that like other forms of sensual pleasure, sexuality is an inherently inferior form of human activity, which must be kept in its place and subject to strict rational control.

However, the final criticism of the liberal stress on reason and rationality is that this is said to be misguided, for reason is *not* necessarily applicable to all areas of life. Thus its application to sexuality may lead to an unattractive calculating hedonism, and it cannot take into account the power of such 'irrational' emotions as jealousy, which may be easier to ignore in theory than in practice (as earlier feminists such as Wollstonecraft and Goldman discovered; see Chapters 1 and 5 above). It may also be that an inability to 'switch off' mental processes will limit physical pleasure. Similarly, some have argued that the application of rational principles to child-rearing is quite simply inefficient, for very different principles are involved than in the world of paid employment; thus many women have discovered that the experience of childbirth can generate complex and unpredictable emotions, and that the needs of children cannot be neatly packaged into pre-planned slots of 'quality time'. Here again, it is argued that instinct and intuition may prove superior to logical assessment and academic knowledge; other women of course continue to insist that intelligent mothering can combine these at first sight incompatible approaches, and certainly need not involve the suspension of reason.

The public/private distinction

All these arguments suggest that, at the very least, the liberal perspectives on the state, equality, human nature and reason may pose problems for feminist analysis and politics, and be less readily applicable to women than they at first sight appear. For some radical feminists, however, it is liberalism's distinction between the 'private' and the 'public' that is its basic flaw, for this means that it devalues the former, it is unable to understand how this may affect the latter and it cannot see that such apparently 'private' areas of life as the family may in fact be the site of sexual politics or oppression (see in particular Pateman, 1986a and 1987, and Okin, 1990).

The possibility that 'the "separate" liberal worlds of private and public are actually interrelated, connected by a patriarchal structure' (Pateman, 1987, p. 118) has until recently not been considered by liberal feminism which, as we have seen, has failed to come to terms with either the ways in which the domestic division of labour militates against equality in public life or the vested interests men may have in maintaining it. More recently, Susan Moller Okin (discussed in more detail below) has attempted to combine a broadly liberal position with the recognition that it is impossible to extend liberal principles to women without challenging the family, for 'the personal *is* political, and the public/private dichotomy is a misleading concept which obscures the cyclical problem of inequalities between men and women' (Okin, 1990, p. 124). Her position is, however, exceptional, and in general liberal feminism has had no way of conceptualising the possibility that the family itself may be an institution that oppresses and exploits women physically, emotionally and sexually, or of understanding the ways in which sexuality and sexual experiences may be related to the dominant power structure; domestic violence is therefore rendered invisible, rape becomes an unfortunate personal experience and sexual activity and orientation are simple matters of individual choice.

The liberal concept of a private area of life, free from power struggle and political interference does therefore seem to pose major problems for feminists, and it is incompatible with the radical feminist view (discussed in the next chapter) that all existing social institutions and relationships are part of a patriarchal power structure. As Eisenstein argues, this does not mean that radical feminists are attacking privacy as an ideal or *advocating* political involvement in personal and family life; rather they are claiming that 'the relations of the family *are* political and *should not be*' (Eisenstein, 1984, p. 215). It is, however, far from clear that in a future gender-equal society the problem will be solved and that the boundaries between the private and the public will become plain. Rather, it seems likely that precisely what is to be regarded as a matter of public or collective concern will continue to be debated: it may be that in a communally organised society the very concept of privacy could disappear, but it may also be that it could be extended to acknowledge an individual need for privacy *within* personal life that includes a right to time and space away from parents, partners, children and friends.

Richards, Okin and a feminist theory of justice

As I said at the beginning of the chapter, most modern liberal feminism has been expressed in terms of political action and campaigns, and there has been little attempt to defend its theoretical premises against the kinds of criticism that have been discussed so far. Attempts to provide a modern theory based on a relatively critical application of liberal ideas have however been made by Wolgast (1980) and Midgley and Hughes (1983); rather more innovative contributions have been made by Janet Radcliffe Richards (1982) and Susan Moller Okin (1980, 1987, 1989, and 1990).

In *The Sceptical Feminist* Richards provides a robust defence of liberal feminism against both anti-feminists and radical feminist 'extremists', which provides a much-needed corrective to some current woolly thinking; despite the philosophical rigour of her arguments, however, the book also reveals some of the problems inherent in the liberal approach. Her prime concern is, she says, with justice, which she sees as bound up with an individual's freedom to pursue his or her own destiny, and which she believes women are at present systematically denied. Like Okin, she uses the idea of the modern contract theorist, John Rawls, to provide a model of the just society in which women will be as free to explore their own potential as men. In *A Theory of Justice* (1971), Rawls had discussed the kind of society that might have been planned by individuals who did not know in advance which social positions they were to occupy. Here he argued that the only kind of inequality that would be agreed to by those behind this 'veil of ignorance' would be that which in fact benefited the *least* well off members of society; this 'difference principle' was the principle for the just distribution of resources in society and meant that inequality could not be defended in terms of the needs or merits of those already advantaged. Pateman has forcefully criticised all contract theory including Rawls' as a patriarchal device designed to conceal the realities of sex oppression behind a spurious equality (Pateman, 1988). Certainly in its original form Rawls' theory supports her accusations, for he assumed that his anonymous individuals were in fact the male heads of households (*Justice*, p. 128), and that justice within the family already existed. However Richards argues that a more consistent application of Rawls' principle, according to which knowledge of one's sex would also be firmly behind the 'veil of ignorance', and family structures could be questioned, would lead to a fundamental challenge to the gender divisions in society. She argues in particular that a sexually just society would require a radical restructuring of work and childcare arrangements that would increase the choices available to women and ensure that the benefits and burdens of having children were shared more equally between the sexes.

In *Justice, Gender and the Family*, Okin too says that Rawls' ideas can be extended to the family, and she claims that this is essential if the interests of women and children are to be defended. At present, she says, women are systematically disadvantaged in all areas of life, and 'Underlying all these inequalities is the unequal distribution of the unpaid labour of the family'. Her ideal is therefore a society in which child-rearing and domestic work are shared equally; this equality within the home would make possible gender equality in all other areas of life, so that 'A just future would be one without gender. In its social structures and practices, one's sex would have no more relevance than one's eye colour or the length of one's toes.' In order to achieve such a future, she advocates the introduction of both state-subsidised nurseries and much greater flexibility in employment patterns, so that paid work and nurturing can be readily combined by both men and women. In accordance with Rawls' principle that all interests must be considered when planning the just society, she also argues that those who choose to continue to base family life on traditional patterns must be protected. She therefore suggests that both partners should have an equal legal entitlement to all earnings coming into the household and that neither should be disproportionately disadvantaged in the event of divorce (*Justice*, pp. 25 and 171).

Okin further argues that justice within the family is integrally bound up with justice in the wider society in two other ways. Firstly, like J.S. Mill a century earlier, she says that it is within the home that children learn the values on which they will base their adult life, and that the virtues of democratic citizenship cannot be learned in a family based on domination and inequality. Secondly, her proposed redistribution of all forms of work will not simply free women from domestic responsibilities, but means that men as well as women will develop qualities of nurturing and caring and that top decision-makers of both sexes will have had experiences which she believes will improve their capacity to act justly:

> The experience of *being* a physical and psychological nurturer – whether of a child or of another adult – would increase that capacity to identify with and fully comprehend the viewpoints of others that is important to a sense of justice (p. 18).

All this represents an important step away from the classic liberal insistence on the non-political nature of the family which at the same time rejects the idea that the family is essentially oppressive and must be destroyed: the family, Okin argues, can and should be reorganised according to rational principles of justice, for it is only if we achieve justice here that women can be treated justly and a just society created.

The problem with the ideas of Richards and Okin, as with Friedan's less theoretically based demands, is that the writers make no attempt to explain *why* it is that women are at present treated unjustly, or to understand the forces that militate against their proposed changes. In an earlier book Okin did acknowledge the problem; she expected her proposals 'to be resisted strongly by those with economic power and an interest in maintaining the status quo', and she questioned whether they are in fact achievable within the structures of capitalism (Okin, 1980, p. 303). The implications of this are, however, never explored. Richards seems blissfully unaware of such considerations. For her, the prime task is to demonstrate the philosophical requirements of justice, and her main enemies are therefore careless thinking and faulty logic. The possibility of opposition to her proposals based on self-interest is not even considered, and she makes no attempt to explore the very real motives that powerful groups may have in perpetuating injustice. The logic of her arguments also leads her to some conclusions which many feminists find unacceptable: for example, she defends prostitution and disagrees with state-funded maternity benefits (unless these are part of a deliberate attempt to increase the population). These particular conclusions, however, remain contestable in principle, and are much less important than her underlying approach which fails to see that 'the terms of moral debate do not exist in a remote philosopher's heaven' (Grimshaw, 1982, p. 6), but in a world characterised by gender, race and class divisions and in which outcomes are likely to be determined by power, rather than by the sweet voice of reason.

Here then we have one of the major problems of liberal feminism: that in trying to discover through reason a universally valid concept of justice, it cannot understand the realities of social existence and the power relations of society. This does not mean that the task of identifying goals is meaningless, but unless this is combined with an attempt to understand the history and causes of women's oppression and the very real forces opposing liberation, feminist proposals will remain merely utopian, academic exercises incapable of realisation.

It now seems clear that unmodified liberal principles cannot provide an understanding of the nature and causes of women's oppression, and that they are therefore unlikely to provide an adequate strategy for ending it; as discussed in this chapter, the attempt to extend these principles to women also poses problems and has led to a certain amount of theoretical confusion. However this does not mean that all liberal demands and values need be rejected by feminists. In the past, the struggle for legal and political equality was clearly progressive, and was bound up with the achievement of concrete improvements in the lives of women of all classes (here the sceptical reader is referred to Chapter 2 above, for an account of the situation of women in the nineteenth century). Now at the very least, these equal rights provide us with a better starting point for future struggle and must be defended against any attempts to remove or weaken them. It may be too that reform and 'piecemeal social engineering' are the best way forward for women, but this is only likely to succeed if it is based on an understanding of society's complex power structures and the interrelationships between 'public' and 'private' life. Radical and Marxist feminists provide very different theoretical approaches to these problems; it is to these that we now turn.

10

Modern radical feminism: the theory of patriarchy

The radical feminist label has been applied in recent years to a confusingly diverse range of theories. Far from constituting a coherent body of political thought, it is the site for far-ranging disagreements at all levels of theory and practice. Nevertheless, there is a clear theoretical starting-point which distinguishes it from other approaches and provides a unifying framework within which diverging ideas have been developed. In the first place, it is essentially a theory of, by and for women; as such, it is based firmly in women's own experiences and perceptions and sees no need to compromise with existing political perspectives and agendas. Secondly, it sees the oppression of women as the most fundamental and universal form of domination, and its aim is to understand and end this; here 'patriarchy' is a key term. From this it follows that, thirdly, women as a group have interests opposed to those of men; these interests unite them in a common sisterhood that transcends the division of class or race, and means that women should struggle together to achieve their own liberation. Finally, radical feminist analysis insists that male power is not confined to the public worlds of politics and paid employment, but that it extends into private life; this means that traditional concepts of power and politics are challenged and extended to such 'personal' areas of life as the family and sexuality, both of which are seen as instruments of patriarchal domination.

The origins of radical feminism

As we have seen in earlier chapters, such ideas are not new, but it was not until the late 1960s that they began to be developed systematically as a self-conscious theory. The impetus towards this development came from women's experiences in the Civil Rights, anti-war, New Left and student movements in North America, Europe and Australia. In these, young women were to find that left-wing groups were not immune from the 'feminine mystique' that Betty Friedan had identified in mainstream American life, and that their role was essentially that of secretary, housewife or sex object, servicing the political, domestic and sexual needs of male activists; any attempt at raising the subject of women's exclusion from decision-making was met with silence, ridicule or contempt. Such sexism has by now been well documented (see for example Evans, 1980, and Sargent, 1986); it is perhaps also worth recording that my first sight of a 'Women's Lib' banner was at a student sit-in in 1970, and that it was produced as a reaction to the proposal that the 'girls' clean up while the 'men' discussed strategy. In America, the irony of a movement that seemed to promise freedom to blacks while denying it to women soon became apparent, symbolised in the often quoted comment of the black leader, Stokely Carmichael, who refused to discuss the position of women in the movement beyond saying that it should be 'prone'. As in the nineteenth century, parallels between the situation of blacks and women were readily drawn (see, for example, Gayle Rubin, 'Woman as Nigger', 1970) and when after 1964 sections of the black movement shifted away from liberal civil rights ideas to more radical and militant concepts of black power, white imperialism, black separatism and liberation through revolution, some women saw this as a clear model for a female liberation that went far beyond the equal rights ideas of liberal campaigners like Betty Friedan. From this new perspective, women were involved in a revolutionary struggle against men that could not be won by polite requests for equal opportunities or changes in the law; far from seeking respectability and acceptance within the system, feminists were now committed to its overthrow.

Despite these origins in black movements, many critics claim that from its inception radical feminism has been rooted in racist assumptions. There had always been social, racial and sexual

tensions between black and white women in the civil rights movement, and although black women had been to the forefront of
early complaints about sexism, they rapidly became invisible in a
movement that contrasted the demands of *blacks* and *women*, as
if *black women* did not exist (see Evans, 1980, and Spelman,
1988). Insistence on the oppression shared by all women also
obscured the very real differences that existed amongst women,
and seemed to deny the possibility that women could also oppress
each other.

The articulation of a black feminist critique lay however in the
future, and in the first heady years of the new movement such
problems could easily be ignored. In 1967 the first radical women's
groups were formed in America. Influenced by Maoist ideas current in left-wing circles, these used the Chinese communist idea
of 'speaking bitterness' to express and share personal experiences
so as to bring out their political implications and to develop a
political strategy for change. This approach became known as
'consciousness raising' and was of central importance in this period
as women broke years of silence to discover the shared nature of
problems which they had assumed to be theirs alone. Later, some
women tended to use consciousness raising as a form of therapy
which articulated problems to which individualistic solutions could
be found; originally, however, it was a self-consciously political
strategy, based on the premise that women's problems were
shared and that they could only be ended by collective political
action (see Morgan, 1970, and Brooke, 1978). As new groups
spread rapidly, the key message was that 'the personal is political',
and that a new theory and strategy for women's liberation could
only be based on women's shared experiences, not on abstract
speculation. From this perspective, no aspect of life lacked a
political dimension and political struggle could therefore take
many new forms; women's struggle could not be postponed until
'after the revolution' but was a matter for immediate political
action, and was to be waged against the universal oppressor –
man. Such views are epitomised by the New York Redstockings
manifesto of 1969:

> Women are an oppressed class. Our oppression is total, affecting every
> facet of our lives. We are exploited as sex objects, breeders, domestic
> servants, and cheap labor. We are considered inferior beings whose

only purpose is to enhance men's lives . . . we have been kept from seeing our personal suffering as a political condition . . . the conflicts between individual men and women are *political* conflicts that can only be solved collectively . . . We identify the agents of our oppression as men. Male supremacy is the oldest, most basic form of domination . . . *All men* receive economic, sexual, and psychological benefits from male supremacy. *All men* have oppressed women (in Morgan, 1970, p. 598).

Kate Millett and the theory of patriarchy

By the early 1970s these new ideas were reflected in a substantial body of literature that included Kate Millett's *Sexual Politics*, Shulamith Firestone's *The Dialectic of Sex*, Germaine Greer's *The Female Eunuch* and Eva Figes' *Patriarchal Attitudes* (all first published in 1970); anthologies of some of the new manifestos, speeches and articles were also published in Betty and Theodore Roszak's *Masculine/Feminine* (1969), Robin Morgan's *Sisterhood is Powerful* (1970), Leslie Tanner's *Voices from Women's Liberation* (1970) and Michelle Wandor's *The Body Politic* (1972). While all of these were important manifestations of the new movement, it is the second chapter of Millett's *Sexual Politics* that is of the most theoretical importance, as it introduced into modern feminist thought the key concept of *patriarchy*. Although Millett describes her work as simply 'notes towards a theory of patriarchy' (*Sexual Politics*, 1985 edition, p. 24), it provides a starting-point from which many later theories have developed and encapsulates many of the central concerns of radical feminist thought; her discussion of the concept is also considerably more rigorous and thoughtful than that of many later writers who have seized upon the term without fully examining its implications, so that many of the criticisms that have been made of the concept do not in fact apply to her original analysis.

The term patriarchy is not of course new to political theory, but the use to which Millett put it certainly was. Derived from the Greek *patriarches*, meaning 'head of the tribe', it was central to seventeenth-century debates over the extent of monarchical power; here supporters of absolute rule claimed that the power of a king over his people was the same as that of a father over his family, and that both were sanctioned by God and nature.

Millett seems to take such familial power as her starting-point, so that 'the principles of patriarchy appear to be twofold: male shall dominate female, elder male shall dominate young' (*Politics*, p. 25). It is, however, only the first of these principles that she explores, and she does not distinguish between male power within the family and in society as whole; despite the efforts of some writers to restrict the term to strictly family-based power (see Randall, 1987, p. 20, and Cocks, 1989), its use as a shorthand for a social system based on male domination and female subordination has become standard amongst feminists.

Millett's central claims are simple, and they essentially represent a formalisation of the ideas that were already current in the new women's movement. She argues that in all known societies the relationship between the sexes has been based on power, and that they are therefore political. This power takes the form of male domination over women in all areas of life; sexual domination is so universal, so ubiquitous and so complete that it appears 'natural' and hence becomes invisible, so that it is 'perhaps the most pervasive ideology of our culture and provides its most fundamental concept of power' (*Politics*, p. 25). The patriarchal power of men over women is therefore basic to the functioning of all societies and it extends far beyond formal institutions of power. It overrides class and race divisions, for economic dependency means that women's class identity is a 'tangential, vicarious and temporary matter', while 'sexism may be more endemic in our society than racism' (*Politics*, pp. 38 and 39). Patriarchy is primarily maintained by a process of conditioning which starts with childhood socialisation within the family and is reinforced by education, literature and religion to such an extent that its values are internalised by men and women alike; for some women this leads to self-hatred, self-rejection and an acceptance of inferiority. Despite the success of this 'interior colonisation', patriarchy also rests upon economic exploitation and the use or threat of force. This means that its history is a record of man's inhumanity to woman and that the thousands of women who die in the United States each year as a result of illegal abortion are victims of the same system as the Indian woman forced to die on her husband's funeral pyre, the Chinese woman crippled by foot-binding and the African girl whose clitoris is cut out. In all societies too, patriarchy relies upon sexual violence and rape. In this context, sexual relations between men and women are but an expression of male power, and Millett devotes a large section of her book to 'deconstructing' the portrayal of sex in the work of four major twentieth-century writers (D. H. Lawrence, Henry Miller, Norman Mailer and Jean Genet) so as to reveal the crude sexual domination involved. Love, too, can be but a confidence trick, part of a patriarchal ideology designed to hide the realities of power; not until patriarchy has been overthrown and sexuality radically transformed can men and women relate in any way as equal human beings.

Criticisms of the theory of patriarchy

Such a view of power and politics is completely new to political theory, which has never seen the power gap between men and women as central, and which has been unable to see that political power relations may be involved in 'private' life. It brings together ideas that we have found scattered throughout the work of earlier feminist writers, and transforms them from isolated notions into a systematic theory; it also makes sense of the opposition encountered by earlier feminists and their failure to achieve all the changes for which they had hoped, by showing the vested interests and power structures involved. However, although as we shall see in Chapter 13, the concept of patriarchy has also been utilised by many Marxist and socialist feminists who find existing theories inadequate or incomplete, its use by radical feminists has been heavily criticised. These criticisms centre upon four interrelated points. Firstly, the radical feminist theory of patriarchy is said to be descriptive rather than analytical, unable to explain the origins of male power and therefore unable to provide an adequate strategy for ending it. Secondly, some see it as based on a false idea of 'man as the enemy' that leads logically only to lesbian separatism and that can have little appeal or relevance for the majority of women. Thirdly, the theory is said to be ahistorical and based on a 'false universalism' that reflects only the experiences of white middle-class women and obscures the very different problems faced by working-class, black and third world women. Finally, in describing the wrongs done by men over the centuries, it sees women simply in the role of passive victims, rather than the comakers of history and the agents of change in the future. What therefore needs to be established is whether these criticisms are justified, and if so, whether the flaws in the theory are inherent and insurmountable, or whether, as Walby has recently claimed in *Theorizing Patriarchy* (1990), they are merely contingent.

Whereas Marxist and socialist feminists see the existence and origins of patriarchy as inextricably bound up with class society (the exact nature of this relationship being a matter of intense debate), radical feminists see it as either autonomous or itself the cause of other forms of oppression. Either way, it is agreed that patriarchy is *not* a mere derivative of economic power or class society, and that it cannot be reduced to other forms of domination but must be understood in its own terms. This, however, leaves open the huge question of how patriarchy first arose, or of whether it has always existed in all human societies. Millett's original theory is decidedly hazy on this, refusing to become involved in 'the evanescent delights afforded by the game of origins', on the grounds that 'Conjecture about origins is always frustrated by lack of evidence. Speculation about pre-history . . . remains nothing but speculation' (*Politics*, pp. 28 and 27). Other writers have been less reticent, and there now seems to be a fairly widespread consensus that a matriarchy in which women were in positions of power and domination has never existed, but that some very early societies have been much more woman-centred than our own and that some may have been based on matrilineal descent and a degree of sexual equality (see Lerner, 1986). For some radical feminists, the original shift to patriarchy was a simply consequence of men's greater strength, stemming from women's weakness during pregnancy, childbirth and lactation; for others, it is above all men's ability to rape that enables them to dominate women (Brownmiller, 1977). Some however claim that it was the discovery of the male role in reproduction that was critical and first led men to seek to control women. Thus Rich writes that

> A crucial moment in human consciousness arrives when man discovers that it is he himself, not the moon or the spring rains or the spirits of the dead, who impregnates the woman; that the child she carries and gives birth to is his child, who can make *him* immortal (Rich, 1977, p. 60; see also Figes, 1970, and O'Brien, 1981).

Yet others see the development of patriarchy as rooted in the early development of hunting by men, which both gave them a new source of power and led to the development of a value system based on violent conquest (see French, 1985, and Collard, 1988).

There is therefore no radical feminist agreement as to the causes or origins of patriarchy. Spender, however, does not think this matters:

> We do not need definite evidence of the first cause to know that men have power, that they have had it for a very long time, that they seem to have had it in every known human society, and that they now use it to keep their power (Spender, 1985b, p. 42).

From this perspective, what is important is to identify and understand the structures and institutions that maintain patriarchy *today* in order that these may be overthrown, and this Millett and later writers have attempted to do.

Although the point is not developed by Millett as much as by some later theorists, a central message of her work must be that it is not unjust laws or economic systems that are responsible for women's oppression but MEN, that men as a group have interests opposed to those of women and that it is therefore against the power of men that the battle must be fought. For many critics such a position is untenable. Many men, they point out, are not in positions of power over women but may in fact be subordinate to them, and despite the general imbalance of power, loving and non-exploitative relationships between men and women can and do exist in our society. Men, too, they say, may suffer in a sexist society: for example, they are forced into the role of breadwinner and denied an active role in bringing up their own children, and, by having to repress unacceptably 'feminine' aspects of their personality, they are alienated from their own full humanity. Many men, they say, would therefore be willing to help women in their struggle, and their support should not be rejected. Moreover, men cannot be simply 'killed off' in the same way as a class enemy might conceivably be; quite apart from humanitarian considerations, this would be a biological impossibility. Such criticisms, however, miss the point that the theory of patriarchy does not necessarily imply that all individual men oppress all women, that each and every male person is to be considered an enemy incapable of reform, or that the total elimination of the male sex would be the desired consequence of an improvement in sperm-bank technology. Indeed an important aspect of the theory is that it enables us to distinguish between the structures of male domination on the one hand and individual men on the other (Dahlerup, 1987, and Walby, 1990); the enemy is male *power* in all its manifestations, but this power is seen to be socially con-structed rather than embodied in all biological males.

It remains true that some radical feminists have developed a position which rejects all association with men, whether this be social, sexual or political, and that for some this is based on a belief that there is a fundamental, inevitable and biologically based conflict of interests between the sexes. Separatist ideas must, however, be disentangled from the original theory of patri-archy, which need not imply that differences between the sexes are biologically determined or that they are in principle unresolv-able. Male power can therefore be seen as analytically distinct from male persons, and although the concept of patriarchy can be developed in this direction, man-hating and separatism are not inherent in it.

Another alleged problem with the theory of patriarchy is that in insisting on women's universal and shared oppression, it obscures the changes that have taken place throughout history, the differ-ences between one society and another and the realities of class and race. Such criticisms seem true of some writers. Thus for example Adrienne Rich's account of patriarchy explicitly abstracts the position of women from any social context:

> Under patriarchy, I may live in *purdah* or drive a truck; I may raise my children in a *kibbutz*, or be the sole breadwinner for a fatherless family . . . I may serve my husband his early-morning coffee within the clay walls of a Barbar village or march in an academic procession; whatever my status or situation, my derived economic class or my sexual preference, I live under the power of the fathers, and have access only to so much of privilege or influence as the patriarchy is willing to accede to me, and only for so long as I will pay the price for male approval (Rich, 1977, p. 58).

Similarly, Dworkin has linked the pre-revolutionary Chinese prac-tice of foot-binding to the girdles, high heels and eyebrow plucking dictated by American fashion, claiming that for all women 'Pain is an essential part of the grooming process and that is not accidental . . . [it] serves to prepare women for lives of child-bearing, self-abnegation and husband-pleasing' (Dworkin, 1974, p 115). Mary Daly too claims that such horrors as foot-binding, witch-burning, genital mutilation and modern American gynae-cology are all essentially similar manifestations of the universal system of male tyranny, so that the situation of women is basically the same whether they live in Saudi Arabia or Sweden, and 'Even outer space and the future have been colonized' (Daly, 1973, and 1978, p. 1).

At one level, such analyses may have an intuitive appeal and contain a kind of truth. It is not necessary to believe in the immutable and biologically based 'badness' of men to agree that women in radically different societies or situations do frequently have experiences in common involving sexual exploitation, lack of reproductive freedom and marginalisation or exclusion from 'male-stream' economic, social, political and intellectual life; these experiences may reflect the systematic exercise of power by men over women. Nevertheless the idea that all women are therefore united in a common sisterhood that transcends all man-made divisions can be dangerously misleading. In the first place, a too-easy comparison of women's experiences across the centuries and within and between modern societies may trivialise the depth of suffering experienced by some women. Thus the oppression experienced by a modern American 'fashion victim' (even one who diets herself to death) is qualitatively different from the suffering of the generations of Chinese women who were from childhood deliberately and systematically crippled in the name of erotic attraction, able only to totter painfully

> on the outside of toes which had been bent under into the sole of the foot. The heel and instep of the foot resembled the sole and heel of a high-heeled boot. Hard callouses formed, toe-nails grew into the skin; the feet were pus-filled and bloody; circulation was virtually stopped (Dworkin, 1974, p. 101).

Similarly, attempts to compare the experiences of women in very different twentieth-century societies that are based on the premise that these are essentially 'the same', conceal the vast gap in experience that may also be involved. For example, lack of reproductive rights means something very different to the Romanian woman forced to bear at least six children, the Chinese woman forced by the 'one child' policy to abort her second, the white American career woman whose contraception has failed and the Puerto Rican woman sterilised against her will. Moreover, the attempt to universalise women's experience may conceal other forms of oppression based on race or class or belittle their importance, as from the perspective of the global and transhistorical oppression of women, racism, militaristic nationalism and economic exploitation can seem but trivial squabbles amongst men. According to some critics, therefore, the feminist assumption that the concerns of white, middle-class Western women can be equated with the experiences of all women everywhere is itself a form of cultural imperialism that seeks to disguise the particularity of its own world-view by the use of spuriously general concepts. This means that 'patriarchy' and 'sisterhood' may be mystifying devices that conceal divisions in society in much the same way as male perspectives have concealed the oppression of women, so that 'There are disturbing parallels between what feminists find disquieting in Western political thought and what many black women have found troubling in much of Western feminism' (Spelman, 1988, p. 6; see also Moraga and Anzaldua, 1983, especially the article by Lorde; Davis, 1982 and 1990; *Feminist Review*, no 17, 1984; Collins, 1990; Ramazanoglu, 1986).

Forceful as these criticisms are, it is, however, far from clear that such problems are inherent in the concept of patriarchy as opposed to some of its less cautious exponents. Millett herself never argued that patriarchy was an unchanging system of oppression, and there seems no reason why in principle the recognition of the existence of patriarchy need involve denial of other forms of oppression; this can mean that the vast question of the interconnections and possible causal relationships between the gender, race and class systems can be opened up for exploration rather than reduced to one simple cause.

A similar response is possible to the final main criticism that has been made of the radical feminist concept of patriarchy. This claims that it is essentially ahistorical, and that too often it sees women solely as passive victims of male injustice, so that 'Women's powerlessness, victimisation and lack of resources . . .

constitute women's timeless history' (Segal, 1987, p. xi). Again, however, the idea that society is structured by male domination need not in itself preclude the possibility of change. Millett's original theory saw the importance of women's struggles in the past and argued that these had made 'monumental progress' and provided the basis for future change (*Politics*, p. 64); by making patriarchy visible and identifying the battles that have to be fought she sees her own work as itself a part of that struggle. Some writers have therefore attempted to produce a more sophisticated theory which argues that, far from being unchanging, patriarchal domination takes a number of different forms which are the product of particular historical situations. Thus Ferguson and Walby have both recently argued that in Western societies there has been a general shift away from private patriarchy based on individual control within the household to a public patriarchy based on structures outside the home – although Walby cautions that this is 'a continuum rather than a rigid dichotomy' and that different groups have been affected in different ways (Walby, 1990, p. 180; Ferguson, 1989; see also Dahlerup, 1987). Although she challenges some radical feminists' use of the term 'patriarchy', Cocks similarly argues that there has been a decline in traditional patriarchal power within the family; she claims that this has been accompanied by a rise in what she calls *phallic* power, that is, sexual domination and exploitation (Cocks, 1989). Such views do not see patriarchy as an unchanging and monolithic structure of oppression, but allow for the possibility that patriarchal power may be challenged and feminist victories won. This means that changes in the nature or degree of patriarchy become visible, as do women's challenges to it.

It seems therefore that the basic principles of the radical feminist approach and its theory of patriarchy must be disentangled from the conclusions that have been drawn from them, and genuine disagreements separated from misunderstandings and differences in emphasis. Its starting point is that women are central; their needs and experiences are not to be appended or assimilated into a pre-existing theory, but provide the basis of a woman-centred understanding of the world. From this perspective, a central shared experience is domination by men. This domination is experienced not only in the public worlds of politics and employment, but also in the family and in personal relationships. Power and politics are therefore redefined, and seen to pervade the whole of life. The task of radical feminist theory is therefore both to expose this domination and to analyse how it is maintained in order that it may be successfully challenged. Here different writers have focused upon very different aspects and sources of male power and have reached some at first sight very different conclusions. At one level, many of these conclusions are in fact complementary, and can be combined to provide a more comprehensive analysis of gender relations than has existed hitherto, rather than being presented as 'rival' explanations. Genuine differences do, however, remain, and these centre upon the split between those who, like most liberal and socialist feminists, stress men and women's shared humanity, and those who believe that there are essential and irreducible biological differences that shape men and women's nature. The latter position frequently involves a belief in women's inherent superiority which has led some to an extreme separatist position and others to the development of an 'eco-feminist' analysis. The following two chapters will explore the main structures that have been seen as important to the workings of patriarchy: the state, the economic system, the family, reproduction, sexuality and violence, and male control of language and knowledge. To a considerable extent these overlap with the structures recently identified by Walby (1990), and like her I argue that a satisfactory understanding of patriarchy cannot be reduced to an examination of any one structure but must explore their interrelationships.

11

Modern radical feminism: public and private patriarchy

Patriarchy and the state

Unlike most conventional political theory, radical feminism does not see state power as the central political issue. From this new perspective, the state is but one manifestation of patriarchal power, reflecting other deeper structures of oppression, and women's well-documented exclusion from its formal institutions is a symptom rather than the cause of gender inequality. Therefore although the radical feminist analysis of the state has tended to be implicit rather than fully developed in its own right, this neglect itself embodies a theory of state power which is seen as neither autonomous nor as reducible to the needs of the economy, but as inextricably connected to areas of life such as the family and sexuality that have usually been seen as private and non-political, but which are now seen as basic to all power relationships in society.

As discussed in Chapter 9, liberal feminists see the state as an essentially neutral institution from which women have been unfairly excluded in the past, but which can in principle be used to their advantage; equal legal and political rights are therefore key demands, legislation and state provision of services are seen as a means of improving women's situation, and women have organised themselves politically in much the same way as other conventional pressure groups. For radical feminists, however, the exclusion of women from power is no unfortunate and easily remedied accident, for the structures and institutions of the state have been made by men and embody their interests rather than those of women. This means that feminist demands will never be readily conceded by the state but will encounter opposition that the liberal perspective has no means of understanding. It also means that legislation on its own can do little to improve the real situation of women, although it may disguise or legitimise their oppression by combining it with a formal equality. Indeed state intervention that is ostensibly aimed at improving the situation of women may in fact dangerously increase the power of this male state; for example, state provision of welfare services may involve new forms of subordination rather than independence for women, while legislation to outlaw pornography may be used to censor lesbian literature or to outlaw sex education. For some radical feminists the whole idea of the competitive pursuit of power is rejected as an embodiment of male values, and conventional politics is abandoned: organisational hierarchies are avoided, political struggle is relocated from the ballot-box to the bedroom, and separatism is favoured over participation in existing organisations or institutions, which are seen as a mere playground for male egoists. For others, however, the identification of patriarchal power within the state is an insight that can further the feminist cause by providing a more realistic assessment of political possibilities than that provided by the liberal approach. From this perspective, the state is seen as an arena of conflict which is systematically biased against women but within which important victories can nevertheless be won; it is essential to understand the power relations that are involved and the tremendous obstacles that women face, but this need not lead to the pessimistic abandonment of conventional politics. Such an approach can also in principle recognise the existence of cross-cutting race and class conflicts that will help determine political outcomes and which interact with gender struggles in highly complex ways.

The radical feminist approach to the state can therefore give us a simplistic picture of a monolithic institution that can be written off by feminists as an instrument of patriarchal oppression; it can also provide the basis for a more sophisticated approach that recognises the complex nature of the power struggles involved and the interconnectedness of the different patriarchal structures. This allows us to recognise both the importance and the limitations of conventional politics and legislation. For example, a law that gives a woman the right to leave an abusing husband is not in itself enough to protect her from marital violence, for it will be enforced by a sexist police force within a culture in which sexuality and domination are inextricably linked, and she is unlikely to have the economic resources to maintain herself. If, however, the law is passed in the context of feminist struggles to make such violence visible and unacceptable, to increase the accountability of the police, to provide safe houses for battered wives and to improve educational and employment prospects for women, then it can represent a significant victory.

For radical feminists, therefore, state power is not to be understood in its own terms, but as part of a ubiquitous system of patriarchal power. This means that it is not a neutral tool equally available for women and men, and that it will not automatically respond to the dictates of reason or justice; it also suggests that its nature cannot be changed by simply changing the incumbents of the positions of power, for political outcomes are structured by society-wide power relations, not by individual decisions. For some, the patriarchal domination of women by men is the central and defining feature of state power; for others however the concept of patriarchy allows scope both for conventional political struggle and for an analysis of related structures of class and race oppression.

Patriarchy and the economic system

As we have seen in earlier chapters, the classic Marxist position on women's oppression is that it is a product of class society that will disappear with the overthrow of capitalism and the establishment of a classless communist society. For radical feminists such reductionism is completely unacceptable, for it ignores the non-economic bases and the ubiquity of male power, and it denies the shared experiences of all women and the vested interests of men in maintaining their oppression. From this perspective, economic change on is own can never change the deeply-rooted structures of patriarchal power, and a socialist revolution 'would be *no* revolution; but only another coup d'etat among men' (Morgan, 1970, p. *xxxvi*); the failure of past revolutions to liberate women is seen as proof of the hollowness of the Marxist promise.

For radical feminists, women are economically exploited as

women, rather than as gender-neutral members of the proletariat. The exploitation of their labour both in the paid workforce and in the home is but one dimension of their oppression by men, and the global nature of this exploitation is summed up in the 1980 United Nations report that

> Women constitute one half of the world's population, perform nearly two thirds of its work hours, receive one tenth of the world's income and own less than one hundredth of the world's property.

More specifically, the well-documented lower pay and marginalisation of women in advanced capitalist economies is seen as a means of maintaining women's dependence upon men and hence forcing them to service their domestic and sexual needs. This dependency cannot be ended by equal pay or opportunities legislation or by economic struggle alone, for it is inextricably linked with other aspects of patriarchal domination: for example, women cannot achieve full economic independence and equality in the paid workforce if they are also expected to run the home and this domestic work is unwaged, and, even when they escape the worst effects of sexual harassment, women will not be taken seriously as workers in a culture that sees them primarily as sex objects or nurturers. Economics cannot therefore be isolated as an autonomous arena of struggle or as the prime cause of women's oppression; struggles for economic independence may be important, but they cannot on their own bring an end to patriarchy.

The problem with all of this is that if applied too simply it falls into the trap of 'false universalism' discussed above, denying the diversity of women's situations, the specific forms of economic exploitation experienced by black and third world women and the class ties that may cut across gender divisions; it also ignores the worldwide exploitation of most men's labour. Nevertheless it does offer important insights into the nature of women's economic situation which, as we shall see in Chapter 13, have forced modern Marxist feminists into a re-examination of their own assumptions. In particular, it has opened up a whole area of debate as to the relationship between patriarchy and capitalism and made visible the domestic labour performed by women in the home. In agreeing that women's oppression cannot be seen as a simple product of capitalist class society it must however also be understood that an understanding of the economy and class relations cannot simply be reduced to the needs of men. The economy may be an important structure of patriarchy, in and through which men dominate women; it is also rather more.

Patriarchy and the family

According to Millett, 'Patriarchy's chief institution is the family' (*Sexual Politics*, p. 33), and later radical feminists have agreed that, contrary to the assumptions of conventional political theory, the family is indeed a central part of society's power structure; as such it both sustains patriarchal power in the 'public' world and is itself a source of women's oppression. Far from being a 'natural' arrangement based on mutual love and respect in which the emotional, sexual and domestic needs of adult partners are met and their children cared for, it is a social institution in which women's labour is exploited, male sexual power may be violently expressed and oppressive gender identities and modes of behaviour are learned.

Domestic labour

Like liberal feminists, many early radical feminists saw all domestic work, including childcare, as inherently unfulfilling and degrading; unlike liberal feminists, however, they did not see women's responsibility for the home as a kind of unfortunate accident that could be rectified by an obliging husband and a cleaning lady. With the insights provided by the concept of patriarchy, it was argued that men benefited from present arrangements both in terms of domestic comfort and through handicapping women who attempted to compete with them in politics and paid employment. From this perspective, men's resistance to change and their refusal to help with domestic chores which liberal feminists found surprising or 'unfair' were only to be expected, and quarrels about who should do the washing were not individual disagreements but part of a wider power struggle. For some, the solution was simply to refuse to continue to perform domestic services for men, and this implied separatist women-only households. Others believed that men could be forced or persuaded into accepting domestic responsibilities, but saw that this would not be an automatic consequence of pointing out the injustice of present arrangements, but must be consciously and continuously struggled for. For many, the solution lay not simply in abolishing the division of labour within the family, but in abolishing the family itself; this was bound up with a more widespread counter-culture rejection of traditional values and an experimentation with alternative lifestyles. Experience, however, was to show that the sexual division of labour could flourish in communes as well as in the nuclear family; 'progressive' men might pay lip-service to feminist principles, but in practice they too benefited from patri-archy and could dismiss women's complaints as petty and trivial; many feminist women too found that years of training in domestic skills and expectations could be hard to put aside.

The most formal radical feminist analysis of women's domestic work as a source of oppression has been provided by the French feminist Christine Delphy, who argues that because they perform unpaid housework all women share a common economic position: 'As a group effectively (at any given time) subject to this relation of production they constitute a *class*; as a category of human beings *destined by birth* to become a member of this class, they constitute a *caste*' (Delphy, 1980, p. 35). She claims that marriage is a labour contract through which men exploit women's labour and become their economic masters, and that because most women perform this unpaid labour, the position of all women in the employment market is depressed and marriage continues to appear their most viable economic option. This domestic exploita-tion takes place outside the capitalist mode of production, and she therefore argues that a genuinely materialist analysis of women's oppression shows that this is not simply derived from class struggle and capitalism, but that it has an independent material basis in women's unpaid domestic labour. Delphy's analysis has been heavily criticised by socialist feminists who accuse her of a woolly misuse of Marxist concepts and of a failure to explore changes in marriage over time and between classes; they also dislike the implication that it is at the level of domestic exploitation rather than paid work or ideology that feminists should be struggling (see Barrett and McIntosh, 1979). Clearly there are problems in universalising from a particular historical moment and in seeing domestic labour as the sole or even the prime source of women's oppression, and, as Chapter 13 will show, recent attempts to extend orthodox Marxist economic categories to women's work in the home have also run into difficulties. Exploitation of women's labour in the home is entangled with other aspects of patriarchal power which it may both reflect and maintain; it is also bound up with other dimensions of economic and social life. As such it is not an unchanging source of oppression, and although household tasks are still not shared equally, some increase in male involvement in the home, combined with a reduction in family size and increased availability of domestic appliances, may mean that it is less important than formerly in modern industrial societies. Delphy's analysis does focus our attention on an important area neglected by earlier feminist theorists; on its own however it does not provide a full understanding of the multi-faceted nature of women's oppression.

Sexual exploitation

For other radical feminists, it is sexual rather than domestic exploitation within the family that is important. As we shall see in later sections, some argue that patriarchy is based primarily upon male violence and control of women's sexuality; here it should be noted simply that increased awareness of domestic violence and the sexual abuse of both women and children within the home mean that for many feminists the family is seen as the cutting edge of patriarchal oppression where many women face male power in its crudest and most aggressive form. The connection between individual acts of violence and wider patriarchal power is underlined by the reluctance of authorities to interfere in 'private' domestic affairs and the fact that in some American states marital rape is not a crime and it has only very recently become one in Britain; the demand made by Stanton and other nineteenth-century feminists for sexual autonomy within marriage has therefore still not been fully won either in law or in reality. Even for those women lucky enough to escape the worst manifestations of patriarchal aggression, marriage does not, it is argued, provide sexual or emotional freedom, but perpetuates a form of domination disguised by love. Thus Firestone argues that 'Love, perhaps even more than child-bearing, is the pivot of women's oppression today' (Firestone, 1979, p. 121), and that love in a patriarchal society cannot be based upon equality, but reflects women's economic and social dependency and ensures that they will not challenge their subordinate position; although expressed very differently, this claim is remarkably similar to the analyses of Thompson and J. S. Mill who had argued a century earlier that men were not content with women's obedience, but demand their love as well (see Chapters 1 and 2 above).

Parenting and the acquisition of adult sexual identity

For Millett, the family's main importance is as an agent of socialisation, the primary social institution through which young children learn the values and expectations of their society. Thus it is within the family that boys and girls first encounter patriarchal power and the sexual division of labour, and it is through the example and admonitions of their parents that they are first taught the role, temperament and status appropriate to their sex. Such lessons are reinforced by peer groups, schools and the media, and having been learned at such an early age they are particularly resistant to later challenges.

For some writers, however, the question of sexual identity goes even deeper and can only be understood by using insights derived from psychoanalytic theory. Freud has had an extremely hostile feminist press; indeed his whole theory has been ridiculed and seen as a patriarchal tool designed to reconcile women with an oppressive reality (see de Beauvoir, 1972; Figes, 1970; Friedan, 1986; Greer, 1979; Millett, 1985). Some recent feminist writers have, however, attempted to rehabilitate him and claim that his concepts of the unconscious and of infantile sexuality can be used to understand adult behaviour; for such writers it is important to understand how infant experiences mould adult attitudes and behaviour if these are to be challenged and changed (for a lucid discussion of such writings, see Sayers, 1986). This means that child-rearing practices are seen as having a political dimension; here the work of Nancy Choderow and Dorothy Dinnerstein has been particularly influential (see Choderow, *The Reproduction of Mothering*, 1978, and Dinnerstein, *The Rocking of the Cradle and the Ruling of the World*, 1987, first published as *The Mermaid and the Minotaur*, 1976).

Although their theoretical starting-points differ, both these writers have concluded that it is the female monopoly of childcare that is at the root of our present problems – indeed Dinnerstein claims that the resulting psychological damage has brought the human race to the very edge of extinction. Their solution is therefore the involvement of men in parenting; this will make possible new forms of gender identity freed from ideas of domination and submission and the development of a fully integrated and responsible adult personality for both sexes; the consequences of this will be to end women's exclusion from public power and to transform the entire gender arrangements of society.

Even if this analysis has some truth, it leaves a number of problems unresolved. Neither writer tackles the huge question of how the economy would resist or adapt to the changed work patterns that shared parenting would require, and it is quite unclear how mother-raised men and women are to break out of the vicious circle of which they are a part. Some critics further complain that, like many radical feminists, they have based a supposedly universal theory on the experiences of white, middle-class Americans. Their assumptions are also challenged by other schools of psychoanalytic thought. In particular, French writers have linked the acquisition of gender identity to the child's acquisition of language; debates here have involved complex arguments as to whether sex differences are acquired via the Oedipal recognition of sex difference or whether they in fact pre-date it and are essentially rooted in the body, while some query the whole notion of a stable adult identity. These arguments suggest that it is not simply patterns of infant care that are important in forming the (possibly ever-changing) adult psyche, but that this may be rooted in the structures of language and thought processes available to the child, or that as some claim it is inescapably linked to biological difference (see Chapter 12 below).

Pro-family arguments

While early radical feminists were extremely hostile to the family, Choderow and Dinnerstein attacked the current sexual division of labour rather than the family as such. Other feminists have recently positively defended traditional values and roles (see Stacey, 1986, for a critical assessment of such theories). Thus Germaine Greer, whose earlier *The Female Eunuch* (1970) had done much to popularise radical feminist ideas, argued in 1984 in favour of the kind of extended family to be found in southern Italy and India: 'The Family offers the paradigm for female collectivity; it shows us women cooperating to dignify their lives, to heighten each other's labour . . . growing in real love and sisterhood' (Greer, 1984, p. 241). Elshtain similarly defends traditional 'womanly values' to be found within the family and insists that stable family life is an essential prerequisite for a civilised society: 'Not every neglected and abused child becomes a Charles Manson [a notorious mass murderer], but every Charles Manson was an abused and neglected child' (Elshtain, 1981, p. 332). She therefore objects both to collective childcare, which she sees as a form of neglect, and attempts to politicise family life or to devalue nurturing and domestic skills. Others have argued that traditional family structures did allow women a certain degree of control and autonomy, but that this is now being eroded and undermined by the state (Stacey and Price, 1981); yet others see the family as an essential bastion against class or race oppression, a part of life in which non-capitalist relationships survive and emotional needs are met (Humphries, 1982).

A problem with all of this is that it ignores the power relationships that exist both within the family and in the wider society of which it is a part. It tends to confirm women's confinement to the 'private' realm and hence their economic dependency and exclusion from public decision-making, it denies that violence, emotional manipulation and sexual exploitation may be as typical of family life as love and mutual support, and it does not even consider the possible negative effects of the traditional female monopoly of parenting. It does have the advantage of rejecting the uncritical adoption of male values and the devaluation of skills and attributes traditionally associated with women. The danger, however, remains that this traditional association will be confirmed as 'natural', inevitable and desirable, and that it will be used by anti-feminists as an excuse for a rigid gender division of labour that combines veneration of women's alleged qualities with a refusal to allow these to be 'corrupted' by public power, free choice or financial reward.

Despite its problems, the pro-family approach can usefully caution us against seeing 'the family' as an unchangingly oppressive entity which all feminists must automatically reject. Clearly the family has different meanings for different groups, and it cannot be isolated from its wider social context; it may help determine other social institutions but it is also partly determined by them.

Patriarchy and reproduction

Reproductive technology

Although many of her conclusions are out of line with current feminist thinking, the most notorious radical feminist analysis of reproduction remains Shulamith Firestone's *The Dialectic of Sex* (first published 1970, reference here to the 1979 edition). In this, Firestone argues that it is their role as reproducers that has handicapped women over the centuries and made possible men's patriarchal power: 'The heart of women's oppression is her childbearing and child-rearing role.' It is, she says, this biological reality rather than economic structures that forms the material basis for the most fundamental division in society, that between men and women. She therefore attempts to rewrite the Marxist theory of history, combining it with what she sees as the positive aspects of Freudian analysis, and substituting 'reproduction' for 'production' and 'sex class' for 'economic class', so that

> The sexual-reproductive organisation of society always furnishes the real basis, starting from which we can alone work out the ultimate explanation of the whole superstructure of economic, judicial and political institutions as well as of the religious, philosophical and other ideas of a given period.

Although rooted in nature, this biological basis is not unchanging. With the development of effective contraception and new reproductive technology, the possibility exists for the first time of breaking the link with biology and freeing women from their reproductive role, and she sees future artificial reproduction outside the womb as the basis for women's liberation. Such liberation will not, however, be the automatic consequence of the new technologies, for men's interest in maintaining patriarchy will continue, and the new technology, especially fertility control, may be used against women to reinforce the entrenched system of exploitation. Women therefore constitute an oppressed class which must rise up and seize control of the means of reproduction (which includes the social institutions of child-bearing and child-rearing as well as the new technologies), with the ultimate goal of eliminating not just male privilege but the sex distinction itself, so that 'genital differences between human beings would no longer matter culturally'. She assumes that this will be accompanied by a proletarian revolution which will eliminate social class and, through the use of cybernetics, make possible the elimination of labour itself; it is, however, the women's revolution that she sees as the ultimate human revolution, for this will end not just a particular form of power, but the psychology of power itself (*Dialectic*, 1979, pp. 73, 21 and 19).

As a political programme, such sweeping and grandiose proposals are clearly inadequate, and Firestone offers no suggestions as to how or when her revolutions are to occur, how they interact with each other and how feminists should start organising. She also fails to disentangle the biological and social aspects of childbirth and child-rearing, and her whole theoretical framework has been attacked as confused and simplistic (see, in particular, O'Brien, 1981). Nevertheless, the central idea that a feminist theory of women's history and oppression must start with human reproduction and that modern technology may be the basis of liberation, is shared by a number of writers. For example, Mary O'Brien in *The Politics of Reproduction* (1981) argues that reproduction is not an unchanging biological fact, but a process related to human consciousness and the basis of human society. From this perspective, the two key moments of human history are the first early discovery of paternity, and the modern contraceptive technology which has for the first time made possible the rational control of reproduction. Both of these are 'world historical events', which 'create a transformation in human consciousness of human relations with the natural world' and change the whole structure of society. Most of human history has occurred between these two events, and has been characterised by a male supremacy that is in fact based on men's *failure* to establish absolute control over reproduction: 'The social relations of reproduction are relations of dominance precisely because at the heart of the doctrine of potency lies the intransigent impotency of uncertainty . . .'. Now however 'The institutions of patriarchy are vulnerable because the Age of Contraception has changed the *process* of reproduction, and the social relations of reproduction must therefore undergo transformation' (O'Brien, 1981, pp. 189, 22, 121 and 62). Badinter too sees contraceptive technology as of extraordinary importance. Although she argues that patriarchy has been in gradual decline for the last two centuries, she says that within the last twenty years women have won the right to control their own fertility and that this has dealt the coup de grace to male power, making possible the creation of a whole new world order in which men and women increasingly come to resemble each other, and in which the age-old sexual division of labour is being abandoned for the first time in the whole of human history (Badinter, 1989).

Clearly modern contraception and reproductive technology have already had a major effect on the lives of many women. The ability to plan and control fertility has a potentially liberating effect, and has made possible a kind of freedom undreamed of by earlier generations. However the real choices available to women are also constrained by economic, social and political circumstances and by prevailing ideologies and moralities, and in a patriarchal society new developments are more likely to be used to control than to liberate women; they are also particularly likely to be abused in relation to poor, black or third world women, who may face forced sterilisation or be the unwitting guinea pigs for contraceptive experiments. Therefore although feminists have increasingly come to see free access to contraception and abortion as key feminist demands, some have also come to understand their potential dangers, arguing that they can endanger women's health and lead to an increase in sexual exploitation, and that they may be used to limit the reproductive capacities of women deemed 'unfit' to become mothers (blacks, the poor, the single, lesbians, the mentally subnormal . . .). Similarly, although modern medicine can greatly decrease the risks involved in pregnancy and childbirth, it can also become unnecessarily interventionist, and involve a transfer of power from female friends, relations and midwives to male doctors, while the mother herself may be unable to participate actively in the birth of her own child. Recent developments in reproductive technology have also, it is argued, been used against women to consolidate male power and make patriarchy for the first time absolute: 'Here is man's control of the awesome power of woman; the last stronghold of nature which he can finally dominate' (Arditti, 1984, p. 265). Thus access to AID (artificial insemination by donor) or IVF (in vitro fertilisation) programmes may be limited to those the authorities consider 'respectable' and all forms of surrogate motherhood are likely to involve the exploitation of poor or third world women, while the social conditions that may drive women to see pregnancy as their only source of worth or fulfilment remain unexamined. Even more sinister, pre-birth diagnosis of sex had led in some circumstances to selective abortion of female foetuses, and some writers fear that this and other developments mean that women may ultimately become dispensable, or that 'there will be a new kind of holocaust, as unimaginable now as the Nazi one before it happened . . . men will finally have the means to create and control the kind of women they want . . . There will be domestics, sex prostitutes, and reproductive prostitutes' (Dworkin, 1983, p. 151; see also Corea, 1985, and Stanworth, 1987; for fictional explorations of the possible effects of reproductive technology, see Fairbairns, 1979, and Piercy, 1979).

All this is a far cry from Firestone's belief in the liberating possibilities of artificial wombs, and suggests that in a patriarchal society 'seizing the means of reproduction' might be a neat reformulation of Marx, but that it can have little practical meaning. Once again, the issue must be related to other areas of patriarchal control, and the struggle over reproductive rights must be fought in this context, rather than isolated as a simple cause of oppression or key to liberation. This means that the whole area of contraception, childbirth and the new reproductive technologies can be seen as yet another site in which power is exercised but in which it can also be resisted. The outcome of such struggle is crucially important, but it cannot be simply determined, for it is tied in with power relations elsewhere.

Mothering, sexual difference and eco-feminism

For some feminists, the central problem with Firestone's analysis is not simply her naive assumption that reproductive technology can be readily used by women, but the underlying belief that pregnancy, childbirth and child-rearing are essentially humiliating and oppressive activities from which women should be liberated. On this Firestone (who was heavily influenced by de Beauvoir) is quite explicit. Pregnancy, she insists, is *not* a fulfilling and creative experience but 'the temporary deformation of the body of the individual for the sake of the species', while childbirth simply hurts ('like shitting a pumpkin', she was told by a friend), and with its attendant possessiveness and emotional manipulation, it is psychologically damaging to both mother and child (*Dialectic*, p 189). The problem with this analysis of course is that it is contradicted by the perceptions and experiences of those many women who have found joy and fulfilment in motherhood, and that, like much liberal feminism, it rests upon an uncritical acceptance of a scale of values which rates traditional male activities above those associated with women. It also fails to distinguish between conditions of mothering as they actually exist and as they might be. This point is elaborated by Adrienne Rich in *Of Woman Born* (1977), in which she argue that it is not the biological fact of giving birth that oppresses women, but the fact that they reproduce in a patriarchal society in which motherhood is seldom freely chosen and is controlled by men. This means that unlike much earlier feminist writing her book 'is not an attack on the family or on mothering, *except as defined and restricted under patriarchy*' (Rich, 1977, p. 14); although she agrees with Firestone's rejection of the current institutions of mothering, she also affirms the positive values associated with the experience of motherhood, and sees these as a potential source of power for women.

Rich's ideas have led to a more general re-evaluation of motherhood which Segal has described as 'maternal revivalism' (Segal, 1987, p. 145) and which is particularly influential in America. This strand of thought has long been present in the women's movement, and it sees motherhood and the care of the young as positive experiences to be celebrated and as giving rise to 'womanly values' to do with nurturing, co-operation and peace. These are contrasted with male attributes of self-interest, competition and aggression and have led to the development of 'eco feminist' theory. Such writers as Susan Griffin (*Woman and Nature*, 1984), Andrée Collard (*Rape of the Wild*, 1988) and Caldecott and Leland (eds, *Reclaim the Earth*, 1983) equate men's treatment of women with their treatment of nature, seeing both as the result of male domination and claiming that both have been raped, exploited, abused and hated; they insist that it is only women's values that can save the planet from ecological disaster, and that 'The identity and destiny of women and nature are merged. Accordingly, feminist values and principles directed towards the ending of the oppression of women are inextricably linked to ecological values and principles directed towards ending the oppression of nature' (Collard, 1988, p. 168). Such ideas have also been extremely influential in the peace movement, where women have explored new forms of opposition to militarism, most famously the women-only peace camp at Greenham Common in Britain.

The idea that women and men embody respectively the values of peace and war, nurturing and destruction, is not new, but is embedded in the assumptions of Western culture. It has been used both by feminists demanding that women's voices be heard and by anti-feminists arguing that women's essential purity must not be sullied by the sordid realities of public life. Many modern feminists are therefore extremely wary of alleging any natural differences in aptitude or moral outlook between the sexes, fearing that in a patriarchal society this will always be used to the detriment of women. Others argue that differences *do* exist, but that they are acquired rather than innate, and that what must be done is to ensure that women's present superior qualities are properly valued and acquired by men as well. As we saw in the previous section, Choderow and Dinnerstein argue that men's involvement in child-rearing could change the psyche of the adult male, and Gilligan claims that it is the experience of boys and girls that leads them to develop different moral outlooks (Gilligan, 1982; see Chapter 9 above). Ruddick also suggests that distinctive ways of thinking arise out of the work that mothers do, and she argues in particular that the values required for good 'maternal practice' are very different from those of military thought. Despite the accusations of some of her critics, she does not claim for women any natural moral superiority or pacifism arising out of their role as biological reproducers, nor does she deny that many women neglect or abuse their children and that the majority fall far short of any maternal ideal. Rather, she claims that maternal practice identifies certain values as desirable, so that 'Although mothers are not intrinsically peaceful, maternal practice is a "natural resource" for peace politics' (Ruddick, 1990, p. 157) which can be realised when it is combined with feminist politics and understanding. This means that in principle such values can be acquired by men, for she does not think that only women are capable of 'mothering'.

For some writers, however, alleged gender differences are innate. Thus Rich argues that women see the world differently from men because they experience it in relation to their own physicality (an idea developed by writers considered in the next chapter). Griffin similarly sees women as closer to nature than men, and therefore more able to express and identify with its needs, while Collard states that

> Nothing links the human animal and nature so profoundly as woman's reproductive system which enables her to share the experience of bringing forth and nourishing life with the rest of the living world. Whether or not she personally experiences biological mothering, it is in this that woman is most truly a child of nature and in this natural integrity lies the wellspring of her strength (Collard, 1988, p. 106).

One of the many problems with such biological determinism is that it contradicts current scientific thinking, which queries the idea of simple sexual dichotomies by showing that there exists a continuum of chromosomal, hormonal, genital and general anatomical differences (for a discussion of this see Oakley, 1972). It also flies in the face of much historical evidence, for women have frequently supported wars and the despoliation of nature while some men have opposed them. However empowering, it involves 'a-historical abstractions and unreflective celebrations' (Elshtain, 1987, p. 240), and there is a danger that it can lead not to planet-saving action but to fatalism or a retreat into separatism which leaves the structures of patriarchal power intact. As Bacchi has recently argued, insistence on or denial of significant sexual difference may also be based on a false dichotomy that distracts our attention from the need to challenge the dominant values of women *and* men (Bacchi, 1990). Therefore to say that women's traditional role involves life-enhancing values for which they should demand a public hearing is one thing; to say that women's biological attributes give them a monopoly of such values is quite another, for this would seem to confirm traditional roles and divisions, allowing men to continue to destroy the planet while celebrating alternative virtues within the home.

The issue of reproduction is one which profoundly divides radical feminists, and there seems little meeting point between those who see it as a barbaric relic of a lower state of human development from which women can now be liberated and those who insist that it embodies women's superior creativity and virtue. However, these divisions conceal a more general agreement that women's reproductive activities are politically significant and that men's attempts to control them have resulted in a loss of women's freedom which must be resisted. Attempts by women to reassert control over this area of their lives is therefore an agreed radical feminist goal. Those who view motherhood in a negative way may stress the importance of freely available contraception and abortion while others focus on the right of all women to have children if they wish, but both groups are united by the belief that the bearing of children is not a purely private affair, but one which reflects the power relationships between the sexes. This means in turn that the struggle for control over reproduction cannot be divorced from struggle in other areas: as legislative battles over abortion and the uses of new reproductive technology show, it is clearly connected with the control of state power, and economic realities and the structure of family life obviously limit or expand women's reproductive freedoms in practice; the issue is also integrally related to the issues of sexuality and the control of knowledge and values to be considered in the next section and in Chapter 12.

Patriarchy, sexuality and violence

As we have seen in previous chapters, the idea that sexuality is not simply an individual matter but one that is bound up with power structures in society is not new to feminist theory, although it is contrary to the assumptions of mainstream political thought.

Some earlier writers stressed the liberating effects of a freely expressed sexuality, but the majority of feminists have held a much more negative view, equating sexuality with male violence, disease, loss of autonomy and 'animal instincts' and advocating chastity for both sexes. Many modern radical feminists share this hostility to heterosexual intercourse, which they see as inherently oppressive to women; lesbianism rather than chastity is however now the more commonly preferred solution.

For some writers, existing sexuality is a symptom of patriarchal society, the product of a world in which men have authority, women are economically dependent and male needs and desires set the agenda in all spheres. Far from being 'natural', sexual behaviour becomes bound up with the idea of ownership, domination and submission, and is conditioned by a man-made culture in which pornography is all-pervasive, sexual violence is tolerated, women are treated as sex objects and different moral codes exist for men and women. Prostitution therefore becomes a symbol of male power which is both a product of patriarchal sexual relationships and a means of legitimising them, for through prostitution 'the male sex-right is publicly affirmed, and men gain public acknowledgement as women's sexual masters' (Pateman, 1988, p. 208). In this context, sex and love between men and women cannot exist on a basis of equality, but are likely to involve at worst rape and violent humiliation, at best emotional dependency and the neglect of women's sexual needs. Heterosexual relationships must therefore be approached with extreme caution, and feminists must both assert their own needs and challenge the pornographic culture in which they live; lesbianism must also be made more visible and available as a legitimate, or indeed preferable, sexual option. The demand for sexual autonomy and fulfilment is therefore seen as part of the general political struggle against patriarchy, which is both reinforced and reflected by current attitudes and practices.

For other writers, sexuality is not simply one aspect of patriarchal domination, but the main political problem confronting feminists. This 'problem' itself has been seen in three main ways: for some, the denial of sexual freedom involves a 'forced heterosexuality' that is inherently oppressive and unsatisfying to women; for others, it is the violent nature of sexual oppression, especially as manifested in pornography and rape, that is important; a third strand argues that under patriarchy all forms of domination become eroticised, so that male power is inextricably entangled with sexuality.

The attack on heterosexuality

In the early days of the modern women's movement, lesbianism was not a visible option for many feminists, who frequently shared the dominant feelings of suspicion, fear and hostility towards it. Since then much has changed. The publication of Anna Koedt's *The Myth of the Vaginal Orgasm* (1970), which argued that female sexual pleasure was located in the clitoris and that satisfaction therefore did not require penile penetration, created a great stir in some feminist circles. The resulting demand for the 'right to orgasm' led some women to attempt to renegotiate sexual practices with their male partners, but for others it suggested that men could be dispensed with and heterosexual relationships abandoned. For some, the issue was not simply one of sexual pleasure, for heterosexuality itself was declared to be a *political* institution rather than a natural expression of sexual desire (see Rich, 1980); as such it was imposed upon women for the benefit of men, a means of dividing and controlling women and ensuring that they served men domestically and emotionally as well as sexually. From this perspective, 'male domination of the female body is the basic material reality of women's lives; and all struggle for dignity and self-determination is rooted in the struggle for actual control of one's body' (Dworkin, 1981, p. 205). The rejection of heterosexuality is therefore not just a matter of personal sexual orientation, but a political act that strikes at the very heart of patriarchy, and 'Woman-identification is a source of energy, a potential springboard of female power, violently curtailed and wasted under the institution of heterosexuality' (Rich, 1980, p. 657). The British 1978 National Women's Liberation Conference in Birmingham therefore passed a resolution making 'the right to define our sexuality' *the* over-riding question of the women's movement (the hostility engendered during this debate meant that this was in fact the last such conference).

This analysis has led some radical feminists to the idea of 'politically correct' sexual activity which precludes all relationships with men, for all heterosexual intercourse is seen as a form of rape that is irretrievably bound up with the system of domination and oppression to which it is central. This view is well illustrated in a pamphlet issued by the Leeds Revolutionary Feminist Group:

> Only in the system of oppression that is male supremacy does the oppressor actually invade and colonise the interior of the body of the oppressed . . . Penetration is an act of great symbolic significance by which the oppressor enters the body of the oppressed . . . its function and effect is the punishment and control of women . . . every act of penetration for a woman is an invasion which undermines her confidence and saps her strength.

According to this approach, the only feminist solution is therefore to withdraw from sexual involvement with men: 'Men are the enemy. Heterosexual women are collaborators with the enemy' (in Evans, 1982, pp. 64–5; see also the extract in Evans from Jill Johnson's 1974 *Lesbian Nation*, and Jeffries, 1990). In this context 'political lesbianism' becomes the solution for women who identify emotionally and politically with other women and who have withdrawn from men, but who do not engage in actual sexual activity with women (see also Rich, 1980, for the idea of a 'lesbian continuum' which expands the concept of lesbianism beyond that of genital sexual activity).

The idea that sexuality is the most important problem for women and that its solution involves a rejection of all heterosexual activity has been bitterly attacked by other feminists such as Lynne Segal, who asks 'How could such a concrete reductionism, such phallic obsession, have got such a hold on feminism?' (Segal, 1987, p. 97). This 'obsession' is often seen as evidence of radical feminism's narrowly bourgeois horizons and its blindness to other forms of oppression. Marxists and socialists in particular argue that it is only from the perspective of a white middle-class woman that sexual lifestyles and the pursuit of orgasm can appear as central political issues; for women struggling for economic or physical survival, such questions can only be frivolous luxuries which distract energies from the more important issues of economic exploitation and class struggle, while separatism requires a degree of financial independence simply not available to most working-class women.

It is also said that the concept of 'politically correct' sexual behaviour involves an account of heterosexual intercourse which denies the experience of many women who do find it both physically and emotionally pleasurable. The equation of all intercourse with rape is particularly dubious, as it not only denies all possibility of reciprocal tenderness, love and desire between men and women, but by classifying all heterosexual acts together it conceals the horror of actual rape. The idea that women can only be the passive victims of male lust is also suspect: thus Segal reports that it certainly did not feel like that to her during the time in the 1960s 'when I rarely slept alone and devoted much of my leisure time to bedding my favourite man of the moment' (although she admits that her activities earned her more by way of status than physical pleasure, and cautions that 'seducing one's professor was usually the most boring experience of all, and not to be repeated' [Segal, 1987, pp. 77–8]). It may be that current sexual orientations are socially determined and artificially exclude a whole range of possibilities, and that under patriarchy heterosexuality is indeed a dangerous practice; however the idea that it is essentially, inevitably and eternally oppressive is one that only a minority of feminists hold.

For some radical feminists, the advocacy of political lesbianism and separatism is tied in with the ideas of female superiority discussed in the previous section, as well as with the belief that female relationships will be free from the exploitation and manipulation that are said to characterise heterosexual affairs. However power relations are not to be solved so readily, and although some women have doubtless found fulfilment and emotional tranquillity in female partnerships or communal households, others have found that women-only relationships may also involve jealousy, pain and domination. There is also an ongoing debate amongst lesbian feminists as to the political correctness of lesbian pornography and sado-masochistic practices. Such activities are an anathema to those who see them as aping the worst aspects of male sexuality; they are defended by those who see them as a matter of purely private preference, but such a defence makes little sense in the context of the radical feminist insistence that the personal is political. Radical feminist analysis therefore points to agreement with the statement of the black lesbian writer Audre Lorde that

Whatever we do takes place in a social context and has an effect upon other human beings. To degrade someone, even with that person's expressed consent, is to *endorse* the degradation of persons. It is to affirm that the abuse of persons is *acceptable* (quoted in Tong, 1989, p. 122; for a discussion of the issue see Eisenstein, 1984, ch. 12).

The very fact that such debates can take place, however, should be evidence of the dangers of a too simplistic celebration of the joys of sisterhood, and suggests that the problems of power cannot be escaped simply by withdrawing from men.

A radical separatist position also involves a number of practical problems. Most obviously there are extreme difficulties for lesbians who wish to become mothers; here the question of lesbian custody of children and of access to artificial insemination and in vitro fertilisation programmes is a matter of current political concern. As this example shows, the possibilities for 'alternative' lifestyles can be limited by the existing authorities, so that the attempt at total withdrawal from society is likely to be replaced to some degree by struggle within it. The belief that there is for the foreseeable future a total and unresolvable conflict between all men and all women is ultimately a highly pessimistic one, offering little by way of long-term hope or a feasible programme for change. Nevertheless, the analysis does alert us to the risks that may be currently involved in heterosexual relationships and the ways in which these may be used to weaken and manipulate women. The idea that women can be liberated from the need to please men and should not be judged in terms of their ability to attract them is also an empowering one, and the breakdown in many modern industrial societies of traditional patterns of marriage means that for many women life without a permanent male partner is already a reality, although it is often accompanied by poverty; some ideas of female autonomy and independence may therefore be less utopian or class biased than the socialist criticism suggests. Such ideas are moreover not new, but echo those of the seventeenth-century writer Mary Astell discussed in Chapter 1; here it should perhaps be noted that she said of her own advice to reject marriage and establish female communities, that if all women did as she suggested, then 'There's an End to the Human Race'.

Sexual violence, pornography and patriarchal control

The ideas discussed above suggest that sex with men is oppressive because it is unfulfilling, it is not freely chosen and it is used as a means of dividing and controlling women. For other feminist writers, it is more explicitly linked to male *violence* and the idea that patriarchy, like all other systems of power, rests ultimately on force. As Kate Millett says

> We are not accustomed to associate patriarchy with force. So perfect is its system of socialisation, so complete the general assent to its values, so long and so universally has it prevailed in human society, that it scarcely seems to require violent implementation.

Nevertheless, she argues, 'Control in patriarchal society would be imperfect, even inoperable, unless it had the rule of force to rely upon, both in emergencies and as an ever-present instrument of intimidation' (*Politics*, p. 43); such violence may be institutionalised in the law, but it is also directly expressed, and frequently takes the form of sexual violence, particularly rape.

The socially dominant view of rape is that this is an extremely rare act carried out by a tiny minority of abnormal and deviant men, an unfortunate individual experience suffered by a small number of women. Feminists have however recently challenged this orthodoxy by pointing out that clinical tests show that, with rare exceptions, rapists appear to be mentally 'healthy' and normal and that sexual violence in general and rape in particular are far more common than had previously been thought. They point out that, contrary to popular mythology, most rapists are in fact known to their victims. They have helped draw a reluctant public's attention to the scale of sexual abuse of children and they have re-defined sexual violence to include such 'benign' forms as obscene phone calls and sexual harassment in the workplace. This means that rape is not seen as a discrete and isolated experience but as part of a whole culture in which the threat of sexual violence dominates women's lives; Catherine MacKinnon has recently claimed that over 90 per cent of American women have been sexually assaulted or harassed at some point in their lives and that this represents 'the effectively unrestrained and systematic sexual

aggression of one-half of the population against the other half'
(MacKinnon, 1989a, p. 332; see also Lederer, 1980).

Such aggression is, many feminists argue, to do with power
rather than sex; it is a manifestation of men's hatred and contempt
for women rather than of ungovernable lust, and the fear which
it engenders in women is central to their subordination and control
by men. This means that rape is a *political* act, and that although
of course not all men actually rape, all men benefit from the
sexual violence that curtails women's lives and leads them to seek
the protection of one man against all others. The most extreme
expressions of this perspective are provided by Susan Brownmiller
and Jalna Hanmer. The former has claimed that rape 'is nothing
more or less than a conscious process of intimidation by which *all
men* keep *all women* in a state of fear' (Brownmiller, 1977, p.
15), while the latter states that

> The fact that many husbands do not beat their wives, and many men
> do not attack women on the streets . . . is not proof that wife-beating
> and other assaults are irregular, unsystematic practices . . . but merely
> that it is not necessary to do so in order to maintain the privileges of
> the superior group (Hanmer, 1978, p. 229).

This view means that the current policies and attitudes towards
rape which so outrage other feminists are in fact only to be
expected; state connivance or indifference, the myth that victims
are 'asking for it' and the tendency to treat it as a joke are all
seen as evidence of male interest in perpetuating a system of
domination based on fear.

For many, a cornerstone of this system is pornography. At the
most straightforward level, it is argued that the existence and
availability of violent pornography leads to sexual violence against
women, so that 'pornography is the theory; rape is the practice'
(see *Pornography and Sexual Violence: Evidence of the Links*). It
is however not simply that men are led to imitate what they see
depicted, but that they are desensitised to acts of violence and
that the pornographic lie that women enjoy pain, humiliation and
domination is heard while women's voices are silenced; women
too therefore internalise a false view of their own sexuality (Griffin, 1981; Dworkin, 1981 and 1988). Feminist arguments are not
on the whole directed against sexual explicitness as such, but
against the association of this with violence and domination (for

a distinction between erotica and pornography, see Steinem, 1984; she argues that the former, which involves mutual pleasure, is acceptable, but that the latter, which is based on force, violence and power is not). They have also been extended to object to any depiction of women as passive and sexually available, claiming that the distinctions between 'hard' and 'soft' pornography and the more general portrayal of women in our society are false ones that conceal the all-pervasiveness of pornography throughout our culture.

Andrea Dworkin is one of the best known and most determined of radical feminist anti-pornography writers and campaigners. She sees pornography as both symptom and cause of the male hatred and contempt for women that has led to their systematic abuse over the centuries, and that affects their behaviour and treatment in all areas of life, so that 'at the heart of the female condition is pornography; it is the ideology that is the source of all the rest' (Dworkin, 1983, p. 223). With Catherine MacKinnon, she succeeded in having anti-pornography ordinances passed in two American cities (Minneapolis and Indianapolis). These would have enabled individual women to bring a legal action against the producers or distributors of pornographic material on a number of grounds including that of violating their civil rights by degrading women as a group and causing them to be treated as second class citizens. Other feminists have, however, opposed such attempts at censorship, arguing that they lead to an unhealthy alliance with the right-wing 'moral majority', that they are likely to be used against sexually explicit feminist material, that they involve a dangerous increase in the power of the state and that, because of the problems to do with definition and provability, they will be unworkable. Partly because of pressure from feminist anti-censorship groups, the MacKinnon-Dworkin ordinances were declared unconstitutional by the Supreme Court (For a discussion of the arguments involved see Tong 1989, pp. 111–21 and Chester and Dickey (eds), 1988).

The radical feminist analysis of sexual violence and pornography is an important advance upon earlier approaches as it reveals both the extent of these and the underlying power structures to which they are related. Most feminists would not however accept the idea that all men *consciously* collude or participate in sexual violence, that such violence is biologically determined by male hormones or that men can have no motivation for helping to end it. The possibility is therefore opened up for achieving change through direct action, legislation or by challenges to prevailing sexual orthodoxies that seek to delegitimise many current practices. Such attempts must be based on a realistic assessment of the interests and influences involved, but they need not always involve writing off the possibility of any genuine support from men, or of achieving changes in male behaviour.

A rather different and more pessimistic analysis is provided by Catherine MacKinnon (MacKinnon, 1983 and 1989a). She rejects the feminist orthodoxy that rape is an expression of violence rather than sexual desire, by arguing that in a patriarchal society it is impossible to disentangle the two. The gender identity and sexuality of both men and women are she says learned in a context of domination and submission from which they become inseparable. Sexual pleasure for women is therefore masochistic, while for men power is eroticised. Indeed, she suggests that men's prime motive for oppressing women may be the sexual satisfaction derived from domination: 'Part of the male interest in keeping women down is the fact that it gets men up' (MacKinnon, 1989, p. 335). In this context pornography does not simply create oppressive sexual needs, it reflects them; it gives men what they already want, and this is

> Women bound, women battered, women tortured, women humiliated, women degraded and defiled, women killed – or, to be fair to the soft core – women sexually accessible, have-able, there for them, wanting to be taken and used, with perhaps just a little of light bondage (MacKinnon, 1989, pp. 326–7).

Although there is she says no 'irreducible essence' to sex, which is a social construct, it is hard to see how such pervasive oppression can be challenged or the vicious circle of domination and masochism broken into, rooted as they have become in the very psyche of every man and woman. This means that MacKinnon's own anti-pornography campaigns are hard to explain (why does she not submit with pleasure to her own humiliation?) and appear more as an act of faith than a realistic basis for significant change, for her position leaves little room for optimism.

It is not necessary to accept the most extreme radical feminist claims, to see that sexual violence and pornography may be important aspects of patriarchal power, and to believe that women's sexuality has become distorted or curtailed. To see this as the sole or prime cause of patriarchy is however to be guilty of a crude reductionism that ignores the interaction of sexuality with other patriarchal structures and systems of domination: thus for example, women's economic dependency upon men may be the cause as well as the consequence of their sexual subordination, while the growth of pornography into a multi-billion dollar industry could only have been possible in a particular economic context. The analysis can also imply an over-general and ahistorical perspective which obscures changes in the nature of patriarchy and the different ways it is experienced by different groups of women. Thus a modern student pressured into 'permissive' sexual activity is sexually oppressed in a very different way from the 'respectable' nineteenth-century woman whose sexuality was entirely denied, or the slave repeatedly raped by her owner. Similarly, the whole area of sexuality and violence may increase or decrease in importance as patriarchy changes: here Ferguson argues that the recent increase in pornography reflects 'a shift from private to public patriarchy which requires a more collective, impersonal, male control of women's bodies' (Ferguson, 1989, p. 115), while Walby similarly sees modern sexual permissiveness as involving an increase in sexual dependency on men in general, although attachment to any individual man has declined (Walby, 1990, p. 124). Many feminists of course also dislike the total hostility to male sexuality shown by some radical feminists, and the denial that this may sometimes be expressed in terms favourable to women, while lesbian separatism does not seem to provide a political programme or a long-term solution for the majority of women. In general, sexuality and male violence seem to be means of patriarchal control that can be contested directly, but which cannot be isolated from other areas of women's experience. Thus struggles over legislation, economic dependency, family organisation and reproductive rights are clearly related to demands for sexual autonomy and the control of sexual violence; the claim that women are denied knowledge of their own sexuality and that they lack the language in which to express it is also tied to the arguments discussed in the next chapter, in which the claim that knowledge and language are also areas of patriarchal control and domination is examined.

12

Modern radical feminism: knowledge, language and patriarchy

'Man-made language' and feminist challenges

For many radical feminists, the basis of women's oppression lies not in social organisation or physical domination, but in a male control of culture, religion, language and knowledge that limits the ways in which we can think and causes patriarchal assumptions to be internalised by women as well as by men. As we saw in Chapter 9, feminists have challenged the claims of philosophy and political theory to embody reason and universality, arguing that these are based on a male paradigm that ignores or devalues experiences and ways of thinking associated with women, so that 'objectivity' in fact means the subjective perception of men. The whole of cultural and academic life is therefore seen by some feminists as a political arena in which male biases must be exposed and female knowledge asserted: for example, feminist literary criticism reveals the assumptions and power structures embodied in literary texts, while feminist historians are reclaiming women's history and proclaiming women's right to knowledge of their past.

At one level, this approach is most clearly expressed in the work of Dale Spender, who argues that women's knowledge and understanding of their own situation has been suppressed over the centuries, so that 'every 50 years women have to re-invent the wheel' (Spender, 1983a, p. 13). In *Women of Ideas (and what men have done to them)*, she documents part of the long and forgotten heritage of feminist ideas, arguing that the discovery of our feminist foremothers is both exciting and empowering, and in *For the Record*, she provides an account of recent theories which she sees as part of a feminist struggle to prevent these too from 'disappearing'. In *Man-Made Language* she argues that male control is also exercised at the level of the very language we use, for this is not a neutral medium of communication, but involves a way of structuring our thought that is based on men's perceptions and cannot accommodate women's experiences. Thus for example there is no word to describe the activities of the 'non-working' mother whose time- and energy-consuming chores therefore disappear from public consciousness. Further problems arise from the 'male includes female – sometimes' rule in many languages, whereby words such as 'he', 'his' and 'man' can be understood as containing their female equivalent; this reinforces the view that man is the norm and woman a kind of 'optional extra', and there is empirical evidence to suggest that people do 'think male' when confronted with such labels as 'economic man', even though this can in principle mean 'economic people'.

Such analysis finds it unsurprising that Friedan could only describe the discontents of American housewives as 'the problem that has no name' (see Chapter 9 above), and *labelling* their situation becomes a vital first step for feminists seeking to understand and change it. Terms like 'sexism' or 'sexual harassment' are therefore not simply 'feminist jargon', but involve a redefinition of reality from a female perspective. For example, many women today will say they dislike pornography because it degrades women; twenty years ago such language was not available, and as it seemed that pornography could only be opposed from the standpoint of sexual puritanism, much of the unease which it generated went unarticulated.

Other writers take the idea of challenging male knowledge and use of language further by creating alternative methodologies and linguistic structures which, they claim, escape the confines of male logic and enable us to reach a higher and fuller understanding of the world. Andrea Dworkin, in an Afterword to her first book, *Woman Hating*, records that she had wanted to have the text printed in lower case letters only, in the belief that

> reading a text which violates standard forms forces one to change mental sets in order to read . . . to permit writers to use form to violate conventions just might permit writers to develop forms which could teach people to think differently: not to think different things, but to think in different ways (Dworkin, 1974, p. 202).

Her publisher was, however, unconvinced, and she was not permitted to make this feminist experiment. Robin Morgan has also attempted to experiment with new forms: in *The Anatomy of Freedom* she combines conventional academic argument and grammatical forms with poetry, private correspondence, imaginary dialogues and discursive asides. Eschewing the trappings of formal logic and escaping at times into the wilder shores of fantasy, she claims to be providing an open-ended approach in which the disparate elements are complementary parts of a multi-dimensional whole.

The most famous of such feminist practitioners of new forms is however Mary Daly. In *Beyond God the Father*, *Gyn/Ecology* and *Pure Lust* she develops a new language and mode of writing and thinking which she sees as leading to a new female consciousness and culture that is remote from and inaccessible to men. Men have, she says, stolen the power of *naming* from women, who must therefore fight against the deceptions of language and logic, the 'gang-rape of minds as well as bodies' (Daly, 1973, p. 9), and by inventing new words and forms discover new ways of being. This involves an inversion of dominant values and a dramatic assertion of the power of Hags, Crones, Harpies, Furies, Amazons and Spinsters to resist the power of men by flying above and beyond their understanding. Eisenstein calls *Gyn/Ecology* 'An extraordinary synthesis of poetry, history, philosophy, literary criticism and diatribe' (Eisenstein, 1984, p. 107), and the power, wit and imagination of her work is undeniable. However it rests upon a number of dubious assertions: that women are wholly good while men are wholly bad, that women's energies must be directed towards an inner transformation rather than an engagement with power structures, that most women (including in particular 'successful' feminists) are collaborators with the existing order and that only a small elite can or deserve to be free. Daly has therefore been accused of advocating a withdrawal from all practical struggle into a woman-only culture to which only a few middle-class women could hope to have access. Like the other writers discussed above, but to a greater degree, she is said to want a purely idealist solution which would leave material conditions and bases of power unchanged, and to accept a false dichotomy between male and female culture that ignores shared values, changes over time and divisions between women. Such possible shortcomings must be disentangled from the underlying analysis of language and knowledge as sites of political struggle; this need not imply that these are the causes or most important aspects of patriarchy, but simply recognition that although new ways of thinking may not in themselves end women's oppression, they must constitute an important weapon against it.

Post-modernism and feminist thought

The above writers' arguments rest upon a relatively straight-forward analysis that can be readily understood even when it is disagreed with. Feminist attacks on philosophy and man-made language have however also coincided with a crisis in 'male-stream' philosophy and with developments in linguistic and psychoanalytic analysis that seem to some to offer radically new ways of understanding that may be of use to feminists. These new theories involve a plethora of overlapping schools of thought which can be highly confusing to the layperson, and which have been variously labelled as post-structuralist, discourse, decon-structionist, psychoanalytic, linguistic or 'French' theory; although they do not constitute a unified body of thought, all of these are sometimes subsumed under the general heading of *post-modern-ism* (for discussion from a feminist perspective, see Alcoff, 1988; Cameron, 1990; Duchen, 1986; Flax, 1986 and 1990; Grosz, 1990; Lovibond, 1989; Nicholson, 1990; Ragland-Sullivan, 1991; Saw-icki, 1991; Tong, 1989; Tress, 1988; Weedon, 1987).

At first sight, post-modernism seems to have much in common with some aspects of radical feminist thought. It sees 'modernism' as a movement that started with the Enlightenment's celebration of reason, and it rejects the idea since dominant in Western culture that everything is in principle knowable through human reason, and that society can be ordered in accordance with reason, knowl-edge and justice. As we have seen throughout this book, these Enlightenment ideals inspired many earlier generations of femin-ists and remain central to liberal feminism today. The whole concept of reason has, however, been attacked by modern radical feminists (see Chapter 9 above). For post-modernists, the search for certainty is seen as misguided, for truth, they say, can only be provisional; the search for a single all-encompassing theory is therefore rejected in principle, as is the very possibility of objectivity. Western philosophy's quest for truth and certainty (described as logocentricism) is therefore abandoned, and is seen as the product of a particular historical era that is becoming inappropriate in a post-modern society that is increasingly characterised by fragmentation, diversity and diffuseness in all spheres of life. Existing theories, particularly Marxism, which claim to embody certainty and objectivity are rejected as totalitarian; here it is not simply the conclusions that are rejected, but the quest for truth itself.

This critical position is derived from developments in psychoanalytic and linguistic theory associated in particular with Derrida, Foucault and Lacan. These male writers argue that because reality is mediated by language and experience it is different for each of us; there can be no impersonal, objective 'God's eye view', only particular individual subjectivities. Here language is of crucial importance, for it not only determines how we see the world, but how we exist and who we are; the meaning of words is not however fixed and unchanging, but is constantly being modified, and therefore so too is our subjectivity or sense of self and our perception of the world. In this context, Foucault further argues, disputes over the meanings of words are critical in determining social consciousness, and are tied in with actual power structures, so that the 'discourses' of dominant groups will be privileged, although they may be challenged or subverted by marginal groups. This view would seem to fit well with the feminist ideas discussed earlier in this section, and for a part of the French women's movement the struggle over language and for ways of defining and articulating womanhood that have not been formulated by men is seen as a key issue. From this perspective, we cannot get rid of patriarchy unless we can think as women; freedom from oppressive thought therefore becomes a prime goal, and experiments with language, speech and writing are central feminist activities.

However for such writers, of whom the most famous are probably Julia Kristeva, Luce Irigaray and Helene Cixous, male control over language is not simply a question of the meaning of words, but is central to all its structures. Lacan draws on psychoanalytic theory about the acquisition of gender identity to argue that this stage occurs when a child resolves the Oedipal complex and enters the 'Symbolic Order' of language, laws and social pressures. Because the meaning of language is constantly changing, the acquisition of subjectivity and sexual identity is never complete, and it is experienced differently by every woman. Sexual identity is therefore inherently precarious, and the term 'woman' itself is not a constant and unified category, but one that conceals the different subjectivities of all female persons. Nevertheless, the acquisition of gender identity is fundamentally different for boys and girls, for at the most basic level, beyond human consciousness or intervention, the Symbolic Order involves masculine structures which can never conceptualise the feminine, which is outside of and permanently excluded from 'phallic discourse', and therefore incapable of articulation. Some French feminists have accepted Lacan's starting-point, but argue that the feminine *can* be brought into an existence that challenges the male order and structures of thought (in this context, 'feminine' does not have the negative connotations usually attached to it in feminist theory). In particular, it is argued that the female body can give rise to specifically feminine ways of thinking that defy the logical forms and binary oppositions of 'phallogocentric' thought, and that are based on women's experience of sexual pleasure (*jouissance*) – for unlike men, women's sexual pleasure is said to be diffused throughout the body, giving rise to a plurality of experiences and sensations that cannot be comprehended within male discourse.

'French feminism' is certainly not a unified body of thought, and it is not restricted to this kind of analysis, which has been described by its opponents as elitist, intolerant and deliberately inaccessible; particular anger was generated amongst other feminist groups by the decision of the Psych et Po (Psychoanalyse et Politique) group with which Kristeva, Irigaray and Cixous have all at times been associated, to register for its own exclusive use the logo MLF (Mouvement de Libération des Femmes [Women's Liberation Movement]; see Duchen, 1986). There are also complex and deep-seated disagreements amongst these writers as to whether there is a pre-Oedipal condition and source of energy to which we can, through *jouissance*, return, whether there is an essential femininity based in biology and whether only women can in principle express themselves in 'feminine' ways. Nevertheless they are united by their insistence on the need to explore the relationships between language, sexuality and power and to develop 'non-phallogocentric' ways of thinking, sharing 'what seems a common desire to think nonbinary, nonoppositional thought, the kind that may have existed before Adam was given the power to name the animals' (Tong, 1989, p. 233).

There are a number of problems with these writers. In the first place, they tend at times to imply not only biological essentialism, but a sexual reductionism that lacks a social context, that ignores the fact that we also experience our bodies in non-sexual ways and that involves some questionable assertions about the inevitably limited nature of male sexuality; it also disregards the ways in which other social groups too may be disadvantaged in language. There are, moreover, problems in translating their conclusions into any kind of coherent political action. Not only do they imply that feminist practice should be critical or literary rather than directly political, but any kind of engagement with existing male structures is frequently rejected in favour of developing a separatist feminine discourse. Perhaps more fundamentally, post-modernism's stress on subjectivity can reduce everything to the level of the individual, so that any possibility of collective political action or understanding of what women share is lost; indeed some writers have rejected the terms 'woman', 'man' and 'feminist' as misleading labels that seek to fix and conceal the shifting, variable realities they claim to represent. Other critics claim that the post-modernist refusal to ask 'big' questions about the nature or desirability of social arrangements (on the grounds that there can be no objective answers) is politically convenient for those who have already been advantaged by the 'project of modernity', but who now rule all further questions of 'right' and 'justice' out of order. Thus Lovibond asks

> If there can be no systematic political approach to questions of wealth, power and labour, how can there be any effective challenge to a social order which distributes its benefits and burdens in a systematically unequal way between the sexes? (Lovibond, 1989, p. 22).

For such critics, post-modernism is an essentially conservative theory, that turns feminism from a subversive social movement into an inward-looking elite activity, and that in rejecting the possibility of wholesale transformation discredits all movements for social change. This means that, to use its own terms, post-modernism itself may be a discourse of power, imposing a particular world-view in the guise of rejecting all (like the Cretan who said 'all Cretans are liars', it seems to insist on the truth of the statement that 'there are no truths').

At its best, post-modernism can demonstrate how language and subjectivity are socially constructed and so open them up for change, and by stressing the specificity and partiality of all experience it can guard feminists against generalising about all women on the basis of white, middle-class western experience (see Nicholson, 1990). It can challenge the legitimacy of male perspectives and reveal the falsity of their claims for objectivity and universality; it can also show how power is constructed through discourse, how oppression works, and where resistance is possible. Such an approach is advocated throughout Chris Weedon's admirably lucid *Feminist Practice and Poststructuralist Theory*, in which she affirms that

> An understanding of how discourses of biological sex difference are mobilized, in a particular society, at a particular moment, is the first stage in intervening in order to initiate change

and concludes that

> It is a framework that can be applied to all forms of social and political practice. It is my hope in attempting to make this framework accessible that others will take it up and use it in the fight for change (Weedon, 1987, pp. 87 and 175).

At its worst, however, it constitutes an impenetrable jargon-ridden rhetoric of oppression that, by denying all validity to such concepts as 'right', 'justice' and 'reason' ends up with a total relativism that is unable to differentiate between freedom and slavery and that therefore denies legitimacy to feminist attempts to change society.

It would seem, therefore, that while it is important to recognise language and knowledge as sites of struggle, feminists must approach them with extreme caution. They must avoid being seduced by an esoteric idealism divorced from daily life and inaccessible to most women, and they must be wary of throwing out concepts of reason and justice in their entirety. It is important to develop new feminist theories that take women as their essential starting point and refuse to remain entrapped in the structures of male discourse. Nevertheless, as Weedon warns 'we cannot afford to abandon reason entirely to the interests of patriarchy. Reason, like experience, requires both deconstruction and reconstruction in the interests of feminism' (Weedon, 1987, p. 10).

It is clear that radical feminism offers a fundamental challenge to the whole of traditional political theory. Not only is this re-written with women and their oppression as the new focal point, but the nature of politics itself is re-defined as the public/private distinction is declared invalid and power is said to exist in the most intimate private relationships. Although this basic position brings together ideas that we have found scattered throughout earlier feminist writings, radical feminism is a very new theory, and many of its insights are embryonic rather than fully developed. Therefore although it offers exciting new possibilities, its propositions need to be treated with caution. In particular, it is essential to avoid simplistic explanations that seek to reduce the whole of women's oppression to a single cause, or that too readily generalise about the condition of *all* women in *all* societies in *all* historical epochs. The interdependency of all patriarchal structures must be recognised; in terms of feminist politics, this means that different forms of action can be seen as complementary rather than alternative, for changes in one structure may both determine and be determined by changes in others. To be effective, such action must be based upon a realistic assessment of power, through which the structures of patriarchy can be seen not as monolithically oppressive, but as arenas of struggle within which opportunities may exist and gains be won. It is also necessary to explore the relationships of patriarchy to other forms of inequality: women's struggles may have their own dynamic, but they do not exist in isolation, and ties of race and class may unite women with men, at the same time as their gender interests divide them.

If it develops in this kind of way, radical feminism may perhaps be synthesised with some aspects of other approaches to provide a more sophisticated theory than has hitherto been possible. Such a theory would continue to see women as central, but would explore the interrelationships between class, race and sex oppressions, and although it would be suspicious of liberal and humanitarian values it would not reject these out of hand. It would recognise the ubiquity of male power and men's interests in continuing present arrangements, but in distinguishing between the structures and agents of oppression it would see men as potential allies as well as adversaries. This would involve seeing men as persons motivated by values other than power who, as Thompson and Mill had argued in the nineteenth century, might find pleasure in equal companionship rather than domination, and who might even be on occasion amenable to considerations of 'right' or 'justice'. For radical separatists such proposals are anathema. For them, the differences and conflicts between women and men are not social constructs but based in biology; as such they are a permanent feature of human society, and the most that women can hope for is to create their own space within patriarchal society. This position represents a dead-end for political theory and action. However although it is clearly derived from the central principles of radical feminism, it is *not* the only ways in which these can be developed. The ideas discussed in the last three chapters cover an extremely wide area and do not point to easy solutions; they may however provide a starting-point for a theory that is both more comprehensive than any that has gone before and self-consciously aware of its own inevitable limitations.

13

Modern Marxist and socialist feminism

A central tenet of all forms of Marxist and socialist feminism is the belief that women's situation cannot be understood in isolation from its socio-economic context, and that any meaningful improvement in the lives of women requires that this context be changed. As we have seen in previous chapters, this approach goes back at least as far as the early nineteenth century, and socialist feminist ideas are to be found in all periods; many early writers and ideas have however disappeared from history and are only now being rediscovered. Marxism adds to this basic position the idea that society will not be changed by appeals to reason and justice, but by collective class struggle that can only succeed at a particular stage of economic and social development. This means that women's oppression is given a history and that it can only be ended in the context of a socialist revolution that is itself the product of a specific historical situation. In the hands of later Marxists such as Engels, Bebel and Zetkin, this idea was in danger of being reduced to a crude economic determinism; although Alexandra Kollontai attempted to produce a more radical and sophisticated analysis, her ideas too were soon forgotten.

After the 1920s, so-called communist societies made little contribution to the debate, but tended to follow the official Soviet line that the 'Woman Question' was a product of capitalist society which had therefore since been solved. Although from the 1960s it was acknowledged that there were still problems facing women, and Soviet sociologists documented at length the tremendous burdens faced by women combining paid work with domestic responsibilities, such problems were deemed to be 'non-antagonistic contradictions', resolvable within the existing socio-economic system and not requiring basic structural change. More recently the twin policies of *Glasnost* (openness) and *Perestroika* (restructuring) again placed women's issues on the political agenda in the Soviet Union. However the classic Marxist position that women's liberation required economic independence and full participation in the economy was increasingly rejected in favour of a renewed emphasis on their traditional role within the family (here cynics might note that this emphasis on family life both provided a potentially stabilising force in a rapidly changing society and conveniently 'mopped up' some of the unemployment that would otherwise have resulted from economic restructuring). Contrary to the classic Marxist position, it was argued that women's double burden should not be resolved by collective housework and childcare, but by increasing their opportunity for part-time and flexible working arrangements; the underlying sexual division of labour remained unchallenged, and the official Soviet line now emphasised natural differences rather than equality between men and women and argued that, both for their own benefit and for that of society as a whole, women should be enabled to fulfil themselves in the traditional roles of mother, wife and homemaker (see Buckley, 1989; Rosenberg, 1989; Waters, 1989). Although a few Soviet sociologists said that feminists should try to re-examine Marxist concepts and use them in their analysis (see Voronina, 1989), most recent thinking in the Eastern block represented an abandonment not only of the radical ideas of Alexandra Kollontai but also of any kind of Marxist or socialist approach to women's situation; this retreat from Marxism was completed by the collapse of communism throughout Eastern Europe and the disintegration of the Soviet Union. It is to the West that we must therefore look for any advances in socialist feminist theory since the Second World War.

Here the apparent paucity of socialist and Marxist feminist thought meant that left-wing activists in the late 1960s were quite unprepared for the new radical feminist attack which denounced their political practice as sexist, and claimed that their theories were patriarchal ideologies that served to conceal the reality of women's oppression. Some initially responded with ridicule, or argued that feminism can only be a bourgeois deviation that divides the workers and distracts them from the class struggle; others have consistently attempted to ignore feminism, apparently in the belief that it will somehow 'go away'. Nevertheless, the last twenty-five years have seen many serious attempts to respond to feminist ideas and to develop socialist and Marxist theories that see women's situation as a central political issue.

In discussing such theories, confusion often arises from the number of different ways in which the terms 'Marxist feminist' and 'socialist feminist' have been used. Some writers use both terms interchangeably and apply them to all those who see socialist and feminist goals as interrelated. Others use them more precisely to distinguish Marxists from those left-wing feminists who do *not* base their analysis on Marxist theory (such as the utopian socialists, Charlotte Perkins Gilman or some feminists within the British Labour Party); the term 'socialist feminist' is, however, also used today to refer to recent attempts to synthesise the insights of Marxist and radical feminisms to build a new theory combining the best of both (see Jaggar, 1983). Throughout this book I use 'Marxist feminist' fairly loosely, to refer to all feminist theories which use Marxist analysis, even if this has been modified by radical feminist ideas. I use 'socialist feminist' as an inclusive category covering all feminists who believe that women's liberation requires the socialist transformation of the socio-economic system; as such it includes but is not confined to Marxist feminism. In practice, the line between Marxist and non-Marxist socialist feminists is frequently blurred, and there has been a tendency for writers to move away from a strictly Marxist position as the difficulties of achieving a 'happy marriage' between Marxism and feminism have become more apparent. I have not therefore based this chapter upon any rigid classification; in general, it traces a development from the most 'orthodox' Marxist approaches to those that argue for a greater flexibility in both theory and practice, and that see gender and, increasingly, race as key categories that cannot be simply explained in terms of class analysis.

Marxist theory and feminism

Such development does not simply reflect the impact of feminism upon Marxist dogma, but is also bound up with changes within Marxist theory itself. For much of the twentieth century, Marxism has been seen as a rigid theory of economic determinism, but from the 1960s the ideas of the 'New Left' and the rediscovery of the 'young Marx' and his idea of alienation have led to a looser interpretation which at times has more affinity with liberal humanitarianism than with Stalinist dogma. The ideas of the inter-war Italian Marxist Gramsci have been developed by writers such as Althusser and Poulantzas to argue for the importance of ideo-logical and political struggle and their relative autonomy from economic determinants, and there has been a fairly widespread move away from an analysis that sees class as central and towards a more pluralistic approach that can encompass other forms of struggle (for a critique of such 'revisions' of Marxism, see Wood, 1986). These trends have been reinforced both by the recent collapse of Marxist orthodoxy in Eastern Europe and by the increasingly fashionable post-modernist critique of the whole Marxist endeavour, which rejects any idea of certainty or simple causation and stresses instead complexity, diversity and fragmen-tation (see Chapter 12 above). There have also been attempts to synthesise Marxism with the insights of psychoanalysis (most famously by Wilhelm Reich in the 1930s, and by Herbert Marcuse in the 1960s); these extend Marxist concerns beyond the econ-omic, and see the importance of sexuality and the workings of the unconscious for any understanding of society and social change. All this means that there is now scope for a variety of approaches within the Marxist tradition, which is in many ways much more open and friendly to feminist concerns than in the past. There is however a danger that an uncritical acceptance of such developments will sacrifice the intellectual rigour and clarity of the original theory, or be based on over-simplification or misun-derstanding of complex Marxist concepts; here it is necessary to retain a critical awareness of the methodological assumptions underlying Marxist theory and of the ways in which these may contribute to or limit feminist understanding.

Catherine MacKinnon has argued in a much quoted article that although both feminism and Marxism are concerned with analysing power, the former is based on an understanding of sexuality and its exploitation, while the latter focuses upon work: 'Sexuality is to feminism what work is to Marxism: that which is most one's own yet most taken away'. She therefore claims that as the two theories have such radically different starting-points, they cannot easily be reconciled, and that attempts at synthesis 'have not recognised the depth of the antagonism or the separate integrity of each theory' (MacKinnon, 1983, pp. 227, 228 and 236). However, her assertion that women's identity and oppression can be reduced to sexuality is highly dubious and certainly not accepted by all radical feminists; it is moreover far from clear why she thinks that the identification and analysis of two power structures need in principle result in theories that are contradictory rather than complementary. She further claims that the theories are incompatible because feminist method and knowledge is based on women's lived experience, and that it therefore posits a new and different relationship between thought and life as through 'consciousness raising' (see Chapter 10 above) the distinction between knowing subject and known subject is rejected, and 'women grasp the collective reality of women's condition from within the perspective of that experience, not from outside it' (MacKinnon, 1983, p. 268). However, Marx also argued that revolutionary theory cannot be deduced from abstract speculation or outside observation, but can only result from concrete practices which it both reflects and informs; indeed Harstock has claimed that through consciousness raising feminists have re-invented the original Marxist method, which insists that theory be based on experience, and integrates personal and political transformation, arguing that both are part of the same process of revolutionary practice (Harstock, 1979).

It seems therefore that at this level there is no inherent reason why Marxism need contradict basic feminist assumptions. For those who insist on the absolute primacy of either class or sex divisions there are however clearly problems. Here it is necessary to disentangle Marx's own failure to develop his ideas in relation to women from the possibilities of wider understanding to which they may give rise. In particular, it must be remembered that although they failed to explore the implications of this, Marx and Engels did say that reproduction as well as production was a part of the material basis of society. In the *German Ideology* they wrote of 'the production of life, both of one's own in labour and of fresh life in procreation', and Engels stated that

> The social institutions under which the people of a particular historical epoch and a particular country live are conditioned by both kinds of

production: by the state of development of labour on the one hand
and of the family on the other (*The Origin*, p. 4).

This means that in principle there may be reciprocal interaction
rather than one-way causation between the two spheres, opening
up the possibility that patriarchy may have a material base autonomous from that of class oppression, rooted in reproduction and
the family rather than in conditions of productive labour. This
provides Marxism with a conceptual tool that can analyse conflict
between men and women without assuming that this is essentially
secondary to economic class divisions. The arguments involved
here are complex and are explored below; for some writers, however, a necessary starting-point has been the attempt to extend
Marx's economic concepts and to use these to analyse the particular situation of women; here analysis has concentrated upon the
so-called 'domestic labour debate' and on the idea of women as
a 'reserve army of labour', to which we now turn.

The domestic labour debate

At first sight the domestic labour debate, much of which was
conducted in the pages of the British Journal *New Left Review*
during the 1970s, might appear to be an example of the tedium and
inaccessibility of modern Marxist thought, involving nit-picking
terminological disagreements of interest only to sectarian Marxists
and far removed from the real interests and concerns of women.
However, as Vogel says, it was not simply 'an obscure exercise
in Marxist pedantry' (Vogel, 1983, p. 21), but an attempt to
make visible the work done by women within the home and, by
exploring its relationship to the capitalist economy, to assess its
strategic importance and the possible implications of this in achieving socialist change (for summaries and discussion of the debate
see Foreman, 1978; Coole, 1988; Vogel, 1983; and Burton, 1985).

As assumption of classic Marxism was that as capitalism
developed, women and children would increasingly be drawn into
the paid labour market, and that this would represent an increase
in exploitation through a depreciation in the value of the male
worker's labour power, as he need no longer be paid the cost of
maintaining his family as well as himself. Marx never explored

either the possibility that this process might be reversed and the 'family wage' become widespread, or the economic significance of the unpaid work that continued to be done by women at home, whether or not they were in paid employment. The protagonists in the domestic labour debate were agreed both that such omissions were a serious limitation on Marxist understanding and that Marxist concepts could nevertheless be employed to fill the gap. They disagreed however as to whether women's domestic work should be seen as some kind of precapitalist mode of production outside of the money economy; whether it is essential to the reproduction of labour power under capitalism and whether it does in fact produce exchange value in the strict Marxist sense (in the form of the labour power of the adult male worker, sold like any other commodity on the market, with his overalls neatly pressed and his sandwiches in his pocket). Such disagreements are not 'merely academic', for the centrality of domestic labour to capitalism is related to the kind of political action that might be taken by women. Thus some writers argue that because domestic labour does produce value in the same way as other forms of productive labour, then the role of the housewife is as strategically important as the factory worker, and the home itself can be seen as a site of anti-capitalist struggle, for 'woman is the slave of a wage-slave, and her slavery ensures the slavery of her man' (James, quoted in Malos, 1980, p. 178; see also Dalla Costa, 1973). From this perspective, women should not enter the paid workforce as earlier Marxist analysis had suggested, but they should demand that housework itself be paid for. The international 'Wages for Housework' campaign has been heavily criticised for alleged misunderstanding of Marxist concepts, for perpetuating the assumption that housework is women's responsibility and for the impracticality of its demands. Its opponents however argue that it corresponds to the real needs of working-class women who will never be liberated by the kind of paid work available to them, and that to demand that housework be paid for by the capitalist state is both to make visible its importance as part of the class struggle and to challenge the assumption that its performance is some kind of natural attribute of womanhood. Most writers do not go so far, but as the debate developed there appeared to be a general agreement that the housework done by women does not simply represent a personal service to individual men, but that it serves the interests of the capitalist economy by reproducing and maintaining the workforce in a particularly cheap and efficient way; this in turn implies that male supremacy within the home is not simply a matter of personal patriarchal oppression, but is embedded in economic structures.

What the debate did therefore was to show that the unpaid work performed by women in the home is connected to the wider economy and to explain that the family under capitalism continues to perform important economic as well as ideological and psychological functions which any overall strategy for change must take into account. It therefore in principle allowed the actual economic situation of women to be addressed rather than assuming that domestic work is an unimportant issue that will automatically be resolved 'after the revolution'. What it notably failed to do, however, was to ask why it is that domestic labour is overwhelmingly performed by *women* or to explore the pre-existing structures or patriarchal attitudes that produced the present gender division of labour; any idea that men as well as capitalism benefit from present arrangements therefore tended to disappear. It also failed to explore cross-class differences in women's situation or to see the dynamic interrelationship between gender divisions and the capitalist economy, with the need for domestic services often conflicting with the demand for women's paid labour, and outcomes being determined not simply by the abstract 'needs of capitalism' but also by organised labour's defence of the family wage or feminist pressures for increased male participation within the home. Further problems arise from a concentration on housework that fails to consider the related and possibly more important questions of childcare, and from an assumption that a woman's economic identity is primarily based upon her role as housewife rather than paid worker. Perhaps most fundamentally, the debate was in danger of providing a new form of economic determinism that argued that because present arrangements can be shown to be advantageous to capitalism, they are also somehow caused by it and unchangeable within it. However, although it may be more expensive and less convenient, there seems no reason in principle why domestic work *could not* be shared equally with men or provided either commercially or by the state. There are of course enormous political difficulties in the way of this, for the family clearly performs important psychological and ideological functions, and it may be that capitalism would be dangerously destabilised by such changes. This argument needs however to be disentangled from a purely economic analysis and shows that the significance of domestic labour cannot be understood in economic terms alone; as Molyneux concluded in her discussion of the debate in 1979, the issues it raises are clearly important but need to be understood in a wider context, for 'Neither an understanding of women's subordination nor the politics for overcoming it, can be derived from the analysis of domestic labour alone' (Molyneux, 1979, p. 22).

Women and the labour market

For some writers, the significance of women's domestic labour lies not so much in the ways in which this integrates the family into capitalism, as in the ways in which it structures women's relationship to the paid economy. This means that, contrary to Engels' prediction that women's employment would end their oppression, women enter the labour market from a position of subordination which is both reflected and reinforced by their conditions of employment. The arguments involved here are complicated, and at times shift from one explanatory level to another. A central starting-point, however, is that women's assumed dependency on a male breadwinner depresses their wages relative to men's, for employers need not pay them directly either for the entire cost of reproducing their own labour power or for reproducing the next generation; this low pay in turn reinforces both their economic dependency within marriage and the economic necessity of finding a husband. This dependency also means that women can more easily than men be made unemployed at a time of recession, and here writers have used the concept of the *reserve army of labour*, which Marx saw as essential to the workings of the capitalist economy, to analyse women's economic situation. According to Marx, capitalism's need for labour inevitably fluctuated as the economy went through cycles of expansion and recession. It therefore required the existence of a group of workers who could be treated as marginal to the economy and dispensed with at times of recession; although he treated this 'reserve army' as an 'empty' category, some Marxist feminists have argued that it is particularly applicable to the employment of women. Although perhaps intuitively appealing, this analysis is not however entirely supported by the available empirical evidence. In particular, the relative cheapness of women's labour creates a contrary pressure to employ them in preference to men, while current employment patterns mean that they are less likely than men to be found in those occupations most vulnerable to the effects of recession (mainly manufacturing industry); in many nations too, state provision of at least minimal welfare services may have made male unemployment a more politically viable option than in the past.

However it seems clear that women's domestic responsibilities do mean that they are less able than men to defend their own economic interests. In particular, their labour is more likely than that of men to be labelled 'unskilled' and therefore worthy only of low pay and status. Marx had claimed that as capitalism developed, employers would increasingly seek to simplify the labour processes and replace skilled with unskilled workers, and that the entry of women and children into the workforce was a reflection of this process. Phillips and Taylor have however argued persuasively that, far from being objective and neutral, 'skill' is frequently an ideological category, arising from the struggle of men to maintain their dominance in the sexual hierarchy, and that men have frequently been able to resist the 'deskilling' process and to displace this onto women. From this perspective, women are not paid less simply because they are unskilled, but because working-class men have succeeded in protecting their own interests at women's expense; they have been able to do this because dominant attitudes label any work done by women as inherently inferior to that done by men. This means that there has been conflict between men and women workers, and that it is to the activities of men, particularly as organised in the trade union movement, that we should look if we are to understand women's lower pay and inferior conditions of employment.

This does not mean that gender struggle is always overt, clear-cut and unambiguous, for prevailing gender ideologies may be accepted by women themselves as well as by both employers and male workers; indeed such ideologies are likely to be internalised at the deepest emotional and psychological level, so that women's sense of identity and expectations of fulfilment are bound up with family and personal life rather than paid work, and they are therefore likely to welcome forms of employment, particularly part-time working, that do not involve high levels of commitment or time. Moreover as Humphries has argued, there may be times when the demand for the 'family wage' or protective legislation can be seen as part of a general class struggle to improve working-class standards of living, rather than a move to reinforce male domination (Humphries, 1982). It does mean, however, that positions in the labour hierarchy have always reflected the struggle between men and women as well as that between labour and capital, so that capitalism's need for a marginal or reserve army of cheap, docile and unskilled labour has been met in gender-specific ways.

The idea that gender issues may have a degree of independence from class has been explored by Michelle Barrett, who has been strongly influenced by the ideas of the French Marxist Louis Althusser on the 'relative autonomy' of ideology. This approach argues that, contrary to many traditional interpretations of Marx, ideas are not simply determined by economic relationships, but may have a certain independence. In terms of political activity and outcomes, this means that the 'battle of ideas' is important in its own right, and that social arrangements may be a consequence as well as a cause of the dominant ideology. In *Women's Oppression Today* (first published in 1980), Barrett applies this to women's situation, and argues that women's oppression cannot be reduced to the needs of the capitalist economy, but that it is also the product of a specific pre-existing gender ideology; as such it may be extraordinarily useful to capitalism, but it was certainly not caused by it. Against those critics who claim that this oppression must have had a material basis and that this was located in the biological facts of reproduction and the need for women to organise their paid employment around childbearing, she insists that biological 'facts' are in practice always socially mediated (so that, for example, the birth rate halved during the nineteenth century in America but not in Britain) (see Brenner and Ramas, 1984; Barrett, 1984; Lewis, 1985). Women's disadvantaged position in the nineteenth-century paid workforce was, she says, therefore in no way inevitable, but the result of particular struggles, including that of working-class men for protective legislation and the family wage. This of course leaves open the whole question of where the original gender ideology came from.

Although Marx would agree with Barrett that ideology is not mechanically determined by the economy, he did not see socially dominant ideas as 'free-floating' but as reflecting real social relations, albeit in a distorted form; Barrett seems at times to accept this, but she never really examines the precapitalist conditions that might have given rise to her gender ideology, which is therefore taken as given rather than explained. She does, however, think that oppressive relationships have become so entangled with the capitalist economy that they are now virtually inseparable, so that

> the oppression of women, although not a functional pre-requisite of capitalism, has acquired a material basis in the relations of production and reproduction of capitalism today (Barrett, 1988, p. 249).

Two systems or one? 'Dual systems' v. 'capitalist patriarchy'

For some writers, the interaction of class and gender inequalities suggests that there are two dynamic forces at work in history, which must therefore be understood in terms of both class and gender struggle. This has been the assumption behind much recent socialist feminist analysis, which has sought to 'marry' the insights of Marxism with the new perspectives opened up by radical feminism. In particular, Heidi Hartmann has argued that modern society must be understood as both capitalist and patriarchal. Although they have become bound up with each other, neither of these 'dual systems' can, she says, be reduced to the other, and although at times they are mutually reinforcing, they may also come into conflict (most notably when capitalism's need for women's labour power is opposed by the patriarchal demand for personal services within the home). She says that Marxist analysis forgets that men as well as capitalism benefit from present arrangements, and claims that because they 'have a higher standard of living than women in terms of luxury consumption, leisure time and personalised services', men of all classes have at least a short-term material interest in maintaining women's oppression, which pre-dates capitalism and could continue beyond it (Hartmann, 1986, p. 9). Ann Ferguson has similarly argued that there is a semi-autonomous system of patriarchy, and that as traditional

Marxism cannot fully understand women's oppression, new concepts derived from radical feminism must be developed. She says that in addition to its economic mode of production, society is based on a mode of 'sex affective production'. By this somewhat clumsy term she understands the social bonding, the physical and emotional interactions that arise in such areas as sexuality, parenting, family and friendship, and she argues that 'the form of human organisation which a society develops to meet the human material needs for such connection will be as important in understanding these societies as their economic systems' (Ferguson, 1989, p. 83). Like Hartmann, she therefore insists both that the concept of patriarchy must be given a history and that this is not reducible to economic change as traditionally understood by Marxists. In particular, she argues that modern American society must be understood as a public and capitalist patriarchy, but that the contradictions between capitalist and patriarchal interests provide a potential for disruption and the pursuit of both socialist and feminist goals.

Other writers have rejected such 'dual systems' approaches, and argue that what we now have is a unified system of capitalist patriarchy. For Young, patriarchy is based on men's control over women's labour, but this is itself a part of the productive process. This means that she wants the Marxist understanding of production and class to be transformed so as to include the gender division of labour with which these are bound up; from this perspective the analysis of gender relations is not some kind of 'optional extra' for Marxists, but is central to the understanding of any economic system and hence basic to the whole of society (Young, 1986). Jaggar too says that patriarchy and capitalism are inseparable, but she argues rather differently that the key to understanding women's oppression must lie in extending the Marxist idea of the economic foundation of society to include reproduction as well as production. This means that sexuality and conditions of procreation can be analysed as part of the economic base rather than as being determined by it, although she concedes that we do not yet understand the nature of the interconnections involved (Jaggar, 1983).

In *Marxism and the Oppression of Women*, also published in 1983, Lise Vogel develops a similar argument along more 'orthodox' lines. She builds upon Marx's unexplored recognition that the maintenance and reproduction of the working class are essential requirements of capitalism, to argue that the material basis of women's oppression is to be found in *social reproduction*, that is, in the reproduction of the conditions of production, including the supply of labour power. Although in principle labour power can be renewed through immigration, this is of course normally done through generational reproduction, and it is here that Vogel claims to have found the key to women's oppression in class society. Most obviously, the biological fact of childbearing imposes a basic division of labour, and means that the economic productivity of reproductively active women is temporarily reduced. This involves a contradiction for the ruling class, whereby its interest in extracting the maximum profit from women's labour conflicts with the need for efficient generational replacement of the workforce. It resolves this by taking advantage of pre-existing kinship relationships to institutionalise the support by working-class men of less productive women, so that although historically conditions of reproduction and forms of the family have varied:

> In virtually all cases, they entail men's greater responsibility for provision of material means of subsistence, women's greater responsibility for the ongoing tasks of necessary labour, and institutionalised forms of male domination over women (*Marxism*, p. 149).

In other words, in class society women's biological role as childbearers almost always involves an economic dependency upon men and also an extended division of labour whereby women are disproportionately responsible for the domestic labour necessary to maintain the workforce, and men for that which involves the production of a surplus. Under capitalism, the separation of home and work and the system of wage labour increases and formalises both the distinction between domestic and production work and women's economic dependency upon men; however in a socialist society, in which production is for use rather than profit, the economic imperative to extract a surplus from women's labour will no longer be operative, childcare and domestic labour will be socialised and the biological division of labour will no longer involve an oppressive economic dependency. All this means that it is

> their differential role in the reproduction of labour power that lies at

the root of women's oppression . . . it is the provision by men of subsistence to women during the child-rearing period, and not the division of labour itself, that forms the material basis for women's subordination in class society (*Marxism*, pp. 145 and 147).

It is important to recognise that Vogel is not saying simply that men can exploit women because they have babies, but that their subordination solves an economic problem for the ruling class that stems from their role in the reproduction of labour power; she is therefore arguing that, contrary to the classic Marxist analysis, working-class women do suffer from sex-specific oppression and that Marxist concepts can be used to understand it. Here her argument that oppression constitutes a resolution of contradictions within capitalism itself avoids the need to posit an autonomous system of patriarchy with interests potentially opposed to that of capitalism; working-class women are, she says, oppressed as women, but they are oppressed by capitalism, not by working-class men.

Although Vogel's understanding and knowledge of original Marxism are much greater than that of many would-be Marxist feminists, her analysis gives rise to problems at a number of levels. Firstly, she makes no attempt to substantiate her claims with reference to anthropological evidence or to an examination of precapitalist societies; the whole argument that it is only in class society that the sexual division of labour becomes oppressive therefore remains a theoretical deduction wide open to empirical challenge. Secondly, her use of the concept of social reproduction is an unhelpfully narrow one that remains confined by classic Marxist perceptions and fails to include any examination of sexuality or of changes in contraceptive knowledge or reproductive technology. Women's responsibility for social reproduction is therefore seen as unproblematically constant, and changes in the material conditions of reproduction and of social relations based upon them disappear from history; the possibility that new reproductive technology might radically change women's childbearing role is not even considered.

Thirdly, as Hartmann had earlier complained (Hartmann, 1986), any attempt to reduce women's oppression to the needs of class society completely ignores the way in which it may also benefit men, and fails to understand that even working-class and socialist men may have an interest in maintaining gender inequalities. Vogel therefore reports that 'existing socialist societies . . . have been unable to confront the problems of domestic labour and women's subordination in any systematic way' (*Marxism*, p. 174), without even considering the possibility that this 'inability' is in fact a *refusal* stemming from continued male dominance in all spheres; similarly she blithely states that in the transition to a socialist society domestic work will be both socialised and shared with men, ignoring all likelihood of male opposition. Finally, her blindness to the existence of male vested interest means that whole areas of oppression identified by radical feminists again disappear, and she has nothing to say on male violence, sexual exploitation or the control of language and knowledge (Young, who as we saw also argues against a 'dual systems' approach, does mention sexual harrassment and pornography, but insists that these can be explained in terms of the hierarchical relationships and the drive for profit that are basic to the capitalist economy; see Young, 1986). Such theoretical omissions have profound implications for feminist politics, for in refusing to see that working-class women's interests may be opposed to as well as shared by men they provide no basis for autonomous women's organisations or for understanding the sexism and marginalisation of women's issues in mixed groups. They therefore also downplay the importance of feminist struggles and are in danger of a fatalism that assumes that because women's subordination serves the needs of capitalism, then no significant improvements in their situation can be achieved until it is overthrown.

All this means that to label western societies as 'capitalist patriarchies' is not simply to provide a shorthand label describing a system in which two systems of domination have become inextricably entangled. Rather it implies a kind of economic determinism which, even if it is extended to include 'reproduction of the conditions of production', ignores important areas of women's lives and denies that the material basis of patriarchy in reproduction may itself be subject to change, and that it may at times provide an independent dynamic and an arena of struggle in which women's interests may be opposed to those of men.

The family, ideology and Mitchell's 'structures of oppression'

The kind of Marxist 'orthodoxy' discussed above not only fails to come to terms with major issues raised by radical feminists, but has also become increasingly out of tune with much modern Marxist thinking which, as discussed at the beginning of this chapter, is becoming much more open-ended and willing to explore non-economic factors. Some Marxist feminists are therefore attempting to move away from a purely economic analysis of women's oppression to one that incorporates and allows a certain autonomy to areas of life traditionally considered 'private' and non-political.

Here a pioneering and influential contribution was made by Juliet Mitchell, whose *Women, The Longest Revolution*, first published in 1966, has been described as 'really the first written text of the British Women's Liberation movement' (Wilson, 1980, p. 196). In this essay and in *Women's Estate* (1971) and *Psychoanalysis and Feminism* (1974) she seeks to 'ask the feminist questions, but try to come up with some Marxist answers' (*Estate*, p. 99), and argues that although earlier Marxists were correct in seeing women's relation to production as of key importance, their analysis did not go nearly far enough and ignored the crucial ways in which women's subordination is maintained within the family. More specifically, she claims that four structures are involved in determining women's situation: in addition to the structure of production, traditionally analysed by Marxist theory, feminists must examine the family-based structures of reproduction, sexuality and the socialisation of children. This leads her to an analysis of the ways in which subordination is internalised and consent engineered, which in turn involves an examination of the workings of the unconscious and of the ways in which adult identity is learned in our society.

There are two key aspects to Mitchell's theory. Firstly, influenced by Althusser, she argues for the relative autonomy as well as the interdependence of her four structures, and for the importance of ideology in understanding the workings of society; secondly, her exploration of psychoanalytic theory has led her to try to rehabilitate Freud and to show that, despite their frequent misuse and the criticisms of feminists, his ideas can be used in feminist analysis. This means that her concerns overlap with radical feminist critiques of the family, sexuality and men's control over knowledge, although she attempts to give these a history which is still in the last analysis based upon developments in production. She claims that her hopes and predictions for the future are based on an analysis of the present in which economic conditions may be fundamental, but in which political and ideological struggles also have a key role. She therefore avoids the kind of crude economic reductionism to which Marxist analysis is prone; her analysis also leads her to advocate autonomous women's organisations, insisting that as an oppressed group women must work for their own liberation, and to argue that there will be no automatic dissolution of patriarchy without feminist struggle.

As with the later 'dual systems' theories discussed above, the problem remains as to precisely how Mitchell's four structures interact, and there is a danger that her analysis can lead to an artificial distinction between economic and ideological struggles, whereby 'Marxism appears as the theory for class struggle, and psychoanalysis the theory for the analysis of patriarchy' (Wilson, 1980, p. 199; see also Foreman, 1978). A similar problem arises from the analysis of Barrett and McIntosh. In *The Anti-Social Family* (1982) they claim that the main significance of the family in modern capitalist society is ideological rather than economic and, much like Robert Owen in the early nineteenth century, they argue that

> the family embodies the principles of selfishness, exclusion, and pursuit of private interest and contravenes those of altruism, community and pursuit of the common good (Barrett and McIntosh, 1982, p. 47).

The family is, they say, both the product of a selfish, individualistic society and the means by which it is ideologically maintained. As such, its ideology must be challenged by feminists, but as it promises to satisfy real needs for affection and intimacy which are not at present met elsewhere, significant changes can only be achieved through transforming the economic relations of society. This again seems to contrast feminist ideological struggle with economic class struggle, with the success of the former ultimately being dependent on the latter.

This kind of separation can, however, be avoided if we ally this kind of analysis with the previously discussed idea that social reproduction (including procreation and the physical maintenance of the workforce) must be understood as part of the economic basis of society. From this perspective, ideology is a reflection of material conditions within the family as well as of productive life, and changes in family structure are themselves a form of material change that may not be simply reducible to the needs of the capitalist economy. For example, changes in sexual behaviour may result from increased knowledge and availability of contraception, and also from the spread of AIDS. This means that attempts to change family structures can themselves constitute direct economic as well as political and ideological struggle; such developments as increased male involvement in childcare therefore represent real changes in the conditions of social reproduction which may have an independent effect upon production (for example, by decreasing the attractiveness of overtime working). Therefore although the family may itself play an important ideological role in providing an appropriately socialised and motivated workforce, it cannot be reduced to this function; in the same way, concentration on the workplace as part of the process of production should not obscure the fact that it too can play an ideological role, reinforcing not only hierarchical productive relationships but sexist attitudes towards women (for example, through the display of 'girlie' pictures).

Alienation and social reproduction

Some recent feminist theories suggest that the complex interrelationship between family and the paid economy can be further explored by using Marx's concept of *alienation*. As discussed in Chapter 3 above, this was important in Marx's early writings, and it involved a humanitarian critique of conditions of labour under capitalism, arguing that the pursuit of profit and the extreme division of labour meant that work had become an alien activity over which the worker had no control, rather than an expression of human creativity. Both Foreman and Jaggar have extended this idea to argue that for women, alienation is not confined to the world of paid employment and that it is experienced within the family and private life. Here it involves a loss of control over reproduction and sexuality and the provision of emotional and material support to men in a form that denies women's own needs. This means that whereas for the male worker the family is the one area of life where his human needs can be met,

> for women there is no relief. For those intimate relations are the very ones that are the essential structure of her oppression . . . while alienation reduces the man to an instrument of labour within industry, it reduces the woman to an instrument for his sexual pleasure within the family (Foreman, 1978, pp. 102 and 151).

From this perspective, women's personal relationships cannot be understood as the freely chosen expression of their own desires, but are imposed upon them. This alienation is, however, disguised, because relationships within the family are not normally mediated by money, and the dominant ideology denies that they are based on anything other than love. Men benefit emotionally, sexually and economically from this concealed alienation; they will therefore resist any attempts to commercialise women's services, for this would represent a final stage of universal alienation and the ultimate denial of their own humanity. Such a stage would however be progressive, for Marx did not see alienation as simply negative, but as a necessary stage in human evolution, a precondition for full conscious control and fulfilment and man's mastery over nature. Foreman and Jaggar therefore argue that women's alienation is historically specific rather than an unchanging aspect of gender relations. As such, it is a product of women's economic dependency and the impoverishment of human relationships under capitalism; modern physiological knowledge and reproductive technology are at present used to manipulate women, but they can in the future be used to liberate them, so that for the first time in human history reproduction and sexual activity can be freely chosen.

If, as has been argued, we see reproduction and sexuality as part of the material basis of society, such 'private' alienation and its overcoming must be as fundamental as that experienced in production and, unlike the religious and political alienation also identified by Marx, not simply a reflection of it. This means that areas of life traditionally ignored by political theorists can in fact be integrated into Marx's theory of history using one of his original concepts, so that the patterning of the intimate relations of men and women is a vital element in completing the Marxist theory of the development of human consciousness. The changes in their form determine whether human beings express themselves spontaneously as in primitive society; or whether on a level of reality excluded from conscious thought as in capitalist society; or whether men and women are able to express themselves consciously through all their relations as in future communist society (Foreman, 1978, p. 110).

An important aspect of the theory, although not one that has yet been explored by modern feminists, arises from the way in which Marx linked his concept of alienation with a critique of the division of labour in society. Under capitalism, he said, specialisation becomes so extreme that skills are lost and work becomes a denial rather than an expression of human creativity; however in future communist society the positive use of technology to meet human needs will allow the division of labour to be abolished or at least greatly reduced, with individuals enjoying an unprecedented opportunity to choose and move between different occupations; unlike the stunted, impoverished individual of today, the worker of tomorrow will be able to explore his full potential through productive labour, which will be a means of human fulfilment rather than degradation. Unlike the earlier utopian socialists, Marx never applied these ideas to the sexual division of labour. This is, however, central to some modern feminist analysis, which argues both that women must be enabled to do 'men's work' and that men should develop their caring and nurturing qualities through participation in productive life and child-rearing; such change is both an important prerequisite of gender equality and an important goal in itself. This would in fact seem to be a logical extension of Marx's analysis; similarly some radical feminist demands that sexuality be liberated from gender stereotypes and polarities can be seen as the demand for an end to ascribed gender roles; as for Marx, the goal is the fully rounded individual free to express himself or herself in all possible ways. A Marxist perspective, however, does not simply endorse such demands, but gives them a historical context, arguing that they can only be met at a certain stage of human development. It also means that they cannot be isolated from other forms of social change, but are part of a more general social movement. In other words, the ending of women's sex-specific alienation will never be achieved on its own, as liberal and radical perspectives might suggest, for it is integrally bound up with the struggle to end alienation in all its forms.

Modern Marxism, post-modernism and race

All of this is very much in line with more general trends in modern Marxist thought, which seems to be moving away from ideas of economic determinism and class conflict as narrowly understood, and towards a more pluralist approach which both allows a greater independence to political and ideological struggle and can more easily than past orthodoxies accept an interpretation of the social basis of society that includes social reproduction. Some writers argue that these theoretical developments are themselves a reflection of changes in the technological basis and class structure of advanced capitalist society, in which old economic groupings have become fragmented and the fight for socialism must be seen in terms of multiple struggles and sites of resistance rather than straightforward confrontation between opposing classes. In this new context, race and gender become independently important dimensions of struggle, and the fight for ideological domination and control is of central significance (for a particularly clear example of this perspective, see Hall and Jacques (eds), *New Times*, 1989).

Such analysis at times merges with theories of 'post-modernism' which, as discussed in the previous chapter, attack the whole idea of certainty or objectivity in human thought, and purport to show how power is constructed through language and knowledge. Post-modernism also challenges the validity of such categories as 'working class', denying the existence of stable and objectively knowable class interests, and claiming that such crude labels conceal the variety and diversity of human experience and subjectivity. As such, it is diametrically opposed to most traditional interpretations of Marxism, but meshes neatly with some of the concerns of the new 'revisionists'. It has therefore found a ready response from some erstwhile socialist feminists, and Barrett has recently distanced herself from her earlier position to argue in a new introduction to *Women's Oppression Today* that the attempt to construct a Marxist feminist analysis has largely failed, and that 'the arguments of post-modernism already represent, I think, a key position around which feminist theoretical work in the future is likely to revolve' (Barrett, 1988, p. *xxxiv*).

Taken to an extreme, the post-modernist position can collapse into a woolly relativism and an individualistic reductionism that negates all possibility of collective action and paralyses political will. Nevertheless, it can also provide a salutary warning against simplistic certainties and over-inclusiveness. In particular, as Barrett says, it can in principle avoid the incipient racism of much feminist thought, whereby all women are seen as subject to the same processes, and the very different experiences of different groups are ignored.

As we have seen in previous chapters, feminists have always been vulnerable to the accusation that their concerns and priorities reflect those of white middle-class women, and socialist feminism too has tended to base its analysis on advanced industrial societies and to ignore the perspectives of 'non white' women. Here some writers are beginning to acknowledge their own limitations. Thus for example Barrett and McIntosh admit that their study of the family ignored the very different structures and relationships to be found in the Afro-Caribbean and Asian communities in Britain (Barrett and McIntosh, 1985). Critics, however, do not see such 'confessions' as going nearly far enough. The problem is not simply one of acknowledging that differences exist, but of challenging the underlying assumption that white women are the norm, and that the experiences of 'black women', 'women of colour' or 'third world women' are some kind of alien 'problem' or 'optional extra'; this assumption not only denies the validity and primacy of these 'other' experiences, but can often lead to condescending and over-simplistic generalisations or tokenism with regard to all 'non white' women. It can also deny 'the pain, the passion and the power of a racism which is beyond anything that Barrett and McIntosh seem to have imagined' (Ramazanoglu, 1986, p. 84), and the ways in which white feminists are both the beneficiaries and the perpetrators of the racism that many women see as the primary experience of their lives (for an excellent discussion, bringing together a number of different perspectives, see Bulbeck, 1988).

For many writers, the solution is to develop a specifically black feminist approach which is based on black women's own experiences and sees racism as a central issue. This may involve separatist black or black women's movements, for

> Just as women cannot trust men to 'liberate' them, black women cannot trust white women to 'liberate' them during or 'after the revolution'; in part because there is little reason to think that they would know how, and in part because white women's immediate self-interest lies in continued racial oppression (Joseph, 1986, pp. 104–5).

The problem remains, however, that, just as the term 'man' marginalised women and the term 'women' marginalised 'non white' women, so too the term 'black women' (or 'women of colour' or 'Afro-American women' or 'third world women') can marginalise some groups and ignore the vast economic and cultural differences and divisions amongst these the term supposedly encompasses; it can also ignore the class divisions and the racism that may exist within and between 'black' groups, or the ways in which black American women benefit from American imperialism.

The post-modernist approach can therefore usefully remind us of the multiplicity of experiences and subjectiveness that have been forced into such categories. Nevertheless the whole feminist project does insist that the category 'woman' is a meaningful one, and a critical awareness of the problems involved in the use of such terms as 'white women' or 'black women' need not invalidate all use of the terms themselves or of political action based upon them. Here Marxism can in principle point to the historical specificity of the situation experienced by different groups of women and show the ways in which racism, like sexism, is not simply a question of individual wickedness or injustice, but the product of particular historical situations which has become embedded in the structures of society. On a global scale, this means that differences between women cannot be understood outside of the context of colonialism, imperialism and nationalistic struggles for independence; in the case of Afro-American women the legacy of slavery, both economic and psychological, is clearly of pivotal importance. Such analysis would suggest that racism has its roots in colonialism and imperialism, and that like sexism it is now advantageous to capitalism because it divides the working class and provides a marginalised labour force; it cannot therefore be eliminated by appeals to justice or by individual soul-searching and 'correct' political consciousness, but is bound up with the economic and political structures of society. It is, however, also clear that racism today cannot be reduced to the needs of capitalism, for it has become embedded in our language and internalised in the psychology of both blacks and whites; here again it would seem than an 'open' interpretation of Marxism that allows a degree of independence to political and ideological struggle is more useful than one which insists on a narrow economic determinism and the absolute primacy of class struggle.

In terms of political activity, this kind of analysis has led some socialist feminists to insist not only that issues of class, sex and race are inherently interconnected, but that a black feminist perspective is the most truly radical, for 'The necessity of addressing all forms of oppression is one of the hallmarks of black feminist thought' (King, 1988, p. 43). Angela Davis has argued that whereas white middle-class feminists tend to win gains only for themselves, the position of black women at the very bottom of society means that success for them would undermine all existing power structures, so that 'The forward movement of women of colour almost always initiates progressive change for all women' (Davis, 1990, p. 31). From this perspective, the radical feminist idea of *sisterhood*, which implies an oppression shared by all women, gives way to that of *solidarity*, which is based in the understanding that the struggles of all women are interconnected, but that they are not the same (hooks, 1984). Such an approach goes some way in avoiding the politically sterile debate as to whether sex, class or race oppression 'goes deepest', while retaining the Marxist perception that they all have a basis in the material conditions of society.

Socialist feminist strategies

In America, liberal and radical feminism have both had more political impact than any kind of Marxist or socialist approach. In Europe, the greater strength of socialist parties and trade unions has meant that such feminism has become more integrated into mainstream political life, and although it is still often dominated by middle-class 'intellectual socialists', the exclusion of working-class women has been less marked than in America; the marginalisation or exclusion of black women, however, remains. Since the early 1970s, left-wing talk of incipient revolution in advanced industrial societies has faded, to be largely replaced by a more pragmatic approach in which reform within the system and coalitions of 'progressive' groups are preferred to the 'revolutionary overthrow of capitalism' and class struggle. Such changes have been reflected in socialist feminist strategies. The immediate political task for socialist feminists in Britain has therefore become to challenge sexism within trade unions and left-wing parties, to campaign for the election of a Labour government and to organise around particular class, gender, race, community or environmental demands in the belief that these struggles are interconnected and that they can have a cumulative effect upon society. This approach is epitomised in the widely discussed *Beyond the Fragments* (1979), although the mood of the book reflects an optimism which has since been largely undermined by a decade of conservative government. In it, three leading socialist feminist writers and activists (Hilary Wainwright, Sheila Rowbotham and Lynn Segal) attempt to reformulate the socialist project both by challenging the elitism, sexism and hierarchy of existing left-wing organisations, and by building upon new grass-roots movements in the hope of producing a more democratic and participatory movement against all forms of oppression. They argue in particular that feminist critiques of all forms of power are necessarily central to socialism both as a movement for change and as the future form of society, for

> the movement for women's liberation is part of the creation of a new society in which there are no forms of domination. This society cannot be separated from the process of its making (Rowbotham, in *Fragments*, p. 50).

Although such arguments have had a not insignificant effect upon left-wing political organisations, there has, during the 1980s, been a general decline in the self-confidence of socialist feminism (see Segal, 1987; Lovenduski, 1988). This stems in part from years of economic recession and a changed political climate in which socialist values seem to be in general retreat and working-class movements greatly weakened; it also reflects the impact of radical feminist and black feminist critiques, and a guilty self-awareness that charges of elitism may be valid and that many women are alienated by the increasingly esoteric and self-referential nature of the kind of theoretical debates discussed earlier in this chapter.

However, although socialist feminism is now very much on the defensive, the announcement of its death or transmogrification would appear somewhat premature, and it is necessary to disentangle political fashion from theoretical validity. Its central belief remains the idea that socialist and feminist goals are inherently interconnected. For some, this rests on the simple assertion that sex equality can have little meaning in a system in which most men as well as most women are exploited; other writers discussed in this chapter urge further that women's oppression is, or has become, necessary to capitalism, so that patriarchy cannot be ended without fundamental economic change. It is also argued both that women's support is necessary for the achievement of socialism and that the socialist movement must put its own sexist house in order, for a movement that oppresses some of its own members cannot create an egalitarian society. Marxism adds to this general standpoint an analysis that insists that existing material conditions limit or determine what it is possible to achieve in any given situation; increasingly, however, Marxist analysis has moved beyond a crude economic reductionism to a more open-ended approach.

All this gives us an analysis that certainly does not point to any simple solutions and that does offer vast scope for disagreement. It means that the issues of 'personal' oppression identified by radical feminists can be understood within a socio-economic context rather than as ahistorical manifestations of male oppression; this in turn means that the struggle against all forms of oppression involves not only direct confrontation, but a struggle against the social structures from which they arise. Many Marxist and socialist feminists would now argue that women's oppression cannot simply be reduced to the 'needs of capitalism' or subsumed in a general class struggle, for the interests of women may at times conflict with those of men: as Anne Phillips says

> We live in a class society that is also structured by gender, which means that men and women experience class in different ways, and that potential unities of class are disrupted by conflicts of gender.

and

Class and race and gender are *not* parallel oppressions, and the route dictated by one may well diverge from the route dictated by others (Phillips, 1987a, p. 12).

In terms of feminist politics, this implies a flexibility which recognises the historical specificity of any situation and the possibilities to which it gives rise; socialist feminist priorities and tactics are not therefore to be written in tablets of stone, but must be based on a realistic appraisal of existing circumstances. Nevertheless an agreed key area is the struggle over conditions of production, for here socialist feminists are making demands both as women and as workers; as Jaggar says, 'When women workers achieve a living wage, they are not just workers winning a concession from capitalism, they are also women winning economic independence from men' (Jaggar, 1983, p. 328). This struggle must however be extended to include conditions of *social reproduction* and the sexual division of labour; this may include demands for sexual autonomy, 'reproductive rights' and new forms of family organisation. These may in turn involve conflicts with both the state and individual men within the home; such political or 'personal' struggles are not however to be understood in isolation, for gains made at these levels are seen to acquire meaning only in a wider social and economic context. This means that for many modern socialist feminists, legal gains and mainstream political activity are not to be written off as mere formalities that conceal the unchanging realities of capitalist patriarchal oppression. Like the family and the workplace, the law and state institutions are 'arenas of struggle' in which battles may be fought and real gains won; in line with much modern Marxist thought many also see the struggle over ideology as of critical importance. In all of these areas women may find themselves working with men on class issues or supported by men in their feminist demands; many are however prepared to see men as potential enemies in some areas as well as allies in others and therefore advocate autonomous women's organisations as well as participation in existing structures (giving rise to the definition of a socialist feminist as 'someone who goes to twice as many meetings').

Like some of the more sophisticated radical feminist theories, Marxist and socialist feminism is moving away from the idea that there can be a simple solution to the oppression of women. In the process it has lost the easy certainties that gave confidence to earlier writers and it has become in many respects deeply divided; like all forms of socialism it seems to be currently out of political fashion. Partly for this reason, it seems likely that 'socialist feminist' will be less frequently used as a political label than in the past; this need not however mean that its insights are lost, but may rather represent the starting-point for a more comprehensive feminist theory than has existed hitherto.

14

Conclusion: feminist theory in the 1990s

As this book has shown, the history of feminist political theory and practice has not been one of steady advance, and the fortunes of feminism have waxed and waned many times during the past 300 years. In some ways the situation of women in Western societies has obviously improved, and many of the issues for which feminists have fought in the past are now part of the 'common sense' assumptions of our society. Thus few today would challenge the right of women to education, employment or the vote, or advocate a return to the gross inequalities of the nineteenth century. In many nations of the world, however, such rights are still denied, and the benefits of such changes have been far from evenly distributed in Europe and America. Moreover, some modern feminists argue that apparent gains represent a shift in the nature of inequality or oppression rather than its ending, so that legal inequalities and private subordination within the family have been partly replaced by a more diffuse and less tangible form of public oppression in which economic dependency on the male-run state and manipulation of sexuality by a pornographic culture are key aspects, and

> Women are no longer restricted to the domestic hearth, but have the whole society in which to roam and be exploited (Walby, 1990, p. 201).

Even in the most 'advanced' nations, it remains true that positions of public power are overwhelmingly held by men; meanwhile women as a group continue to work much longer hours than men (particularly within the home) and to receive far less financial reward, while fear of sexual violence restricts their lives and they are denied full control over their own reproduction.

In this context, media talk of a 'post-feminist era' is nonsense. Feminism may seem less fashionable than a few years ago, but its assumptions have entered the consciousness of too many people to be easily cast aside. With the possible exception of the United States, feminist political theory has not yet won its place at the forefront of academic or political debate. Nevertheless it continues to flourish; it provides above all a self-consciousness about feminist issues and a knowledge of how these have been misunderstood, manipulated and marginalised in the past that is vital if feminist gains are to be defended and feminist issues kept on the political agenda.

This means that the very diversity of modern feminist political theory is itself a source of strength, a way of keeping issues alive and ensuring that they are not buried under the dead weight of some feminist orthodoxy. However, as I have argued in the preceding chapters, the apparently conflicting assumptions behind the different schools of feminist thought conceal the extent to which these are in important respects converging. This means that although significant differences remain, we can identify areas of agreement that must form the basis for any feminist political theory in the 1990s and beyond.

A starting-point for such a theory must be an expanded conception of politics, based on the understanding that power relations between men and women are not confined to the 'public' worlds of law, the state and economics, but that they pervade all areas of life. This means that, contrary to the assumptions of traditional political theory, the family, reproduction and sexuality must be included in political analysis. This perception that 'the personal is political' is of course central to radical feminism, and it should by now be clear that no theory that claims to take women's needs seriously can ignore it. Although it has no place in traditional Marxism, this understanding has not been entirely absent from the socialist tradition, and some of its implications were explored long ago by the utopian socialists, Charlotte Perkins Gilman and Alexandra Kollontai; today many socialist feminists are attempting to expand, reinterpret or supplement orthodox Marxist concepts so as to apply them to personal life. Liberal feminists too are increasingly arguing that equality and justice require changes in the family as well as in the law and public life. For many, this perception is simply the result of practical experience, as domestic responsibilities conflict with the demands of a career and even Superwomen get tired; at a more theoretical level, Okin has recently developed an important new theory of justice which builds upon liberal ideas but which rejects the public/private dichotomy and treats justice within the family as central.

Feminism therefore challenges not only the conclusions but the content of traditional political theory. It has also discovered that existing concepts and values are not gender neutral but frequently reflect the limited perceptions of men. It cannot therefore use these as ready-made tools for feminist analysis; it may however be able to criticise, modify or build upon them to develop more comprehensive theories. For example, the Marxist concept of productive work has been expanded to include that traditionally done by women, and a more critical approach to liberal values suggests the possibility of a concept of equality which does not exclude the significance of difference, an autonomy that recognises human interdependence and an idea of reason that does not stand in opposition to emotion, intuition or physicality.

Although feminists are increasingly agreed that the values of existing political theory are inadequate, they have not developed an agreed goal of their own, and there seems little common ground between those who seek success in the boardroom, those who preach communist revolution, those who insist that 'womanly virtues' must be envalued and learned by men, and those who would like to replace men by sperm-banks or pathogenesis. A few use arguments based on post-modernist theory to defend this situation, and to reject the whole idea of identifying agreed feminist goals as a totalitarian enterprise that denies the diversity and specificity of women's experiences. Taken to an extreme, this would rob feminism of any meaning or content, denying the significance of shared experiences, the desirability of freedom over slavery or the possibility of collective action; nevertheless it may also serve as a salutary warning of the dangers of confusing particular solutions with universal goals. Certainly there seems little hope of agreement between those radical feminists who believe that gender divisions are biologically ordained and who therefore see lesbian separatism as the only solution, and the majority who continue to believe that men are not beyond redemption and that a sexually egalitarian society is in principle possible. Behind this, however, there are signs that different perspectives are drawing closer together as they move away from their origins in male theory and become increasingly based on the realities of women's lives and struggles. Thus although liberal feminists may hope to change only gender relations and to keep all other social structures intact, in practice their ideas have far-reaching and subversive implications that challenge both conventional family structures and dominant economic thinking. At the same time, socialist feminists are increasingly disinclined to preach the necessity or imminence of anti-capitalist revolution and, like radical feminists, they are now more likely to defend existing legal rights and reforms (such as legal abortions or family allowances) than to dismiss these as 'mere formalities'. At the most general level, there is widespread agreement that the ideal society would be one in which gender inequalities were ended and women were enabled to realise their full potential in all areas of life. It also seems likely that for such a society to exist, activities traditionally associated with women would be more highly valued than in the past. Here liberal feminists might see child-rearing as a potentially fulfilling aspect of life that can be shared with men or professionally trained carers, while an expansion of Marxist concepts allows socialists to understand the importance of domestic work, and all can agree on the need for a more caring and nurturing approach to the resources of our planet. At a practical level, it must also be particularly important to ensure that the bearing and raising of children be made compatible with other activities, so that mothers can also be fully active citizens and workers – this might involve flexible working practices, collective provision of childcare, shared parenting with men, or a combination of all three.

If feminist theory is to establish the basis for political action, it must not only discover the nature of the sexually just society, but it must also analyse the opportunities and problems involved in achieving it. Here it is necessary to understand that because men as a group are privileged by existing gender inequalities, they will have an interest in maintaining them; this is not to say that all men consciously or actively oppress all women, or that they may not be in some ways disadvantaged by present arrangements, but simply to note that at a general level they are systematically favoured over women and that the structures of society support their interests. Such key institutions as the state or the educational system are therefore not neutral, but reflect the perceptions, interests and priorities of the men who control them. Recognition of this need not mean that society is monolithically oppressive or that political struggle should be abandoned, but it allows this struggle to be based on a realistic assessment of the opposition that women are likely to face, and enables us to understand that, contrary to the assumptions of many liberal feminists, the rightness and rationality of feminist demands are not enough to ensure their success. Some men may, however, support feminist goals, either because they are persuaded that they are just, or because they perceive that they too will gain from feminist change. Here good feminist theory should enable us to recognise the possibility of such support by distinguishing between the structures and agents of oppression, so that individual men are not simply or necessarily 'the enemy', but may also be seen as potential allies. This implies that although women will frequently choose to organise autonomously, and must treat offers of male support with great caution, the possibility of working with men to achieve feminist goals should not automatically be rejected.

It is, however, not simply the vested interests of men that may come into conflict with feminist demands, but particular economic interests or indeed the whole of the dominant economic system. Socialist and Marxist feminists have analysed at length the ways in which gender inequality serves the needs of capitalism and the ruling class, and many have argued that women's position cannot be significantly improved without far-reaching economic change. Although in principle liberal feminists reject this analysis and do not wish to challenge capitalist or free market assumptions, the logic of some of their recent demands does precisely this. Thus for example equal pay legislation, the elimination of sexism in education and the monitoring of employment practices all involve an increase in state intervention and planning, while it seems unlikely that an economic system based purely upon the pursuit of profit would provide good quality childcare and the kind of flexible working arrangements that would allow men and women to combine full participation in child-rearing with the pursuit of a career. To understand opposition to feminist demands it is therefore once again necessary to understand the full implications of these and the opposing interests that may be involved; this does not have to mean that no feminist goals can be met unless accompanied by full-scale revolution but it does indicate that to be meaningful they will have to involve quite widespread social and economic changes and that these are likely to be resisted by existing powerful groups.

While quite clearly women must be the starting point for feminist theory, this must also recognise that gender division is not the only significant source of social inequality, and that for many women race or class may be more important. This means that simplistic assertions as to the universality of women's experience must be rejected; these deny the very real differences that exist amongst women and, by invoking a spurious sisterhood that takes white middle-class women as the norm, can constitute a form of racism and elitism. Rather than engaging in a sterile debate as to which is the most important, feminism must develop an analysis that recognises the interaction of different forms of oppression and does not treat women as a unitary group that can be abstracted from all other social relationships. Such an approach allows scope for solidarity with some men in their struggle against race or class oppression, but can also make visible both the sexism of some black and working-class men and the racism and elitism of some white and middle-class feminist women. Ultimately, it may make possible a worldwide feminism based on the understanding that on a global scale there are both underlying patterns of gender inequality and an enormous diversity of needs and experiences that divide as well as unite women.

Above all, modern feminist theory must understand that the problems of gender inequality have no simple explanation or easy solution. It must avoid the kind of reductionism that claims that the economic system (or the family, or the law, or pornography, or reproduction, or language . . .) holds *the* key to understanding or changing the position of women. Instead, it must recognise the multiplicity and the interconnectedness of the forces that maintain present inequalities, the inadequacy of any one-dimensional attempt at change and the impossibility of isolating gender issues from other structured inequalities. Although there is a danger that this recognition will lead to a sense of helplessness and a paralysis of political will, a proper understanding can show that although any kind of action may be inadequate in itself, it gains significance and strength when accompanied by other forms of struggle. This means that there must be flexibility and a plurality of forms of feminist political activity, which should be seen as complementary rather than rival feminist strategies. It does not, however, absolve feminists from the need to assess priorities and possibilities or imply that all actions are equally valid; here good feminist theory must enable us to make effective political choices, and it will not allow pluralism to disintegrate into total relativism.

Feminist political theory must therefore liberate itself from categories that are derived from male priorities and that are dissolving in the light of women's needs and experiences. At present, it is still inevitably the product of Western political thought, but it must also be opened to ideas from outside this tradition: this is not simply a case of 'adding on' the perspectives of different cultures or non-white women, but may involve a reassessment of our understandings as basic as that which Western feminism demands of male-stream theory. It must in addition guard against the kind of self-referential elitism that may further academic careers but is quite inaccessible to the majority of women. Good feminist theory will not be easy, but it must not be needlessly obscure, and if it is to form the basis of collective action and understanding, it must get out of its ivory tower and into the minds of women. Feminism is not a closed book; it is essential that it becomes a readable one.

Bibliography

Abel, E. and Abel, E. (eds) (1983) *The Signs Reader* (Chicago: Chicago University Press).

Alcoff, L. (1988) 'Cultural Feminism versus Poststructuralism: The Identity Crisis in Feminist Theory', *Signs*, vol. 13.

Alexander, S. (1987) 'Women, Class and Sexual Difference', in A. Phillips (ed.).

Alexander, S. and Taylor, B. (1982) 'In Defence of Patriarchy', in M. Evans (ed.).

Amos, V. and Parmar, P. (1984) 'Challenging Imperial Feminism', *Feminist Review* no. 17.

Annas, J. (1977) 'Mill and the Subjection of Women', *Philosophy*, vol. 52.

Anthony, S. B. (ed.) (1987) *The History of Woman Suffrage*, vol. III (New York: Fowler and Wells).

Anthony, S. B. and Harper, I. H. (eds) (1902) *The History of Woman Suffrage vo. IV* (New York: Fowler and Wells).

Appignanesi, L. (1988) *Simone de Beauvoir* (Harmondsworth: Penguin).

Arditti, R. *et al.* (1984) *Test-tube Woman* (London: Pandora Press).

Ashton, F. and Whitting, G. (eds) (1987) *Feminist Theory and Practical Policies. Shifting the Agenda in the 1980s* (Bristol: School for Advanced Urban Studies).

Assiter, A. (1989) *Pornography, Feminism and the Individual* (London: Pluto Press).

Bacchi, C. (1990) *Same Difference. Feminism and Sexual Difference* (London: Allen and Unwin).

Badinter, E. (1989) *Man/Woman. The One is the Other* (London: Collins Harvill).

Badran, M. and Cooke, M. (1990) *Opening the Gates. A Century of Arab Feminist Writing* (London: Virago).

Baker, K. (ed.) (1976) *Condorcet. Selected Writings* (Indianapolis: Bobs-Merrill).

Ball, T. (1980) 'Utilitarianism, Feminism and the Franchise: James Mill and his Critics', *History of Political Thought*, vol. 1.

Banks, O. (1985) *The Biographical Dictionary of British Feminists* vol. I, *1800–1930* (Brighton: Harvester Press).

Banks, O. (1986) *Faces of Feminism* (Oxford: Basil Blackwell).

Banner, L. (1980) *Elizabeth Cady Stanton. A Radical for Woman's Rights* (Boston and Toronto: Little, Brown).

de la Barre, F.P. (1990) *The Equality of the Sexes* translated and with an introduction by D. Clarke (Manchester and New York: Manchester University Press).

Barrett, M. (1984) 'Rethinking Women's Oppression: a reply to Brenner and Ramas', *New Left Review* no. 146.

Barrett, M. (1985) 'Weir and Wilson on Feminist Politics', *New Left Review*, no. 150.

Barrett, M. (1987) 'Marxist Feminism and the Work of Karl Marx', in A. Phillips (ed.).

Barrett, M. (1988) *Women's Oppression Today. The Marxist/Feminist Encounter* (London: Verso).

Barrett, M. Campbell, B., Phillips, A., Weir, E. and Wilson, E. (1986) 'Feminism and Class Politics: A Round-Table Discussion', *Feminist Review*, no. 23.

Barrett, M. and McIntosh, M. (1979) 'Christian Delphy: Towards a Materialist Feminism?', *Feminist Review*, no. 1.

Barrett, M. and McIntosh, M. (1982) *The Anti-Social Family* (London: Verso).

Barrett, M. and McIntosh, M. (1985) 'Ethnocentrism and Socialist-Feminist Theory', *Feminist Review*, no. 20.

de Beauvoir, S. (1968) *Force of Circumstance* (Harmondsworth: Penguin).

de Beauvoir, S. (1972) *The Second Sex* (Harmondsworth: Penguin).

de Beauvoir, S. (1974) *All Said and Done* (London: André Deutsch and Weidenfeld and Nicolson).

de Beauvoir, S. (1987) 'Women and Creativity', in T. Moi (ed.).

Bebel, A. (1904) *Woman under Socialism* translated by D. de Leon (New York: New York Labour Press).

Beecher, J. and Bienveneau, R. (1972) *The Utopian Vision of Charles Fourier. Selected texts on Work, Love and Passionate Attraction* (London: Jonathan Cape).

Beechey, V. (1979) 'On Patriarchy', *Feminist Review* no. 3.

Beechey, V. (1982) 'Some Notes on Female Wage Labour in Capitalist Production', in M. Evans (ed).

Beechey, V. and Perkins, T. (1987) *A Matter of Hours: Women, Part-time Work and the Labour Market* (Cambridge: Polity Press).

Benhabib, S. and Cornell, D. (eds) (1987) *Feminism as Critique* (Oxford: Polity Press).

Benston, M. (1969) 'The Political Economy of Women's Liberation', *Monthly Review* vol. 21, no. 4.

Bernstein, S. (1962) *The First International in America* (New York: Augustus M. Kelly).

Bhavnani, K. and Coulson, M. (1986) 'Transforming Socialist Feminism: The Challenge of Racism', *Feminist Review* no. 23.

Bhavnani, R. (1987) 'Race, Women and Class: Integrating Theory and Practice', in F. Ashton and G. Wittig (eds).

270   *Bibliography*

Bland, L. (1987) 'The Married Woman, the 'New Woman' and Femininity: Sexual Politics in the 1890s', in J. Rendall (ed.).

Boralevi, L. (1987) 'Utilitarianism and Feminism', in E. Kennedy and S. Mendus (eds).

Borchorst, A. and Siim, B. (1987) 'Women and the Advanced Welfare State – A New Kind of Patriarchal Power?', in A.S. Sassoon (ed.).

Bouchier, D. (1983) *The Feminist Challenge* (London: Macmillan).

Boxer, M. and Quataert, J. (eds) (1978) *Socialist Women. European Socialist Feminism in the Nineteenth and Early Twentieth Centuries* (New York: Elsevier North-Holland).

Braidotti, R. (1986) 'Ethics Revisited: Women and/in Philosophy', in C. Pateman (ed.).

Braun, L. (1987) *Selected Writings on Feminism and Socialism* translated and edited by G. Meyer (Bloomington and Indianapolis: Indiana University Press).

Brennan, T. and Pateman, C. (1979) 'Mere Auxiliaries to the Commonwealth: Women and the Origins of Liberalism', *Political Studies*, vol. 27.

Brenner, J. and Ramas, M. (1984) 'Rethinking Women's Oppression', *New Left Review*, no. 144.

Brittan, A. and Maynard, M. (1984) *Sexism, Racism and Oppression* (Oxford: Basil Blackwell).

Brody, M. (1983) 'Mary Wollstonecraft: Sexuality and Women's Rights', in D. Spender (ed.).

Brooke, C. (1978) 'The Retreat to Cultural Feminism', in Redstockings (ed.).

Browne, A. (1987) *The Eighteenth Century Feminist Mind* (Brighton: Harvester Press).

Brownmiller, S. (1977) *Against Our Will* (Harmondsworth: Penguin).

Buckley, M. (1989) *Women and Ideology in the Soviet Union* (New York and London: Harvester Wheatsheaf).

Buhle, M. (1981) *Women and American Socialism 1870–1920* (Urbana, Chicago and London: University of Illinois Press).

Buhle, M. and Buhle, P. (eds) (1978) *The Concise History of Woman Suffrage. Selections from the Classic Works of Stanton, Anthony, Gage and Harper* (Urbana, Chicago and London: University of Illinois Press).

Bulbeck, C. (1988) *One World Women's Movement* (London: Pluto Press).

Burton, C. (1985) *Subordination. Feminism and Social Theory* (London: Allen and Unwin).

Bussey, G. and Tims, M. (1980) *Pioneers for Peace. Women's International League for Peace and Freedom* (London: WILPF British Section).

Caine, B. (1982) 'Feminism, Suffrage and the Nineteenth Century Women's Movement', *Women's Studies International Forum*, vol. 5, no. 6.

Caldecott, L. and Leland, S. (eds) (1983) *Reclaim the Earth. Women speak out for Life on Earth* (London: Women's Press).

Cambridge Women's Peace Collective (1984) *My Country is the Whole World. An Anthology of Women's Work on Peace and War* (London: Pandora Press).

Cameron, D. (1985) *Feminism and Linguistic Theory* (London: Macmillan).

Cameron, D. (ed.) (1990) *The Feminist Critique of Language* (London: Routledge).

Canovan, M. (1987) 'Rousseau's Two Concepts of Citizenship', in E. Kennedy and S. Mendus (eds).

Carter, A. (1988) *The Politics of Women's Rights* (London and New York: Longman).

Carver, T. (1985) 'Engels' Feminism', *History of Political Thought* vol. 6.

Charvet, J. (1982) *Feminism* (London: Dent).

Cheatham, A. and Powell, M. (1986) *This Way Daybreak Comes. Women's Values and the Future* (Philadelphia: New Society Publishers).

Chester, G. and Dickey, J. (eds) (1988) *Feminism and Censorship: The Current Debate* (Bridport, Dorset: Prism Press).

Chodorow, N. (1978) *The Reproduction of Mothering. Psychoanalysis and the Sociology of Gender* (Berkeley, Los Angeles and London: University of California Press).

Cixous, H. (1981) 'The Laugh of the Medusa', in E. Marks and I. de Courtrivon (eds).

Clark, L. and Lange, L. (1979) *The Sexism of Social and Political Theory. Women and Reproduction from Plato to Nietzsche* (London: University of Toronto Press).

Clements, B. (1979) *Bolshevik Feminist. The Life of Alexander Kollontai* (Bloomington and London: Indiana University Press).

Cliff, T. (1987) *Class Struggle and Women's Liberation* (London: Bookmarks).

Coates, J. (1986) *Women, Men and Language* (London and New York: Longman).

Cocks, J. (1989) *The Oppositional Imagination* (London: Routledge).

Collard, A. with Contrussi, J. (1988) *Rape of the Wild. Man's Violence against Animals and the Earth* (London: Women's Press).

Collins, P. (1989) 'The Social Construction of Black Feminist Thought', *Signs*, vol. 14.

Collins, P. (1990) *Black Feminist Thought* (London, Sydney and Wellington: Unwin Hyman).

Condorcet (1976) *Selected Writings* edited and with an introduction by K. Barker (Indianapolis: Bobs-Merrill).

Cook, B.W. (ed) (1978) *Crystal Eastman on Women and Revolution* (Oxford: Oxford University Press).

Coole, D. (1988) *Women in Political Theory* (Brighton: Wheatsheaf).

Coote, A. and Campbell, B. (1982) *Sweet Freedom* (London: Picador).

Coote, A. and Patullo, P. (1990) *Power and Prejudice. Women and Politics* (London: Weidenfeld and Nicolson).

Corea, G. *et al.* (1985) *Man-Made Woman. How New Reproductive Technologies Affect Women* (London: Hutchinson).

Cott, N. (1987) *The Grounding of Modern Feminism* (New Haven and London: Yale University Press).

Cottrell, R. (1975) *Simone de Beauvoir* (New York: Frederick Ungar).

Coulson, M., Magas, B. and Wainwright, H. (1979) 'The Housewife and her Labour under Capitalism: a Critique', *New Left Review*, no. 89.

Coward, R. (1983) *Patriarchal Precedents* (London: Routledge and Kegan Paul).

Dahlerup, D. (1986) *The New Woman's Movement. Feminism and Political Power in Europe and the USA* (London: Sage).

Dahlerup, D. (1987) 'Confusing Concepts – Confusing Reality: A Theoretical Discussion of the Patriarchal State', in A. S. Sassoon (ed).

Dale, J. and Foster, P. (1986) *Feminists and State Welfare* (London: Routledge and Kegan Paul).

Dalla Costa, M. (1973) *The Power of Women and the Subversion of the Community* (Bristol: Falling Wall Press).

Daly, M. (1973) *Beyond God the Father. Towards a Philosophy of Women's Liberation* (Boston: Beacon Press).

Daly, M. (1978) *Gyn/Ecology. The Metaethics of Radical Feminism* (Boston: Beacon Press).

Daly, M. (1984) *Pure Lust. Elemental Feminist Philosophy* (London: Women's Press).

Davis, A. (1982) *Women, Race and Class* (London: Women's Press).

Davis, A. (1990) *Women, Culture and Politics* (London: Women's Press).

Davies, M. (ed) (1978) *Maternity. Letters from Working Women* (London: Virago).

Degler, C. (1966) 'Introduction' to C. P. Gilman, *Women and Economics* (New York: Torchbook).

Delmar, R. (1976) 'Looking Again at Engels' "Origin of the Family, Private Property and the State" ', in J. Mitchell and A. Oakley (eds).

Delmar, R. (1986) 'What is Feminism?' in J. Mitchell and A. Oakley (eds).

Delphy, C. (1977) *The Main Enemy* (London: Women's Research and Resources Centre).

Delphy, C. (1980) 'A Materialist Feminism is Possible', *Feminist Review*, no. 4.

Delphy, C. (1981) 'For a Materialist Feminism', *Feminist Studies*, no. 2.

Delphy, C. (1984) *Close to Home. A Materialist Analysis of Women's Oppression* (London: Hutchinson).

Dietz, M. (1985) 'Citizenship with a Feminist Face. The Problem with Maternal Thinking', *Political Theory*, vol. 13.

Dinnerstein, D. (1987) *The Rocking of the Cradle and the Ruling of the World* (London: Women's Press).

Draper, H. (1972) 'Marx and Engels on Women's Liberation', in R. Salper (ed.).

Draper, H. and Lipow, A. (1976) 'Marxist Women versus Bourgeois Feminism', in *Socialist Register*, ed. R. Miliband (London: Merlin).

Dubois, E. (1979) 'The Nineteenth Century Woman Suffrage Movement and the Analysis of Women's Oppression' in Z. Eisenstein (ed.).

Dubois, E. (1981) *Elizabeth Cady Stanton and Susan B. Anthony: Correspondence, Writings, Speeches* with a critical commentary by E. Dubois (New York: Schocken Books).

Dubois, E. (1987) 'The Radicalisation of the Woman Suffrage Movement', in A. Phillips (ed.).

Duchen, C. (1986) *Feminism in France* (London: Routledge and Kegan Paul).

Dworkin, A. (1974) *Woman Hating* (New York: E. P. Dutton).

Dworkin, A. (1981) *Pornography. Men Possessing Women* (London: Women's Press).

Dworkin, A. (1982) *Our Blood. Prophecies and Discourses on Sexual Politics* (London: Women's Press).

Dworkin, A. (1983) *Right-Wing Women. The Politics of Domesticated Females* (London: Women's Press).

Dworkin, A. (1988) *Letters from a War Zone* (London: Secker and Warburg).

Eastman, C. (1978) *Crystal Eastman on Women and Revolution* edited by B. Cook (Oxford: Oxford University Press).

Eckhart, C. (1984) *Fanny Wright: Rebel in America* (Cambridge, Mass. and London: Harvard University Press).

Edmondson, L. (1981) 'Sylvia Pankhurst: Suffragist, Feminist or Socialist?', in J. Slaughter and R. Kearns (eds).

Edmondson, L. (1984) *Feminism in Russia 1900–1917* (London: Heinemann Educational).

Eisenstein, H. (1984) *Contemporary Feminist Thought* (London: Unwin Paperbacks).

Eisenstein, Z. (ed.) (1979) *Capitalist Patriarchy and the Case for Socialist Feminism* (New York and London: Monthly Review Press).

Eisenstein, Z. (1981) *The Radical Future of Liberal Feminism* (New York and London: Longman)

Eisenstein, Z. (1984) *Feminism and Sexual Equality* (New York: Monthly Review Press)

Elshtain, J. (1981) 'Against Androgyny', *Telos*, no. 47.

Elshtain, J. (1981) *Public Man, Private Woman* (Oxford: Martin Robertson).

Elshtain, J. (ed.) (1982) *The Family in Political Thought* (Brighton: Harvester Press).

Elshtain, J. (1987) *Women and War* (Brighton: Harvester Press).

Engel, B. (1978) 'From Separatism to Socialism: Women in the Russian Revolutionary Movement of the 1870s', in M. Boxer and J. Quataert (eds).

Engels, F. (1973) *The Condition of the Working-class in England* (Moscow: Progress Publishers).

Engels, F. (1978) *The Origin of the Family, Private Property and the State* (Peking: Foreign Languages Press).

Ericson, Y. and Jacobsson, R. (eds) (1985) *Side by Side. A Report on Equality between Women and Men in Sweden* (Stockholm: Gotab).

Evans, J. *et al.* (1986) *Feminism and Political Theory* (London: Sage).

Evans, M. (ed.) (1982) *The Woman Question. Readings on the Subordination of Women* (London: Fontana).

Evans, M. (1985) *Simone de Beauvoir. A Feminist Mandarin* (London and New York: Tavistock).

Evans, M. (1987) 'Engels: Materialism and Morality', in J. Sayers, M. Evans and N. Redclift (eds).

Evans, R. (1977) *The Feminists: Women's Emancipation Movements in Europe, America and Australasia 1840–1920* (London: Croom Helm).

Evans, R. (1980) 'Bourgeois Feminists and Women Socialists in Germany 1894–1914: Lost Opportunity or Inevitable Conflict?', *Women's Studies International Quarterly*, vol. 3.

Evans, R. (1987) *Comrades and Sisters. Feminism, Socialism and Pacifism in Europe, 1870–1945* (Sussex: Wheatsheaf Books).

Evans, S. (1980) *Personal Politics. The Roots of Women's Liberation in the Civil Rights Movement and the New Left* (New York: Vintage Books).

Fairbairns, Z. (1979) *Benefits* (New York: Avon).

Farnsworth, B. (1978) 'Bolshevism, the Woman Question and Alexandra Kollontai', in M. Boxer and J Quataert (eds).

Feminist Review (1984) 'Many Voices, One Chant. Black Feminist Perspectives', *Feminist Review*, no. 17.

Feminist Review (ed.) (1986) *Waged Work. A Reader* (London: Virago).

Ferguson, A. (1981) 'Androgyny as an Ideal for Human Development', in M. Vetterling-Braggin, F. Elliston and J. English (eds).

Ferguson, A. (1989) *Blood at the Root* (London: Pandora Press).

Ferguson, K. (1980) *Self, Society and Womankind. The Dialectics of Liberation* (Westport, Conn.: Greenwood Press).

Ferguson, M. (ed.) (1985) *First Feminists. British Women Writers 1578–1799* (Bloomington: Indiana University Press).

Ferguson, M. and Todd, J. (1984) *Mary Wollstonecraft* (Boston: Twayne Publishers).

Figes, E. (1978) *Patriarchal Attitudes* (London: Virago).

Firestone, S. (1979) *The Dialectic of Sex* (London: Women's Press).

First, R. and Scott, A. (1980) *Olive Schreiner, a Biography* (London: André Deutsch).

Flax, J. (1981) 'Do Feminists Need Marxism?', in *Building Feminist Theory. Essays from Quest* (London: Longman).

Flax, J. (1986) 'Postmodernism and Gender Theory', *Signs*, vol. 12.

Flax, J. (1990) *Thinking Fragments* (Berkeley, California: University of California Press).

Flexner, E. (1959) *Century of Struggle. The Women's Rights Movement in the United States* (Cambridge, Mass.: Harvard University Press).

Florence, M. *et al.* (1987) *Militarism versus Feminism. Writings on Women and War*, edited by M. Kamester and J. Vellacott (London: Virago).

Florent, S. (1988) 'Women and Politics 1830–1850', unpublished MA Dissertation, Manchester Polytechnic.

Foner, P. (1984) *Clara Zetkin. Selected Writings* (New York: International Publishers).

Foreman, A. (1978) *Femininity as Alienation* (London: Pluto Press).

Forster, M. (1984) *Significant Sisters. The Grassroots of Active Feminism 1839–1939* (Harmondsworth: Penguin).

Forster, P. and Sutton, I. (eds) (1989) *Daughters of de Beauvoir* (London: Women's Press).

Freeman, J. (1975) *The Politics of Women's Liberation* (New York and London: Longman).

French, M. (1985) *Beyond Power. Women, Men and Morals* (London: Jonathan Cape).

Friedan, B. (1986) *The Feminine Mystique* (Harmondsworth: Penguin Books).

Friedan, B. (1970) 'Our Revolution is Unique', in M. L. Thompson (ed).

Friedan, B. (1977) *It Changed My Life. Writings on the Women's Movement* (London: Victor Gollanz).

Friedan, B. (1981) *The Second Stage* (London: Michael Joseph).

Gardiner, J. (1975) 'Women's Domestic Labour', *New Left Review*, no. 89.

Garnett, R. G. (1972) *Co-operation and the Owenite Socialist Communities in Britain 1825–45* (Manchester: Manchester University Press).

Garry, A. and Pearsall, M. (eds) (1989) *Women, Knowledge and Reality. Explorations in Feminist Philosophy* (Boston and London: Unwin Hyman).

George, M. (1970) *One Woman's 'Situation': a Study of Mary Wollstonecraft* (Urbana, Chicago, London: University of Illinois Press).

German, L. (1989) *Sex, Class and Socialism* (London: Bookmarks).

Gilligan, C. (1982) *In a Different Voice. Psychological Theory and Women's Development* (Cambridge, Mass. and London: Harvard University Press).

Gilman, C. P. (1904) *Human Work* (New York: McClare, Phillips).

Gilman, C. P. (1906) *Women and Economics* (London: Putnam, and Boston: Small, Maynard).

Gilman, C. P. (1911) *The Man Made World* (London: T. Fisher Unwin).

Gluck, S. (1987) 'Socialist Feminism Between Two World Wars: Insights from Oral History', in C. Scharf and J. Jenson (eds).

Goldman, E. (1979) *Red Emma Speaks. The Selected Speeches and Writings of the Anarchist and Feminist Emma Goldman* edited by A. K. Shulman (London: Wildwood House).

Goldstein, L. (1980) 'Mill, Marx and Women's Liberation', *Journal of the Philosophy of History*, vol. 18.

Goldstein, L. (1982) 'Early Themes in French Utopian Socialism: the St. Simonians and Fourier', *Journal of the History of Ideas*, no. 43.

Goreau, A. (1983) 'Aphra Benn: a Scandal to Modesty', in D. Spender (ed.).

de Gouges, O. (1980) 'Declaration of the Rights of Woman', in E. Reimar and J. Fout (eds).

Greer, G. (1979) *The Female Eunuch* (London: Paladin).

Greer, G. (1984) *Sex and Destiny. The Politics of Human Fertility* (London: Secker and Warburg).

Grewal, S. *et al.* (1988) *Charrting the Journey. Writings by Black and Third World Women* (London: Sheba).

Griffin, S. (1981) *Pornography and Silence: Culture's Revenge against Nature* (London: Women's Press).

Griffin, S. (1984) *Woman and Nature. The Roaring Inside Her* (London: Women's Press).

Griffith, E. (1984) *In Her Own Right. The Life of Elizabeth Cady Stanton* (New York and Oxford: Oxford University Press).

Griffiths, M. and Whitford, M. (eds) (1988) *Feminist Perspectives in Philosophy* (Basingstoke: Macmillan Press).

Grimshaw, J. (1982) 'Feminism: History and Morality', *Radical Philosphy*, no. 30.

Grimshaw, J. (1986) *Feminist Philosophers: Women's Perspectives on Philosophical Traditions* (Brighton: Wheatsheaf).

Grimshaw, J. (1989) 'Mary Wollstonecraft and the Tensions in Feminist Philosophy', *Radical Philosophy*, no. 52.

Gross, E. (1986a) 'Philosophy, Subjectivity and the Body: Kristeva and Irigaray', in C. Pateman and E. Gross (eds).

Gross, E. (1986b) 'What is Feminist Theory?', in C. Pateman and E. Gross (eds).

Grosz, E. (1990) *Jacques Lacan: a Feminist Introduction* (London and New York: Routledge).

Guettel, C. (1974) *Marxism and Feminism* (Ontario: Canadian Women's Educational Press).

Gunew, S. (ed.) (1991) *A Reader in Feminist Knowledge* (London: Routledge).

Hall, S. and Jacques, M. (eds) (1989) *New Times. The Changing Face of Politics in the 1990s* (London: Lawrence and Wishart).

Hanmer, J. (1978) 'Violence and the Social Control of Women', in G. Littlejohn *et al. Power and the State* (London: Croom Helm).

Hardy, D. (1979) *Alternative Communities in Nineteenth Century England* (London and New York: Longman).

Harrison, J. (1969) *Robert Owen and the Owenites in Britain and America* (London: Routledge and Kegan Paul).

Harstock, N. (1979) 'Feminist Theory and the Development of Revolutionary Strategy', in Z. Eisenstein (ed.).

Hartmann, H. (1983) 'Capitalism, Patriarchy and Job Segregation by Sex', in E. Abel and E. Abel (eds.).

Hartmann, H. (1986) 'The Unhappy Marriage of Marxism and Feminism: Towards a More Progressive Union', in L. Sargent (ed.).

Hawkesworth, M. (1988) 'Feminist Rhetoric. Discourses on the Male Monopoly of Thought', *Political Theory*, vol. 16.

Hawkesworth, M. E. (1990) *Beyond Oppression* (New York: Continnuum).

Hayek, F. A. (ed.) (1951) *John Stuart Mill and Harriet Taylor. Their Friendship and Subsequent Marriage* (London: Routledge and Kegan Paul).

Heath, J. (1989) *Simone de Beauvoir* (New York and London: Harvester Wheatsheaf).

Hedman, C. (1990) 'The Artificial Womb', *Radical Philosophy*, no. 56.

Heinen, J. (1978) 'Kollontai and the History of Women's Oppression', *New Left Review*, no. 110.

Hernes, H. (1988) 'The Welfare State, Citizenship and Scandinavian Women' in K. Jones and A. Jonasdottir (eds).

Herstein, S. R. (1985) *A Mid-Victorian Feminist: Barbara Leigh-Smith Bodichon* (London and New Haven: Yale University Press).

Hewlett, S. A. (1988) *A Lesser Life. The Myth of Women's Liberation* (London: Sphere).

Hill, B. (1986) *The First English Feminist. Reflections upon Marriage and other Writings by Mary Astell*, edited and with an Introduction by B. Hill (Aldershot: Gower).

Hill, M. A. (1980) *Charlotte Perkins Gilman. The Making of a Radical Feminist 1860–1896* (Philadelphia: Temple University Press).

Hills, J. *et al.* (1986) *Feminism and Political Theory* (London: Sage).

Holland, B. (ed.) (1985) *Soviet Sisterhood* (Bloomington: Indiana University Press).

Holt, A. (1977) *Alexandra Kollontai. Selected Writings* (London: Allison and Busby).

Honeycut, K. (1981) 'Clara Zetkin: A Socialist Approach to the Problem of Women's Oppression', in J. Slaughter and R. Kearns (eds).

hooks, b. (1981) *Ain't I a Woman. black women and feminism* (Boston: South End Press).

hooks, b. (1984) *Feminist Theory: from margin to center* (Boston, Mass.: South End Press).

hooks, b. (1991) *Yearning. race, gender and cultural politics* (London: Turnaround).

Hull, G. Scott, P. and Smith, B. (eds) (1982) *But Some of Us Are Brave. Black Women's Studies* (New York: Feminist Press).

Humphries, J. (1982) 'The Working-Class Family: A Marxist Perspective' in J. Elshtain (ed.).

Humphries, J. (1987) 'The Origin of the Family: Born Out of Scarcity, not Wealth', in J. Sayers, M. Evans and N. Redclift (eds).

Hunt, K. (1986) 'Crossing the River of Fire: the Socialist Construction of Women's Politicization' in J. Evans (ed.).

Hunt, K. (1988) 'Equivocal Feminists. The Social Democratic Federation and the Woman Question 1884–1911', Unpublished PhD Thesis, University of Manchester.

Inman, M. (1936) *In Woman's Defence* (Los Angeles: Mercury Printing).

Irigaray, L. (1991) 'This Sex Which Is Not One' in S. Gunew (ed.).

Jaggar, A. (1983) *Feminist Politics and Human Nature* (Brighton: Harvester).

James, S. (1980) Introduction to 'The Power of Women and the Subversion of the Community', in E. Malos (ed.).

Janeway, E. (1972) *Man's World, Woman's Place. A Study in Social Mythology* (London: Michael Joseph).

Jebb, C. (ed.) (1912) *Mary Wollstonecroft* (London: Herbert and Daniel).

Jeffries, S. (1982) 'Free From All Uninvited Touch of Man: Women's Campaigns Around Sexuality 1880–1914', *Women's Studies International Forum*, vol. 5, no. 6.

Jeffries, S. (1990) *Anticlimax* (London: Women's Press).

Johnston, J. (1982) 'Lesbian Nation: The Feminist Solution', in M. Evans (ed.).

Jones, K. and Jonasdottir, A. (eds) (1988) *The Political Interests of Gender. Developing Theory and Research with a Human Face* (London: Sage).

Joseph, G. (1986) 'The Incompatible Menage à Trois: Marxism, Feminism and Racism', in L. Sargent (ed.).

Kamm, J. (1966) *Rapiers and Battleaxes: The Women's Movement and Its Aftermath* (London: Allen and Unwin).

Kamm, J. (1977) *John Stuart Mill in Love* (London: Gordon and Cremonesi).

Kanter, S., Lefanu, S., Shah, S. and Spedding, C. (eds) (1984) *Sweeping Statements. Writings from the Women's Liberation Movement 1981–83* (London: Women's Press).

Kauffman, L. (ed.) (1989) *Feminism and Institutions* (Oxford: Basil Blackwell).

Kazi, H. (1986) 'The Beginning of a Debate Long Due: Some Observations on "Ethnocentrism in Socialist Feminist Theory" ', *Feminist Review*, no. 22.

Keefe, T. (1983) *Simone de Beauvoir: a Study of Her Writings* (London: Harrap).

Kelly, L. (1987) *Women of the French Revolution* (London: Hamish Hamilton).

Kennedy, E. and Mendus, S. (eds) (1987) *Women in Western Political Philosophy: Kant to Nietzsche* (Brighton: Wheatsheaf Books).

Kent, S. (1990) *Sex and Suffrage in Britain* (London: Routledge).

King, D. (1988) 'Multiple Jeopardy, Multiple Consciousness: the Context of a Black Feminist Ideology', *Signs*, vol. 14.

King, Y. (1983) 'The Eco-feminist Imperative', in L. Caldecott and S. Leland (eds).

Kinnard, J. (1983) 'Mary Astell: Inspired by Ideas', in D. Spender (ed.).

Klein, V. (1946) *The Feminine Character. History of an Ideology* (London: Routledge and Kegan Paul).

Koedt, A. (1970) 'The Myth of the Vaginal Orgasm' in L. Tanner (ed.).

Kollontai, A. (1977) *Selected Writings*, translated and with an introduction and commentary by A. Holt (London: Allison and Busby).

Komisar, L. (1971) *The New Feminism* (London and New York: Franklin Watts).

Koonz, C. (1987) *Mothers in the Fatherland. Women, The Family and Nazi Politics* (London: Jonathan Cape).

Kraditor, A. S. (1965) *The Ideas of the Woman Suffrage Movement 1890–1920* (New York and London: Columbia University Press).

Kramnick, M. (1978) 'Introduction' to Mary Wollstonecraft's *Vindication of the Rights of Woman* (Harmondsworth: Penguin).

Kristeva, J. (1981) 'Woman Can Never Be Defined', in E. Marks and I. de Courtrivon (eds).

Kuhn, A. and Wolpe, A. (eds) (1978) *Feminism and Materialism. Women and Modes of Production* (London: Routledge and Kegan Paul).

Land, H. (1980) 'The Family Wage', *Feminist Review*, no. 6.

Land, H. (1984) 'The Introduction of Family Allowances' in C. Ungerson (ed.).

Landy, A. (1943) *Marxism and the Woman Question* (New York: New York Workers Library).

Lane, A. (1976) 'Women in Society: A Critique of Frederick Engels', in B. Carroll (ed.). *Liberating Women's History* (Urbana, Chicago and London: University of Chicago Press).

Lane, A. (1983) 'Charlotte Perkins Gilman: The Personal Is Political', in De. Spender (ed.).

Lean, P. (1986) 'The Role of "The Family" in Recent Feminist Thought' Unpublished M A Dissertation, University of Manchester.

Lederer, L. (ed.) (1980) *Take Back the Night* (New York: William Morrow).

Leeds Revolutionary Feminist Group (1982) 'Political Lesbianism: the Case Against Heterosexuality', in M. Evans (ed.).

Lees, S. (1986) 'Sex, Race and Culture: Feminism and the Limits of Cultural Pluralism', *Feminist Review*, no. 22.

Leighton, J. (1975) *Simone de Beauvoir on Women* (London: Associated University Press).

Lenin, V. (1977) *On the Emancipation of Women* (Moscow: Progress Publishers).

Lerner, G. (1986) *The Creation of Patriarchy* (Oxford and New York: Oxford University Press).

Levin, M. (1987) *Feminism and Freedom* (New Brunswick and Oxford: Transaction Books).

Levine, P. (1987) *Victorian Feminism 1850–1900* (London: Hutchinson).

Lewis, J. (ed.) (1983) *Women's Welfare, Women's Rights* (London and Canberra: Croom Helm).

Lewis, J. (1985) 'The Debate on Sex and Class', *New Left Review*, no. 149.

Liddington, J. (1984) *The Life and Times of a Respectable Rebel. Selina Cooper 1864–1946* (London: Virago).

Liddington, J. and Norris, J. (1978) *One Hand Tied Behind Us. The Rise of the Women's Suffrage Movement* (London: Virago).

Lloyd, G. (1984) *The Man of Reason. 'Male' and 'Female' in Western Philosophy* (London: Methuen).

Lockwood, G. (1971) *The New Harmony Movement* (New York: Dover).

Lorde, A. (1984) *Sister Outsider. Essays and Speeches* (New York: Crossing Press).

Lovell, T. (ed.) (1990) *British Feminist Thought. A Reader* (Oxford: Basil Blackwell).

Lovenduski, J. (1988) 'Feminism in the 1980s', *Politics*, vol. 8, no. 1.

Lovibond, S. (1989) 'Feminism and Postmodernism', *New Left Review*, no. 178.

Lutz, A. (1944) *Created Equal. A Biography of Elizabeth Cady Stanton* (New York: John Day).

Luxemburg, R. (1971) *Selected Political Writings*, edited and with an introduction by D. Howard (New York and London: Monthly Review Press).

MacKinnon, C. (1983) 'Feminism, Marxism, Method, and the State: an Agenda for Theory', in E. Abel and E. Abel (eds).

MacKinnon, C. (1989a) 'Sexuality, Pornography and Method: Pleasure under Patriarchy', *Ethics*, vol. 99, no. 2.

MacKinnon, C. (1989b) *Towards a Feminist Theory of the State* (London: Harvard University Press).

Maconachie, M. (1987) 'Engels, sexual divisions and the family', in J. Sayers, M. Evans and N. Redclift (eds).

Malos, E. (1980) *The Politics of Housework* (London: Allison and Busby Ltd.).

Malmgreen, G. (1978) *Neither Bread nor Roses: utopian feminists and the English working class* (Brighton: John L. Noyce).

Mansbridge, J. (1986) *Why We Lost The ERA* (Chicago and London: University of Chicago Press).

Marcus, J. (ed) (1987) *Suffrage and the Pankhursts* (London and New York: Routledge and Kegan Paul).

Marks, E. and de Courtivron, I. (eds) (1981) *New French Feminisms* (Brighton: Harvester Press).

Marsh, S. M. (1981) *Anarchist Women 1870–1920* (Philadelphia: Temple University Press).

Marx, K. (1972) *Critique of the Gotha Programme* (Peking: Foreign Languages Press).

Marx, K. (1963) *Early Writings*, translated and edited by T. B. Bottomore (London: Watts).

Marx, K. and Engels, F. (1982) *The German Ideology* (London: Lawrence and Wishart.)

Marx, K. and Engels, F. (1968) *Selected Works* (London: Lawrence and Wishart).

Marx, K., Engels, F., Lenin, V., and Stalin, J. (1975) *Women and Communism. Selections from the Writings of Marx, Engels, Lenin and Stalin* (Westport, Conn.: Greenwood Press).

Maynard, M. (1989) 'Privilege and Patriarchy: Feminist Thought in the Nineteenth Century', in S. Mendus and J. Rendall (eds).

McLaren, A. (1991) *A History of Contraception* (Oxford: Basil Blackwell).

McMillan, C. (1982) *Women, Reason and Nature. Some Philosophical Problems with Feminism* (Oxford: Basil Blackwell).

McMillan, J. (1981) *Housewife or Harlot: The Place of Women in French Society 1870–1940* (Brighton: Harvester Press).

Meehan, E. and Sevenhuijsen, S. (eds) (1991) *Equality Principles and Politics* (London: Sage).

Mendus, S. (1989) 'The Marriage of True Minds: the Ideal of Marriage in the Philosophy of John Stuart Mill', in S. Mendus and J. Rendall (eds).

Mendus, S. and Rendall, J. (eds) (1989) *Sexuality and Subordination* (London: Routledge and Kegan Paul).

Michels, R. (1962) *Political Parties*, translated by E. Paul and C. Paul (New York: Free Press).

Midgley, M. and Hughes, J. (1983) *Women's Choices. Philosophical Problems Facing Feminism* (London: Weidenfeld and Nicolson).

Mill, J. S. (1971) *Autobiography*, edited by J. Stillinger (Oxford: Oxford University Press).

Mill, J. S. (1900) *Principles of Political Economy* (London: Longmans, Green).

Mill, J. S. (1983) *The Subjection of Women* (London: Virago).

Mill, J. S. (1985) *John Stuart Mill on Politics and Society* edited by G. Williams (Glasgow: Fontana).

Miller, D. (1990) 'The Resurgence of Political Theory', *Political Studies*, vol. 38.

Millett, K. (1985) *Sexual Politics* (London: Virago).

Mirza, H. (1986) 'The Dilemma of Socialist Feminism: A Case for Black Feminism', *Feminist Reveiw*, no. 22.

Mitchell, C. (1989) 'Madame Pelletier (1874–1939): The Politics of Sexual Oppression', *Feminist Review*, no. 33.

Mitchell, H. (1977) *The Hard Way Up* (London: Virago).

Mitchell, J. (1971) *Woman's Estate* (Harmondsworth: Penguin).

Mitchell, J. (1974) *Psychoanalysis and Feminism* (London: Allen Lane).

Mitchell, J. (1984) *Women: the Longest Revolution* (London: Virago).

Mitchell, J. and Oakley, A. (eds) (1979) *The Rights and Wrongs of Women* (Harmondsworth: Penguin).

Mitchell, J. and Oakley, A. (eds) (1986) *What is Feminism?* (Oxford, Basil Blackwell).

Moi, T. (ed.) (1987) *French Feminist Thought. A Reader* (Oxford: Basil Blackwell).

Moi, T. (1990) *Feminist Theory and Simone de Beauvoir* (Oxford: Basil Blackwell).

Molyneux, M. (1979) 'Beyond the Domestic Labour Debate', *New Left Review*, no. 116.

Moon, S. (1978) 'Feminism and Socialism: the Utopian Synthesis of Flora Tristan', in M. Boxer and J. Quataert (eds).

Moraga, C. and Anzaldua, G. (eds) (1983) *This Bridge Called My Back:*

Writings by Radical Women of Color (New York: Kitchen Table, Women of Color Press).

Morewedge, R. (ed.) (1975) *The Role of Women in the Middle Ages* (London: Hodder and Stoughton).

Morgan, R. (ed.) (1970) *Sisterhood is Powerful. An Anthology of Writings from the Women's Liberation Movement* (New York: Vintage).

Morgan, R. (1978) *Going Too Far. The Personal Chronicle of a Feminist* (New York: Vintage).

Morgan, R. (1982) *The Anatomy of Freedom* (Oxford: Martin Robertson).

Morgan, R. (1984) *Sisterhood is Global. The International Women's Movement Anthology* (Harmondsworth: Penguin).

Morrell, C. (1980) ' "Black Friday": Violence Against Women in the Suffragette Movement', *Explorations in Feminism*, no. 9 (London: Women's Research and Resources Centre).

Muncy, R. (1973) *Sex and Marriage in Utopian Communities* (London and Bloomington: Indiana University Press).

Nicholson, L. J. (ed.) (1990) *Feminism/Postmodernism* (New York and London: Routledge).

Nye, A. (1990a) *Feminist Theory and the Philosophies of Man* (London: Routledge).

Nye, A. (1990b) *Words of Power: a Feminist Reading of the History of Logic* (London: Routledge).

Oakley, A. (1972) *Sex, Gender and Society* (London: Maurice Temple Smith).

Oakley, A. (1979) 'Wisewoman and Medicine Man: Changes in the Management of Childbirth, in J. Mitchell and A. Oakley (eds).

Oakley, A. (1983) 'Millicent Garrett Fawcett: Duty and Determination' in D. Spender (ed.).

O'Brien, M. (1979) 'Reproducing Marxist Man' in L. Clark and L. Lange (eds).

O'Brien, M. (1981) *The Politics of Reproduction* (London: Routledge and Kegan Paul).

Okely, J. (1986) *Simone de Beauvoir: A Re-Reading* (London: Virago).

Okin, S. M. (1980) *Women in Western Political Thought* (London: Virago).

Okin, S. M. (1987) 'Justice and Gender', *Philosophy and Public Affairs*, vol. 16, no. 1.

Okin, S. M. (1989) 'Reason and Feeling in Thinking about Justice', *Ethics*, vol. 99, no. 2.

Okin, S. M. (1990) *Justice, Gender and the Family* (New York: Basic Books).

O'Neil, W. (1969) *The Woman Movement. Feminism in the United States and England* (London: Allen and Unwin).

Owen, R. (1972) *A New View of Society and Other Writings*, introduced by J. Butt (London: David).

Owens, R. (1984) *Smashing Times. A History of the Irish Women's Suffrage Movement 1889–1922* (Dublin: Attic Press).

Paine, T. (1894) 'An Occasional Letter on the Female Sex', in *The Writings of Tom Paine*, vol. I, collected and edited by M. D. Conway (New York and London: Putnam).

Pankhurst, C. (1987) 'The Great Scourge and How to End It', in J. Marcus (ed.).

Pankhurst, S. (1977) *The Suffragette Movement* (London: Virago).

Pateman, C. (1986a) 'The Theoretical Subversiveness of Feminism', in C. Pateman and E. Gross (eds).

Pateman, C. (1986b) 'Review of Genevieve Lloyd's "The Man of Reason" ', *Political Theory*, vol. 14.

Pateman, C. (1987) 'Feminist Critiques of the Public/Private Dichotomy', in A. Phillips (ed.).

Pateman, C. (1988) *The Sexual Contract* (Cambridge: Polity Press).

Pateman, C. (1989) *The Disorder of Women* (Cambridge: Polity).

Pateman, C. and Gross, E. (eds) (1986) *Feminist Challenges. Social and Political Theory* (London: Allen and Unwin).

Perry, R. (1986) *The Celebrated Mary Astell* (Chicago and London: University of Chicago Press).

Phelps, L. (1981) 'Patriarchy and Capitalism', in *Building Feminist Theory. Essays from Quest* (London: Longman).

Phillips, A. (1983) *Hidden Hands. Women and Economic Policies* (London: Pluto Press).

Phillips, A. (1987a) *Divided Loyalties: Dilemmas of Sex and Class* (London: Virago).

Phillips, A. (ed.) (1987b) *Feminism and Equality* (Oxford: Basil Blackwell).

Phillips, A. and Taylor, B. (1986) 'Sex and Skill', in Feminist Review (ed.) *Waged Work: a Reader* (London: Virago).

Piercy, M. (1979) *Woman on the Edge of Time* (London: Women's Press).

Pollard, S. and Scott, J (eds) (1971) *Robert Owen, Prophet of the Poor* (London: Macmillan).

Pornography and Sexual Violence. Evidence of the Links: The complete transcript of Public Hearings on Ordinances to Add Pornography as Discrimination Against Women. Minneapolis City Council, Government Operations Committee. Dec. 12 and 13, 1983 (London: Everywoman).

Power, E. (1975) *Medieval Women* (Cambridge: Cambridge University Press).

Quataert, J. (1978) 'Unequal Partners in an Uneasy Alliance: Women and the Working Class in Imperial Germany', in M. Boxer and J. Quataert (eds).

Quataert, J. (1979) *Reluctant Feminists in German Social Democracy 1885–1917* (Princeton, NJ: Princeton University Press).

Ragland-Sullivan, E. (1991) 'Jacques Lacan. Feminism and the Problem of Gender Identity', in S. Gunew (ed.).

Ramazanoglu, C. (1986) 'Ethnocentricity and Socialist-Feminist Theory: a Response to Barrett and McIntosh', *Feminist Review*, no. 22.

Ramelson, M. (1967) *The Petticoat Rebellion. A Century of Struggle for Women's Rights* (London: Lawrence and Wishart).

Randall, V. (1987) *Women and Politics* (Basingstoke: Macmillan).

Rathbone, E. (1927) *The Disinherited Family. A Plea for Direct Provision for the Costs of Child Maintenance through Family Allowances* (London: Allen and Unwin).

Rauschenbusch-Clough, E. (1898) *A Study of Mary Wollstonecraft* (London, New York and Bloomsbury: Longmans Green).

Rawls, J. (1971) *A Theory of Justice* (Oxford: Oxford University Press).

Redstockings (1970) 'Manifesto', in R. Morgan (ed.).

Redstockings (1978) *Feminist Revolution. An Abridged Edition with Additional Writings* (New York: Random House).

Reeves, M. (1979) *Round About a Pound a Week* (London: Virago).

Reid, M. (1988) *A Plea for Women*, introduced by S. Ferguson (Edinburgh: Polygon).

Rendall, J. (1985) *The Origins of Modern Feminism: Women in Britain, France and the United States 1780–1860* (London: Macmillan).

Rendall, J. (ed.) (1987) *Equal or Different. Women's Politics 1800–1914* (Oxford: Basil Blackwell).

Rich, A. (1977) *Of Woman Born. Motherhood as Experience and Institution* (London: Virago).

Rich, A. (1980) 'Compulsory Heterosexuality and Lesbian Existence', *Signs*, vol. 5, no. 4.

Richards, J. R. (1982) *The Sceptical Feminist* (Harmondsworth: Penguin).

Richards, J. R. (1982) 'Reply to Grimshaw. Philosophy and Feminism', *Radical Philosophy*, no. 32.

Riemar, E. and Fout, J. (eds) (1980) *European Women. A Documentary History 1789–1945* (Brighton: Harvester Press).

Robertson, P. (1982) *An Experience of Women. Pattern and Change in Nineteenth Century Europe* (Philadelphia: Temple University Press).

Rogers, K. M. (1982) *Feminism in Eighteenth Century England* (Brighton: Harvester Press).

Romero, P. (1987) *Sylvia Pankhurst. Portrait of a Radical.* (New Haven and London: Yale University Press).

Rose, H. (1986) 'Women's Work: Women's Knowledge', in J. Mitchell and A. Oakley (eds).

Rosen, A. (1974) *Rise Up Women! The Militant Campaign of the Women's Social and Political Union 1903–1914* (London and Boston: Routledge and Kegan Paul).

Rosenberg, C. (1989) *Women and Perestroika. Present, Past and Future for Women in Russia* (London: Bookmarks).

Rossi, A. (ed.) (1970) *Essays on Sex Equality. John Stuart Mill and Harriet Taylor* (Chicago and London: University of Chicago Press).

Rossi, A. S. (ed.) (1973) *The Feminist Papers from Adams to de Beauvoir* (New York and London: Columbia University Press).

Roszak, B. and Roszak, T. (eds) (1969) *Masculine/Feminine. Readings in Sexual Mythology and the Liberation of Women* (New York: Harper Colophon Books).

Rousseau, J. J. (1955) *Emile*, translated by B. Foxley (London: Dent).

Rover, C. (1967) *Women's Suffrage and Party Politics in England 1866–1914* (London: Routledge and Kegan Paul).

Rover, C. (1970) *Love, Morals and the Feminists* (London: Routledge and Kegan Paul).

Rowan, C. (1982) ' "Mothers, vote Labour!" The State, the Labour Movement and Working-Class Mothers, 1900–1918', in R. Brunt and C. Rowan (eds) *Feminism, Culture and Politics* (London: Lawrence and Wishart).

Rowbotham, S. (1972) *Women, Resistance and Revolution* (Harmondsworth: Penguin).

Rowbotham, S. (1973a) *Hidden From History* (London: Pluto Press).

Rowbotham, S. (1973b) *Women's Consciousness, Man's World* (Harmondsworth: Penguin).

Rowbotham, S. (1977) *A New World for Women: Stella Browne – Socialist Feminist* (London: Pluto Press).

Rowbotham, S. (1982) 'The Trouble with Patriarchy', in M. Evans (ed.).

Rowbotham, S. (1983) *Dreams and Dilemmas* (London: Virago).

Rowbotham, S. (1989) *The Past is Before Us: Feminism in Action since the 1960s* (London: Pandora Press).

Rowbotham, S., Segal, L. and Wainwright, H. (1979) *Beyond the Fragments* (London: Merlin Press).

Rowbotham, S. and Weeks, J. (1977) *Socialism and the New Life: the Personal and Sexual Politics of Edward Carpenter and Havelock Ellis* (London: Pluto Press).

Rubin, G. (1970) 'Woman as Nigger', in L. Tanner (ed).

Rubinstein, D. (1986) *Before the Suffragettes* (Brighton: Harvester Press).

Ruddick, S. (1980) 'Maternal Thinking', *Feminist Studies*, vol. 6 no. 1.

Ruddick, S. (1984) 'Preservative Love and Military Destruction: Some Reflections on Mothering and Peace', in J. Trebilcot (ed.).

Ruddick, S. (1990) *Maternal Thinking. Towards a Politics of Peace* (London: Women's Press).

Sabrovsky, J. A. (1979) *From Rationality to Liberation. The Evolution of Feminist Ideology* (Westport Conn. and London: Greenwood Press).

Salper, R. (1972) *Female Liberation. History and Current Politics* (New York: Knopf).

Sarah, E. (1983) 'Christabel Pankhurst: Reclaiming her Power', in D. Spender (ed.).

Sargent, L. (1986) (ed.) *The Unhappy Marriage of Marxism and Feminism: A Debate on Class and Patriarchy* (London: Pluto Press).

Sassoon, A. S. (1987) *Women and the State. The Shifting Boundaries between Public and Private* (London: Hutchinson).

Sawicki, J. (1991) 'Foucault and Feminism: Towards a Politics of Difference', in M. Shanley and C. Pateman (eds).

Sayers, J. (1982) *Biological Politics. Feminist and Anti-Feminist Perspectives* (London and New York: 1982).

Sayers, J. (1986) *Sexual Contradictions. Psychology, Psychoanalysis and Feminism* (London and New York: Tavistock).

Sayers, J., Evans, M. and Redclift, N. (eds) (1987) *Engels Revisited. New Feminist Essays* (London and New York: Tavistock).

Schapiro, J. S. (1978) *Condorcet and the Rise of Liberalism* (New York: Octagon Books).

Scharfe, L. (1980) *To Work and To Wed. Female Employment, Feminism and the Great Depression* (Westport, Conn. and London: Greenwood Press).

Scharfe, L. and Jensen, J. M. (eds) (1978) *Decades of Discontent. The Women's Movement 1920–1940* (Boston: Northeastern University Press).

Schneewind, J. (ed.) (1965) *J. S. Mill. Essays on Literature and Society* (London: Collier-Macmillan).

Schneir, M. (ed.) (1972) *Feminism: the Essential Historical Writings* (New York: Vintage).

Schwarzer, A. (1984) *Simone de Beauvoir Today. Conversations 1972–1982*, translated from the French by M. Howarth (London: Chatto and Windus).

Scott, H. (1982) *Sweden's Right to be Human* (London: Allison and Busby).

Scott, J. (1989) 'French Feminists and the Rights of "Man": Olympe de Gouge's Declarations', *History Workshop*, no. 28.

Seccombe, W. (1974) 'The Housewife and her Labour under Capitalism', *New Left Review*, no 83.

Seccombe, W. (1975) 'Domestic Labour: Reply to Critics', *New Left Review*, no. 74.

Segal, L. (1987) *Is the Future Female? Troubled Thoughts on Contemporary Feminism* (London: Virago).

Sevenhuijsen, S. (1991) 'Justice, Moral Reasoning and the Politics of Child Custody', in E. Meehan and S. Sevenhuijsen (eds).

Shaffer, R. (1979) 'Women and the Communist Party U.S.A. 1930–1940', *Socialist Review*, vol. 9, no. 3.

Shahar, S. (1983) *The Fourth Estate: A History of Women in the Middle Ages*, translated by C. Galai (London and New York: Methuen).

Shanley, M. L. and Pateman, C. (eds) (1991) *Feminist Interpretations and Political Theory* (London: Polity Press).

Shulman, A. K. (ed.) (1979) *Red Emma Speaks. The Selected Speeches and Writings of the anarchist and feminist Emma Goldman* (London: Wildwood House).

Shulman, A. K. (1983) 'Emma Goldman: "Anarchist Queen" (1869–1940)', in D. Spender (ed.).

Sichterman, B. (1983) *Femininity. The Politics of the Personal* (Oxford: Polity Press).

Signs (1981) 'Special edition on French Feminist Theory' *Signs*, vol. 7, no. 1.

Siim, B. (1991) 'Welfare State, Gender Politics and Equality Principles – Women's citizenship in the Scandinavian welfare state', in E. Meehan and S. Sevenhuijsen (eds).

Slaughter, J. and Kern, R. (eds) (1981) *European Women on the Left*.

Socialism, Feminism and the Problems Faced by Political Women 1880 to the Present (Westport, Conn. and London: Greenwood Press).

Smart, C. (1989) *Feminism and the Power of Law* (London and New York: Routledge).

Smart, C. and Smart, B. (1978) *Women, Sexuality and Social Control* (London: Routledge and Kegan Paul).

Smith, H. L. (1982) *Reason's Disciples. Seventeenth Century English Feminists* (Urbana, Chicago and London: University of Illinois Press).

Smith, H. L. (ed.) (1990) *British Feminism in the Twentieth Century* (London: Edward Elgar).

Solaris, V. (1970) 'Excerpts from the SCUM Manifesto', in R. Morgan (ed.).

Sowerwine, C. (1982) *Sisters or Citizens? Women and Socialism in France since 1876* (Cambridge: Cambridge University Press).

Spelman, E. (1988) *Inessential Woman. Problems of Exclusion in Feminist Thought* (Boston: Beacon Press).

Spender, D. (1983a) *Women of Ideas (and What Men Have Done to Them)* (London: Ark).

Spender, D. (ed.) (1983b) *Feminist Theorists. Three centuries of Women's Intellectual Traditions* (London: Women's Press).

Spender, D. (1985a) *Man Made Language* (London: Routledge and Kegan Paul).

Spender, D. (1985b) *For the Record. The Making and Meaning of Feminist Knowledge* (London: Women's Press).

Stacey, J. (1986) 'Are Feminists Afraid to Leave Home? The Challenge of Pro-Family Feminism', in J. Mitchell and A. Oakley (eds).

Stacey, M. and Price, M. (1981) *Women, Power and Politics* (London and New York: Tavistock).

Stanley, L. (1983) 'Olive Schreiner: New Women, Free Women, All Women' in D. Spender (ed.).

Stanton, E. C. and Anthony, S. B. (1981) *Correspondence, Writings, Speeches*, edited and with a critical commentary by E. C. Dubois (New York: Schocken).

Stanton, E. C., Anthony, S. B. and Gage, M. (eds) (1881 and 1882) *The History of Woman Suffrage*, vols I. and II (New York: Fowler and Wells).

Stanworth, M. (ed.) (1987) *Reproductive Technologies* (Oxford: Polity Press).

Steinem, G. (1984) *Outrageous Acts and Everyday Rebellions* (London: Fontana).

Stenton, M. (1957) *The English Woman in History* (London: Allen and Unwin).

Stites, R. (1978) *The Women's Liberation Movement in Russia. Feminism, Nihilism and Bolshevism 1860–1930* (Princeton, New Jersey: Princeton University Press).

Stites, R. (1981) 'Alexandra Kollontai and the Russian Revolution', in J. Slaughter and R. Kern (eds).

Stone, L. (1979) *The Family, Sex and Marriage in England 1500–1800* (Harmondsworth: Penguin).

Strachey, R. (1974) *The Cause. A Short History of the Women's Movement in Great Britain* (Bath: Cedric Chivers).

Strange, P. (1983) *It'll Make a Man of You – A Feminist View of the Arms Race* (Nottingham: A Peace News/Mushroom pamphlet).

Tanner, L. (ed) (1970) *Voices from Women's Liberation* (New York: Mentor).

Taylor, B. (1983) *Eve and the New Jerusalem: Socialism and Feminism in the Nineteenth Century* (London: Virago).

Taylor, D. *et al.* (1985) *Women, A World Report* (London: Methuen).

Taylor, H. (1983) *The Enfranchisement of Women* (London: Virago).

Thatcher, M. (1954) Article in *Onward*, a Conservative Party publication, April 1954. Reprinted in *The Guardian*, 21 March 1990.

Thompson, D (1987) 'Women, Work and Politics in Nineteenth Century England: the Problem of Authority', in J. Rendall (ed.).

Thompson, D. (ed.) (1983) *Over Our Dead Bodies. Women Against the Bomb* (London: Virago).

Thompson, M. L. (ed.) (1970) *Voices of the New Feminism* (Boston: Beacon Press).

Thompson, R. (1974) *Women In Stuart England and America* (London: Routledge and Kegan Paul).

Thompson, W. (1983) *Appeal of one Half of the Human Race, Women against the Pretensions of the Other Half, Men, to retain them in Political, and Thence in Civil and Domestic Slavery* (London: Virago).

Thonnessen, W. (1973) *The Emancipation of Women. The Rise and Decline of the Women's Movement in German Social Democracy 1863–1963* translated by J. de Bres (Bristol: Pluto Press).

Thornton, M. (1986) 'Sex Equality is not enough for Feminism', in C. Pateman and E. Gross (eds).

Todd, J. M. (ed.) (1977) *A Wollstonecraft Anthology* (Bloomington and London: Indiana University Press).

Tomalin, C. (1974) *The Life and Death of Mary Wollstonecraft* (London: Weidenfeld and Nicolson).

Tong, R. (1989) *Feminist Thought. A Comprehensive Introduction* (London: Unwin Hyman).

Tovey, B. and Tovey, G. (1974) 'Women's Philosophical Friends and Enemies', *Social Science Quarterly*, vol. 55.

Treblicot, J. (ed.) (1984) *Mothering. Essays in Feminist Theory* (New York: Rowman and Allenheld).

Tress, D. (1988) 'Comment on Flax's "PostModernism and Gender Relations in Feminist Theory', *Signs* vol. 14.

Trotsky, L. (1924) *Problems of Life*, translated by Z. Venerora, with an introduction by N. Minsky (London: Methuen).

Trotsky, L. (1970) *Women and the Family* (New York: Pathfinder).

Tulloch, G. (1989) *Mill and Sexual Equality* (Hemel Hempstead: Harvester Wheatsheaf).

Ungerson, C. (ed.) (1985) *Women and Social Policy: A Reader* (Basingstoke: Macmillan).

Urbanski, M. (1983) 'Margaret Fuller: Feminist Writer and Revolutionary', in D. Spender (ed.).

Vetterling-Braggin, M., Elliston, F. and English, J. (eds) (1981) *Feminism and Philosophy* (Totowa, NJ: Littlefield, Adams).

Vogel, L. (1983) *Marxism and the Oppression of Women* (London: Pluto Press).

Vogel, U. (1986) 'Rationalism and Romanticism: Two Strategies for Women's Liberation', in J. Evans *et al.*

Vogel, U. (1989) 'Is Citizenship Gender Specific?', unpublished paper presented to the Political Studies Association Annual Conference.

Voronina, O. (1989) 'Women in a "Man's Society" ', *Soviet Sociology*, vol. 28, no. 2.

Walby, S. (1990) *Theorizing Patriarchy* (Oxford: Basil Blackwell).

Walker L. (1984 *The Women's Movement in England in the late Nineteenth and Early Twentieth Centuries*, Unpublished PhD Thesis, University of Manchester.

Walters, M. (1979) 'The Rights and Wrongs of Women: Mary Wollstonecraft, Harriet Martineau, Simone de Beauvoir', in J. Mitchell and A. Oakley (eds).

Waltzer, M. (1983) *Spheres of Justice. A Defense of Pluralism and Equality* (New York: Basic Books).

Wandor, M. (ed.) (1972) *The Body Politic. Women's Liberation in Britain* (London: Stage 1).

Wandor, M. (ed.) (1990) *Once a Feminist: Stories of a Generation* (London: Virago).

Wardle, R. (1951) *Mary Wollstonecraft: a Critical Study* (London: Richards Press).

Ware, S. (1981) *Beyond Suffrage. Women in the New Deal* (Cambridge, Mass.: Harvard University Press).

Warnock, M. (ed.) (1966) *Utilitarianism* (London: Collins).

Waters, E. (1989) 'Restructuring the "Woman Question": Perestroika and Prostitution', *Feminist Review*, no. 32.

Weedon, C. (1987) *Feminist Practice and Poststructuralist Theory* (Oxford: Basil Blackwell).

Weiner, G. (1983) 'Harriet Martineau: a Reassessment', in D. Spender (ed.).

Weir, A. and Wilson, E. (1984) 'The British Women's Movement', *New Left Review*, no. 148.

Wenzel, H. (1986) 'Interview with Simone de Beauvoir', in *Simone de Beauvoir: Witness to a Century* (New Haven, Conn.: Yale French Studies, no. 42).

Wexler, A. (1984) *Emma Goldman. An Intimate Life* (London: Virago).

Wheeler, L. (1983) 'Lucy Stone: Radical Beginnings 1818–93', in D. Spender (ed.).

Whitelegg, E. *et al.* (1982) *The Changing Experience of Women* (Oxford: Martin Robertson).

Willard, C. (1975) 'A Fifteenth Century View of Woman's Role in Medieval Society: Christine de Pizan's "Livre des Trois Vertus" ', in R. Morewedge (ed.).

Williams, G. (ed.) (1985) *John Stuart Mill on Politics and Society* (Glasgow: Fontana).

Wilson, E. (1980) *Only Halfway to Paradise. Women in Postwar Britain 1945–1968* (London and New York: Tavistock).

Wilson, E. with Weir, E. (1986) *Hidden Agendas. Theory, Politics and Experience in the Women's Movement* (London: Tavistock).

Wiltsher, A. (1985) *Most Dangerous Women. Feminist Peace Campaigners of the Great War* (London: Pandora Press).

Winegarten, R. (1988) *Simone de Beauvoir. A Critical View* (Oxford: Berg).

Wittig, M. (1981) 'One is Not Born a Woman', *Feminist Issues*, vol. 1, no. 1.

Wolgast, E. (1980) *Equality and the Rights of Women* (Ithaca and London: Cornell University Press).

Wollstonecraft, M. (1978) *Vindication of the Rights of Woman* (Harmondsworth: Penguin).

Wood, E. M. (1986) *The Retreat from Class: A New 'True' socialism* (London: Verso).

Young, I. (1986) 'Beyond the Unhappy Marriage: a Critique of the Dual Systems Theory', in L. Sargent (ed.).

Young, I. (1989) 'Polity and Group Difference: A Critique of the Ideal of Universal Citizenship', *Ethics*, vol. 99, no. 2.

Zetkin, C. (1984) *Selected Writings*, edited by P. Foner (New York: International Publishers).

Index